PRESCHOOL SCREENING

PRESCHOOL SCREENING
Identifying Young Children with
Developmental and Educational Problems

ROBERT LICHTENSTEIN, PH.D.
Department of Educational Studies
University of Delaware
Newark, Delaware

HARRY IRETON, PH.D.
Department of Family Practice and Community Health
University of Minnesota
Minneapolis, Minnesota

(G&S)

GRUNE & STRATTON, INC.
Harcourt Brace Jovanovich, Publishers
Orlando   New York   San Diego   London
San Francisco   Tokyo   Sydney   Toronto

Library of Congress Cataloging in Publication Data

Lichtenstein, Robert
  Preschool screening

  Bibliography: p.
  Includes index.
  1. Readiness for school. 2. Ability—Testing.
3. Educational tests and measurements. 4. Learning
disabilities. I. Ireton, Harry. II. Title.
LB1132.L52   1983   372.12′6   83-22615
ISBN 0-8089-1625-4

Grune & Stratton, Inc.
Orlando, Florida 32887

Distributed in the United Kingdom by
Grune & Stratton, Ltd.
24/28 Oval Road, London NW 1

Library of Congress Catalog Number 83-22615
International Standard Book Number 0-8089-1625-4
Printed in the United States of America
86 87 88 89   10 9 8 7 6 5 4 3 2

This book is dedicated to all of our teachers, especially our first teachers—our parents.

Contents

Contents

Preface

This book is intended to address the issues and options involved in using screening procedures to identify children who are at risk for school failure. It is written in response to the need of schools and other agencies to create cost-effective systems for reviewing the developmental and educational functioning of preschool children.

In the course of our professional involvements in the area of preschool assessment over the past ten years, we have found ourselves continually being asked the same questions by practitioners and administrators: What test should we use? Can we rely on information provided by parents? When should screening and assessment take place? How should results be interpreted? This book is in large part a compilation of the answers (or observations, where "answers" are in short supply) that we and others have provided.

Our experiences as instrument developers, researchers, consultants, and clinicians have shaped our knowledge and understanding of preschool screening and early identification. In this book, we draw on our own experiences and research, as well as on the work of others, to clarify the issues and obstacles that need to be considered. The result is not a "screening-made-easy" guidebook. We have tried to balance the need to cover practical "how-to" matters against the imperative to take a critical look at the limitations and implications of current practices and policies. It is our impression that workable systems for preschool screening do exist, but that better systems can be created if the task is approached in a clear, systematic way.

The general framework of this book takes us from matters of philosophy and policy (e.g., whether preschool screening is a sound strategy for prevention of school problems) to matters of practice (how a preschool screening program should be implemented) and back again (what an ideal early identification system might look like). Chapter 1 provides an overview of preschool screening and early identification, i.e., definitions, objectives, history, and issues. Chapters 2 through 5 deal with practical and technical considerations that must be addressed in implementing preschool screening programs. In the final chapter, we reflect on the key issues and elements that shape preschool screening and present our recommendations both for tightening up and transcending current screening practices.

We are highly appreciative of the assistance as well as the encouragement we received from the many persons who contributed to this work. Our understanding of the current state of the art was enhanced by input from practitioners in the field: Sue Albert, Patrick Geraghty, Linn Hairston, Rosemary Johnson, Deborah Litman, Kathleen O'Leary, Dennis Peterson, Mary Lou Spies, and Joyce Staples-Hartigan. We are grateful to Sheila Field, Karen Gouze, and Thomas Lombard for their valuable feedback in reviewing sections of the manuscript. And a special thanks is due to Doris Davidson for her extreme care in preparing the final manuscript.

Robert Lichtenstein, Ph.D.
Harry Ireton, Ph.D.

PRESCHOOL SCREENING

c

1
An Overview of Preschool Screening

Professionals in education and related fields have been expressing growing concern about the large number of children who are not progressing well in school, or who are, frankly, failing. An estimated 9.5 million children, 12 percent of the school age population in this country, are impaired by physical, mental, or emotional problems that pose obstacles to their having a successful school experience (Brewer & Kakalik, 1979). Many other children who, as a result of mild problems or economic disadvantage, fail to achieve their potential could also be counted among those who are cause for concern.

Teachers, psychologists, and other professionals, and of course the parents of these children, may find themselves wishing and wondering: "If only we had recognized the problem sooner and done something earlier, maybe the child would not be experiencing the serious problems he or she has now." While this wish is a common one, there is considerable difference of opinion about how early identification and early assistance services should be provided, how much, and even whether services should be provided at all. Prevailing philosophies have changed over time, and practices continue to vary from place to place and from case to case. The following cases illustrate some of the ways in which young children's problems are identified, and what may happen as a consequence of identification.

Jill Green was worried because her 4 year-old child, Jimmy, did not seem to be maturing like her older children had. "I don't know what's going on with him," she told her neighbor, Arlene Thorton. "He doesn't seem to be so 'tuned in.' Sometimes when I tell him something he just ignores me. I used to think it was a case of the 'terrible twos,' but now I'm not so sure."

1

This sounded familiar to Ms. Thorton. When her son Willie was just a toddler, she had suspected that something—she wasn't sure what—was wrong with him. She told Ms. Green how she had hesitated to bring up these concerns with the family pediatrician. To her relief, her concerns were finally addressed when a special program was offered by the local school district. Ms. Thorton described the district's preschool screening program in detail:

> An article in the newspaper gave the number you could call if you wanted the schools to evaluate your child. I called and told them about Willie— how he was slow in starting to walk and talk, and how he didn't seem to learn or remember what he saw on Sesame Street like other kids. I was afraid he might have problems when he started school. They saw him at the high school a couple times, and then set him up with a special preschool program, Early Start, this fall. He's in a small classroom each morning where they teach him lots of stuff to help him get ready for school. Once a month, there's a meeting for parents where we talk about things like how kids can learn at home, and what to do when your kids are driving you up the wall.

The program certainly sounds ideal for Jimmy. And who could object to an educational program that produces such beneficial results?

Ms. Green thought this was worth looking into, and called the schools. She was told that the screening program would take place in the spring. A clerk explained that she could call the Director of Special Education if it seemed to be an urgent problem, or she might consult a pediatrician or psychologist privately.

Ms. Green decided to wait, especially after her husband commented, "I don't think anything is wrong with Jimmy. Just give him some time. You start getting all worried, you'll give him a complex. I'm sure a psychologist would tell us he has problems. For what they charge, I know they'd come up with something." The Greens agreed to have Jimmy checked out with the preschool screening program that spring. When the time came, however, the family was away on vacation and the matter was forgotten.

The earlier discussion between Ms. Thorton and Ms. Green was recalled two years afterward when they met at a party. "Willie's doing fine," Ms. Thorton reported. "He's in the middle reading group at school, and I got a glowing report from his teacher at Open House. How about your son—did he ever get into Early Start?"

"No, but he seems to be doing fine. Just a late bloomer, I guess. He has a wonderful kindergarten teacher. I think he's the artist in the family; you should see the things he brings home."

Maybe Jimmy did not really need special help. Or maybe he did, and still does, and his problems will be worse when they finally become apparent. Ms. Thorton's son Willie seems to have been helped by the Early Start program. But maybe he was just a "late bloomer." Maybe he would have made out all right without Early Start, just as Jimmy seems to have done.

Let us turn to another case in which a parent seeks special services for her children.

Ms. Wilson, a single mother with a limited income, received medical care for herself and her children at a community health care center. When she brought her daughter Jessica, age 3, to the center with a worse than usual episode of one of her frequent colds, a staff pediatrician observed that Jessica seemed to be having some difficulty hearing. The pediatrician, Dr. Eisenstein, also noted that she had a history of serous otitis media (fluid in the middle ear). Beyond treating the illness, he advised Ms. Wilson to bring Jessica in again when she was feeling better. "We'll check her hearing and do a developmental screening test."

"What kind of a test?" the mother asked.

"A developmental screening test." Dr. Eisenstein explained, "The nurse will have her do some things and ask her questions to see how she is coming along with her language development and to see how she is developing otherwise. It won't take long. We use it regularly with young children to see how they are doing, and to spot problems in development. With your daughter's history of ear infections and occasional hearing problems, this is something we need to look at. It's probably not serious, but we would rather be on the safe side."

On the return visit, the hearing test showed a mild hearing loss. The Denver Developmental Screening Test indicated that Jessica's language development was mildly delayed. "It's good to identify this problem now," explained a hearing specialist. "It's not a major problem, but we do need to follow it closely to make sure it doesn't result in any permanent hearing loss, and to see how her language is coming along."

Many children "slipped through the cracks" in the days when various agencies, but no overall system, provided services for children with special needs. Fortunately, Jessica was not one of them. But times change, and so does public policy—as Ms. Wilson discovered.

Ms. Wilson's younger child, Michael, was always in perfect health and had few occasions for visits to the community health care center. Ms. Wilson knew that his vision and hearing were excellent, and she wasn't too concerned about the fact that he spoke very little. "How is he supposed to get a word in anyway, the way Jessica talks all the time?" But when he turned 4 years old, Ms. Wilson decided to ask Dr. Eisenstein for advice.

"You say he's 4 years old?" asked Dr. Eisenstein. "That's being handled by the public schools now because of the new federal law. You could call United Children's Services, but I think they'll tell you the same thing." He was right.

After some delay, since this service was generally provided at a different time of year, the school district arranged an evaluation for Michael. Afterwards, an educational specialist told Ms. Wilson that the schools did not have the kind of language program Michael needed. They hoped to in the future, but funding for all new programs was uncertain. She finally met with the Coordinator of Special Services, who told her, "We can have a speech clinician see Michael for a half hour each week from now, April, until the end of the school year. The only other thing open for preschool children is a class for the moderately and severely mentally retarded, which I would not advise for your son. I really wish we could provide more. The money just isn't there."

Programs and services designed to identify young children with problems vary in their scope and effectiveness. The same preschool screening program that provided a valued service for Willie, whose mother was reluctant to express her concerns to a pediatrician, did not reach Jimmy, whose parents found the timing inconvenient and decided to "wait and see." Jessica was fortunate that her hearing difficulties were discovered through a testing program that was unknown to many parents and mostly relied upon alert professionals like Dr. Eisenstein to provide information about the program. Before special educational services for preschool children were mandated by law, however, many children like Jessica were not identified prior to school age, or if identified, did not have access to affordable services. Yet, comprehensive services are "easier legislated than provided," as Ms. Wilson learned when the school system failed to provide for her son Michael as other agencies had done for Jessica.

While the potential for preschool screening programs to improve services for children is great, results often fall short in actual practice. Questions may be raised along two different lines. First, it could be that failings are primarily due to difficulties in translating principles into practice: Do parents lack knowledge about existing programs, or about their children's right to needed services? Are school administrators short of qualified personnel, or lacking in funds to fully implement programs? Are screening programs planned too hastily, or without adequate knowledge of relevant research?

Or, it is possible that current public policy is misguided, and that there are flaws in the very logic of preschool screening: How can it be determined whether a young child is "going through a stage," or showing early signs of a long-term problem? What are the effects of labeling children at an early age? Do parents and teachers have lower expectations for a "handicapped" or "at risk" child, which are "confirmed" by his or her age-typical problems and eventually result in a self-fulfilling prophecy? Are screening programs that screen large numbers of children able to devote sufficient individual attention to each parent and child? Is it possible to achieve the intended objective of providing comprehensive early services at a price that society is willing to pay?

These are questions that puzzle parents, professionals, and policy makers. The "answers" upon which current practices are based run the gamut from assumptions, to educated guesses, to hard facts. Let us begin to separate one from another.

EARLY INTERVENTION AND EARLY IDENTIFICATION

The primary impetus behind preschool screening is the fact that a substantial number of children are struggling or failing in school. Children with handicapping conditions such as physical and sensory impairment, developmental and learning disabilities, emotional disturbance, etc. who are not receiving an appropriate education make up a large part of school "casualties." According to a survey by the federal government's Office of Special Education (1980), approximately four million U.S. schoolchildren were not receiving the special services they needed, and one million handicapped children were being excluded from school entirely. Added to this are children from educationally deprived environments who fall far short of attaining their academic potential and lag farther behind with each successive year of school. The unmet educational needs of the disadvantaged have become increasingly evident, as federal funding to equalize educational opportunities for this group (e.g., through the Elementary and Secondary Education Act) has not been sustained at the high-priority level of the 1960s and 1970s.

The pattern of failure becomes more firmly entrenched over time. Case histories of children with substantial problems typically reveal early indications of their need for some special assistance. These needs are often disregarded or receive insufficient attention until a crisis state is reached. By then, problems have become severe and prospects for remediation are less hopeful. Self-sustaining cycles develop: the failing child lacks expectations of success, loses motivation, withdraws from academic pursuits, and experiences further failure. The long-term consequences include (1) significant costs to society in terms of services required (e.g., special education, welfare, corrections) and loss of productivity, and (2) immeasurable losses for the individual in terms of intellectual and social/emotional development.

Professionals in schools, clinics, and agencies who come in contact with children whose problems are entrenched often express the regret that "something should have been done for these children sooner." An obvious alternative is to act sooner to provide special help for these children—hence the name *early intervention*. The rationale, as expressed by Hobbs (1975) is that

> Prevention is more effective and more economical, as a rule, than repair;
> it is better to identify problems early and correct them promptly than to
> let them grow until a crisis requires action. Indeed, for many develop-
> mental functions (such as hearing handicap) undue delay in treatment
> may lead to irreversible developmental damage. (pp. 89–90)

Early intervention programs might be designed to provide motoric or
cognitive stimulation, to help a child cope with sensory or physical
impairment, to provide educational enrichment experiences, to teach
social skills and adaptive behavior, to foster positive attitudes towards
learning, to improve the home environment and parenting skills, or to
provide any combination of these services.

In order to pursue a policy of early intervention, children's problems must be identified at an early point so that the intervention can
change the course of the problematic situation or condition. Systematic
efforts to move up the point in time when problems are identified are
referred to as *early identification*. Technically, early identification does
not apply exclusively to the preschool age range. "Early" does not
mean early in the life of the child, but early in the course of the child's
problem. Thus, early identification could also apply to prompt detection of a third grader's reading comprehension problem as the curriculum shifts emphasis from word decoding to reading for meaning. To
borrow from the medical terminology, identification is regarded as
"early" when the condition is still in the incipient, or pre-symptomatic,
stage; that is, when problems are not readily noticeable. The time
interval between the point when early identification takes place and
when problems would otherwise be identified is known as *lead time*.
The greater the lead time, the greater the prospects for producing
benefical effects through early intervention.

In theory, early identification and early intervention for school
problems appear to constitute a perfectly sound and responsible practice. Resources are devoted to "ounces of prevention" rather than
"pounds of cure." Children are strengthened instead of weakened,
professionals feel rewarded instead of frustrated, and parents get as-
sisted instead of blamed. However, this model hinges upon three critical assumptions.

The first assumption is that *early intervention produces a significant
positive effect*. Emphasis on early, rather than subsequent, intervention
implies that there are significant positive consequences of early intervention that cannot occur or are far more costly, if intervention is
delayed until a later point in time. In terms of providing early intervention for young children, this has not been established. Nor has the basic
question been satisfactorily answered. Prior to determining whether
there are critical periods for intervention, the fact that educational

interventions for young children are effective at all must be demonstrated. This has been a point of great contention. Over the past 15 years, while a great number of early intervention programs have been operating, evidence supporting early intervention has accumulated at a modest and uneven rate. The situation has not changed dramatically since Ackerman and Moore (1976) observed,

> No one has yet "proved" the value of various types of preschool educational programming for the handicapped. But one may *assume* the value of preschool intervention, as have hundreds of thousands of parents and professionals. It is this assumption that is presently serving to accelerate the growth of such programs. It is this assumption that will, probably, prove true if adequate measures are ever found to evaluate it. (p. 669)

The practice of providing preschool services under the assumption that their value can and will be proven has been somewhat vindicated by recent research (discussed later in this chapter) that supports the value of preschool intervention programs for environmentally deprived children. However, documentation of the value of services for handicapped children is lacking, largely due to a methodological problem: rigorous research requires that part of a handicapped sample be assigned to a "no-service" control group, which would raise serious ethical concerns regarding deprivation of potentially-beneficial treatment. Therefore, service providers continue to operate on faith by offering intervention programs for a wide range of developmental problems and handicapping conditions.

The second assumption is that *children with developmental problems can be accurately identified as problems are first developing.* Implicit in the practice of early intervention is the expectation that current problems or developmental delays will continue to be cause for concern. In actuality, not all children showing signs of early difficulties prove to have later problems. Developmental changes are especially unpredictable among young children: problems may lessen or disappear over time, just as they may increase or appear. There is only a slight correlation between children's developmental status during the first two years of life and in later years (McCall, 1981; McCall, Hogarty, & Hurlburt, 1972; Rubin & Balow, 1979). With the exception of extremely disabled children, one cannot predict with any accuracy whether developmental delays among infants will disappear in the natural course of maturation or will require special attention. Predictions as to whether children ages 3–5 will experience problems in school are also tenuous, although less uncertain.

Measurement issues introduce further limitations upon early identification of developmental problems. No clear and consistent definitions have been established to determine whether children have "developmental delays," "handicapping conditions," or "intervention needs." This is partly because the adequacy of a child's functioning or behavior is related to situational demands and to expectations of other individuals. It is also due partly to the limitations of assessment procedures for early identification. Identification of school problems may depend upon the methods and measures used in assessment and upon the person making the observation or interpretation. Invariably, some inappropriate identification decisions occur. This has far-reaching consequences for the viability of early identification and intervention.

The third assumption is that *early identification and intervention programs can be implemented without prohibitively exorbitant costs*. The essential question is one of priorities: how much of its resources is this nation willing to devote towards remediation of chldren's problems? While this varies with the times (compare, for example, the high priority given to education in the 1960s with its current low priority), there will always be limits upon the amount of support available for special education and early childhood programs. Trade-offs must always be made between the comprehensiveness and cost of services. Public policy on providing services for children is shaped by perceptions of the value of services and the feasibility of implementing services in a cost-effective manner.

Current public policy largely underwrites the cost of intervention services for preschool children with special needs. Effective delivery of these services depends in large part upon the system used to identify these children. This is not a simple matter; the preschool population is less accessible to identification efforts than a "captive" in-school population. In formulating a system to identify preschool children, the effectiveness and affordability of alternative approaches must be carefully considered.

THE SCREENING APPROACH

In order to provide early intervention for all children in need, early identification must take place on a large scale. Screening, which is one strategy for early identification on a large scale, has been widely used in the field of medicine. Diseases and health problems, which are simple and inexpensive to treat early on but become major problems if left untreated, clearly call for early intervention. However, accurate diagnosis of health problems may require elaborate medical procedures that are prohibitively time-consuming and expensive to use with large numbers of people.

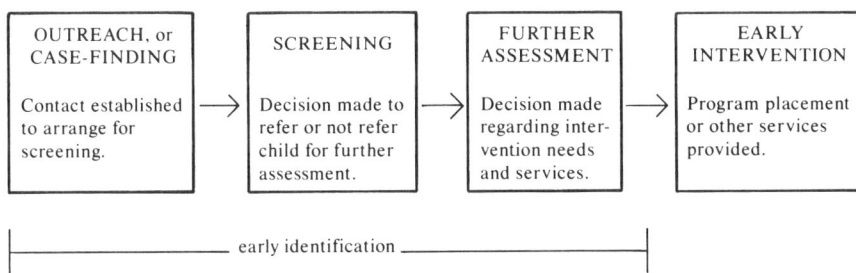

Fig. 1-1.   The screening approach to early identification and intervention.

The screening approach involves evaluating persons in two stages. At the first stage, screening, a large group is assessed with brief, simple, low-cost procedures to sort out those individuals who might have a problem or disease (i.e., who are at risk) from those apparently well individuals who need no follow-up evaluation at the time. Individuals who are referred from screening proceed to the next stage, diagnosis, at which more costly, extensive, and definitive procedures are used to determine whether the problem or problems in question are present. An example of this approach is in early identification of tuberculosis. Rather than subject each individual to a chest x-ray, which is costly and exposes the examinee to radiation, a simple skin-prick test is used. Only those individuals with a "positive" reading on this procedure undergo the more accurate chest x-ray. Another example involves using the familiar Snellen eye chart to screen for vision problems. Those selected out by this screening test are referred for a full optometric examination.

Applying the strategy of screening to early identification of school problems makes it more feasible to identify every preschool child with special educational needs. Of course, screening is of little value unless it is part of a complete system that culminates in the delivery of services. Figure 1-1 illustrates that four components of such a system.

The first component, *outreach*, involves the initial contact with parents, professionals, preschool centers, and community agencies to inform them about the services offered and to arrange for children to participate in the program. Outreach is not only a matter of publicizing a program to parents, but of securing their involvement. Both must take place for a program to have the intended impact upon the target population. Sometimes the name *child find* is used to refer to this initial locating of service-eligible preschool children (Meisels, 1978). Since child find is also used to refer more generally to the overall early identification process, the term is avoided in this book. Barnes (1982) uses the term *case finding,* which, although more explicit in referring to the element of entry into the system, is less widely used than outreach.

The two-stage assessment process, as described earlier, consists of *screening* and a follow-up evaluation stage. The objective at the screening stage is to pick out all those children who in fact have problems. Ideally, this will be accomplished without unnecessarily referring children who are problem-free.

Only those children referred at the screening stage continue on to a more comprehensive evaluation at the next stage. This second-level evaluation stage might be referred to as *further assessment* to distinguish it from assessment in general, of which screening is a part. Two decisions are made at the stage of further assessment: (1) whether or not the referred child is in need of special help, and (2) what intervention services are appropriate for the child.

The first three stages—outreach, screening, and further assessment—constitute the early identification part of the system. The ultimate aim of the system is to provide *early intervention* for children with special needs, which is the fourth and final stage. Intervention programs or services might be provided by an agency other than the one conducting the screening; the exact arrangements are not critical. What is essential for the system to work is that each stage leads directly to the next. This is particularly true for the step from identification to intervention. For every problem or condition that is a target of an early identification program, there should be corresponding intervention services available to children whose needs are identified.

ALTERNATIVE APPROACHES TO EARLY IDENTIFICATION

Children with special needs are identified in various ways—sometimes incidentally and sometimes systematically, sometimes with great uncertainty and sometimes at great cost. It was once a matter of chance, and of economic opportunity, as to whether or not preschool children received the special services they needed. With the movement towards early identification and intervention, mechanisms for identifying preschool children with special needs have become more purposeful.

Formerly, preschool children with developmental problems were identified when parents or relatives, pediatricians, preschool teachers, social workers, or other adults happened to notice that the child was not developing normally. This constituted an informal, or natural, referral system. The major limitation of a natural system is that special services may not be equally available (i.e., affordable) for all families. Parents are discouraged from seeking "non-essential services" (that is; compared to food, shelter, and medical care) if they lack the resources for a professional evaluation—and for whatever is recommended as a result. A natural system is workable for the population at large only if all parents can obtain services for their children, a situation that has been greatly remedied by public funding for special education, pediatric care, and social services.

Subsidizing of services, by itself, however, has not been sufficient, as reflected by the extent to which children's needs have continued to be neglected (Edelman, 1981). Even when services are available, there is no guarantee of delivery. A natural system relies upon one of two mechanisms to operate: the parent perceives a problem and pursues professional help for the child, or some professional (e.g., a pediatrician providing routine medical care) suspects that behavior or development is atypical and raises this concern with the parent. A second precondition for available services to be used as intended is that the services must be accessible and familiar to the public.

An approach that addresses both of these needs is the use of an outreach or public education campaign that provides parents and professionals with information on recognizing developmental problems. Assessment services are provided when parents with concerns about their children respond to the outreach program. In this approach, whether or not parents respond to outreach efforts is analogous to the screening stage of early identification (Figure 1-1). Parents, by responding, select out their children as possibly needing special services and, in effect, refer them on to the next stage of the process.

But what of the children who still fall through the cracks because their parents do not respond to the outreach program? Parents vary greatly in their understanding of developmental problems and in their inclination to seek outside assistance. Thus, some children are identified early while other children receive special attention only when their problems reach a crisis state.

An approach to early identification designed to present these "misses" is *mass screening.* Mass screening refers to a program that has the goal of screening every child in the target population. Effective outreach is still a critical element in this approach; regardless of what the plan is, parents must still be relied upon to arrange for or allow the child to participate. With mass screening, however, the parent does not make an initial stage judgment as to whether or not the child may have special problems. A mass screening program serves an entire preschool population, and there is therefore little stigma associated with the parent's response to the offer of screening services. This is especially true when developmental screening is combined with routine health, vision, and hearing screening. Mass screening introduces the possibility of universal and consistent early identification. As a rule, the cost and effort required by mass screening is considerable.

A precursor of mass screening generally known as *kindergarten roundup* has been a familiar routine in many school systems for decades. Kindergarten roundup was an annual occasion for registration and orientation of those children about to enter school. School personnel checked children's health records and screened for vision and hearing impairments, kindergarten teachers introduced themselves, parents signed up for PTA, school bus schedules were announced, and so on. In recent years, programs of this sort have been modified to serve as preschool screening programs. The school system can then arrange appropriate educational plans for children with special needs from the beginning of their school experience. This single-shot instance of mass screening, however, does not allow the necessary lead time for intervention to be provided *prior* to kindergarten.

A variation of mass screening is to selectively provide direct screening for those demographic subgroups or geographic areas that have a substantial number of unidentified children with special needs. By concentrating on groups that tend to underutilize available services, this *selective screening* approach has potential advantages of cost-efficiency over mass screening. After all, the rationale for more active approaches to early identification is to serve children who would not otherwise be identified. The effectiveness of a screening program in achieving this goal must be judged, not by the total number of children channeled into services, but by the additional numbers identified compared to those identified by simpler approaches (such as outreach/parent referral). In a population where parents tend to take much initiative in seeking services for their children, the advantages of mass screening may be minimal. In effect, selective screening is a mixed model that consists of mass screening for a high-need, underserved subpopulation, and alternative approaches for the remainder of the population.

One strategy involves the mixing of approaches, e.g., mass screening and outreach/referral, along age lines. Many early identification programs use the outreach/parent referral approach to identify children near the lower end of the preschool age range, while conducting mass screening once a year for those children closer to school entry (i.e., 4 and 5 year-olds).

An intermediate course between the outreach/referral system and mass screening is to obtain parental reports on all target population children. A questionnaire or inventory dealing with the child's development and behavior might be distributed to parents by mail. The information that parents provide serves as screening data to determine the need for follow-up assessment. The process is economical and unintrusive, yet has the potential for comprehensive coverage of the target population. Issues regarding the value of this approach are addressed in Chapter 3.

Other variations in screening are introduced by the timing element. Screening may be offered on a one-time basis for each child (as with kindergarten roundup), periodically (e.g., annually), or on a continuously available basis. Ongoing availability of screening services, while requiring greater flexibility by the screening program, can be more responsive to consumers' needs (witness the case of Ms. Green, who was concerned about Jimmy at the "wrong time of year"). Other issues involved in the timing of screening services are discussed in the following chapter.

Alternative approaches to the natural system of early identification proposed in recent years reflect efforts to make special services more widely available to all young children in need. Although mass screening of children ages 3–5 has been the focus of a great many new programs, there is no reason to regard this model as synonymous with preschool screening. Other approaches have untapped potential and may be better suited than mass screening to particular situations. Furthermore, shifts in public funding or legislation or social priorities may lead to emphasis upon different approaches. Given the common objective of alternative approaches to early identification, it is more productive to think in terms of preschool screening, broadly defined, as encompassing all of these alternatives.

HISTORICAL INFLUENCES

To the casual observer, the ever-increasing attention devoted to early identification and intervention over the past 25 years may appear to be the result of a single movement with a unified purpose. This perception leads one to assume that people are all talking about the same thing when they refer to "preschool screening." In actuality, preschool screening has been associated with each of several different movements, each with diverse philosophies and objectives. Three distinct focal points for these separate movements include (1) early enrichment and compensatory education, (2) pediatric screening, and (3) special services for handicapped children. A brief history of these movements should illustrate that much of the confusion and controversy about preschool screening is not simply due to disagreements over methods, but to different views about the purpose of screening.

Early Enrichment and Compensatory Education

Developmental psychologists have long stressed the importance of early child care and environmental stimulation. Skeels (1942, 1966) and Kirk (1958) presented evidence that programs providing special attention and stimulation for young mentally retarded children produced dramatic gains in their intellectual growth, and that these gains were maintained over time. Other researchers (Goldfarb, 1945; Spitz & Wolf, 1946) built a convincing case that development is stymied in the absence of early maternal care.

Several factors coincided to generate an unprecedented interest in early childhood education in the early 1960s. The technological triumph of the Soviet Union with the launching of Sputnik in 1957 triggered a renewed national commitment to education. Exposure of the prevalence of poverty (Harrington, 1962) and racial strife in the early 1960s highlighted the need for large scale social action to break the "cycle of poverty." Johnson's Great Society launched a three-pronged attack to remedy inequities in the interrelated areas of education, jobs, and housing.

At this time when special attention and generous funding were being devoted to education, prominent educational researchers (Bloom, 1964; Hunt, 1961; Kirk, 1958) were stressing the importance of children's early development in shaping their intellectual development and educational progress. Experimental projects providing enrichment experiences and compensatory education for disadvantaged children sprang up in an attempt to demonstrate the beneficial effects of early education. The Institute for Developmental Studies in New York City, the Milwaukee Project, the Perry Preschool Project in Ypsilanti, Michigan, the Early Training Project at George Peabody College in Nashville, the Philadelphia Project, the Florida Parent Education Program, and the Harlem Training Project are examples of such projects. Some model projects with elaborate evaluation components were established as part of Project Head Start, the best known and most wide reaching early childhood program of this era. Head Start, which was founded through the Economic Opportunity Act of 1965, provides educational and enrichment experiences for preschool children ages 4 and 5 in low income areas (see Zigler & Valentine, 1979). Critical to this ambitious experiment in compensatory education is the assumption that environment and education are primary determinants of a child's intellectual functioning, and that enrichment experiences can counteract the effects of deprivation and limited opportunities.

Outcome studies measuring the effectiveness of Head Start and other early childhood education programs on later school performance were awaited with great interest—and received with great consternation. The first major evaluation of Head Start cast serious doubts upon the effectiveness of the program (Westinghouse Learning Corporation, 1969). These findings were widely publicized, and a further controversy developed, when Jensen (1969) referred to this research with the statement that "compensatory education has been tried, and it apparently has failed," thereby supporting his argument that genetic differences rather than education and other environmental factors are the primary determinants of children's intellectual functioning. Hopes were raised as reports of dramatic IQ gains produced by the Milwaukee Project filtered through the media, but these exceptional findings were never documented in any published report and remain clouded in mystery and doubt (Herrnstein, 1982). Follow-up research on other early intervention programs in which children showed impressive initial gains revealed that these gains tend to wash out after the children enter school (see reviews by Bronfenbrenner, 1974; White et al., 1973).

Ironically, early evaluations of the impact of Head Start focused almost exclusively on intellectual and academic gains. This constituted only a limited portion of Head Start program goals, which included social and emotional growth, positive family interactions, and development of self-confidence and high personal expectations. Head Start rebounded from the early evaluation setbacks in two ways. First, in order to have a significant and lasting impact, Head Start expanded its program to begin at infancy and continue into school age. Second, subsequent evaluation studies were designed to investigate a broader range of effects.

The second generation of Head Start evaluation studies provided more encouraging results. Mann, Harrell, and Hurt (1978), summarizing Head Start research from 1969 to 1976, concluded that participation in full-year Head Start programs accounted for gains in cognitive development, social behavior, and health, and had a positive impact on parenting skills, parent-child interactions, and parent participation in school and community programs. Zigler, Abelson, Trickett, and Seitz (1982) demonstrated that positive motivational factors fostered by Head Start allow economically disadvantaged children to sustain an increased level of cognitive functioning.

The most ambitious research project on long-term effects of early intervention involved a collaborative study by the same investigators who conducted the experimental preschool programs in the 1960s and early 70s. The Consortium for Longitudinal Studies pooled long-term follow-up data from 12 experimental programs, and arrived at the following conclusions:

1. " . . . program graduates were significantly less likely to be assigned to special education classes and less likely to be retained in grade than were controls."
2. "There was some indication that program graduates performed better on achievement tests than did controls."
3. Program graduates "were significantly more likely than were controls to give achievement-related reasons . . . for being proud of themselves," and "rated their school performance significantly better than did controls."
4. "Program participation . . . affected maternal attitudes toward school performance and vocation aspirations." (Lazar & Darlington, 1982)

Researchers with one of the programs in the Consortium investigated the additional question of whether early intervention actually produces the long-term economic benefits that have often been proposed. Weber, Foster, and Weikart (1978) demonstrated that, for children in the Perry Preschool Project, the subsequent reductions in special educational and social services more than compensated for the original costs of providing early intervention services.

The controversy is not over. The recent report from the Consortium of Longitudinal Studies (Lazar & Darlington, 1982) found that gains on intelligence measures were not sustained beyond 4 years, and that achievement differences between experimental and control group children were minor.* Subsequent critiques of this research may lead to yet another reversal, as has occured with the early deprivation research. [Researchers (Clark & Clarke, 1976; Rutter, 1980) reanalyzing the early deprivation literature and presenting subsequent research in the area have refuted the finding that young children deprived of attention and stimulation in their early years suffer irreversible developmental deficits.]

While researchers are still far from any clear answers regarding the assumptions underlying early intervention, considerable headway has been made since Ackerman and Moore (1976) observed that proponents of early intervention operate strictly upon faith. The exact nature

---

*As pointed out by Lois Ellin-Data, a researcher intimately familiar with the history of these studies, the original Westinghouse (1969) study and the recent Consortium report (Lazar & Darlington, 1982) differed not so much in actual results as in the way in which the results were presented to and received by the public.

and degree of effects have not been clearly determined, but it seems apparent that modification of early experiences has the potential to produce some effects of educational significance.

Pediatric Screening

Recognizing the scope of children's unmet health needs, medical professionals in the 1960s endorsed screening as a viable approach to providing pediatric services on a large scale. Following in the footsteps of Head Start, federal legislation established a program for delivery of health care services to children from low-income families. (The association with Head Start was more than just temporal; Fred North, one of the designers of this new program, was Senior Pediatrician for Project Head Start.) Established by an act of Congress in 1967, the Early and Periodic Screening, Diagnosis, and Treatment (EPSDT) program was "designed to serve the 13 million young people in this country who are eligible for Medicaid from handicapping conditions that lead to chronic and disabling ailments" (Rojcewicz & Aaronson, 1976, p. 299).

As implied by its name, the EPSDT program employs the screening approach (selective screening, actually) to identify a broad range of health problems, e.g., hematological disease, bacteriuria, growth irregularities, hearing and vision loss, lead poisoning, tuberculosis, and dental problems. Screening is scheduled on a periodic basis, with children returning for visits at specified intervals from ages 0 to 21. Most important, children detected by the program as having health problems are supposed to receive appropriate treatment. Screening should lead to diagnosis and diagnosis to treatment for children with health problems, in keeping with the medical model of screening.

The actual impact of EPSDT has fallen far short of its plan and its potential. The original mandate in the Medicaid provisions of the Social Security Act of 1967 was both far-reaching and vague, providing for "early and periodic screening and diagnosis . . . and such health care, treatment, and other measures to correct or ameliorate defects and chronic conditions discovered thereby" (Public Law 90-248, Sec. 302a). This, however, was virtually all that P.L. 90-248 provided in the way of policy, and it was more than five years before complete regulations were written and the program took effect. Problems in implementation have marked the entire history of EPSDT. Meisels (in press) comments that EPSDT "may be the largest and most expensive public 'secret' in the human services domain," and notes that

> from its inception it failed to ignite the interest of professionals, to
> capture the attention of parents, or most importantly, to provide compre-

hensive services to children. Moreoever, in its first 15 years of existence virtually no programmatic evaluation or research was conducted on EPSDT. Data do not exist that demonstrate its impact, its effectiveness, or its ratio of cost to benefit.

A large part of the explanation is that EPSDT has been variably, and often reluctantly, administered by the individual states. Chang, Goldstein, Thomas, and Wallace (1979) report a range of 1% to 80% of eligible children receiving services in various states. A second major failing is that funding has often been insufficient to provide medical or dental treatment for children whose needs have been identified; in fact, if every eligible child were to be screened, the entire EPSDT budget would be exhausted long before any diagnosis or treatment took place (Divoky, 1977b; Meisels, in press).

In contrast to the actual implementation of EPSDT, the master plan is comprehensive and far-reaching. Its comprehensiveness, in fact, led to a serious controversy. EPSDT guidelines include provisions for developmental screening to identify "children who have significant deviations in psychological, neurological or emotional development" (Frankenburg & North, 1974, p. 139). This was a sensitive area from the start. Rojcewicz and Aaronson (1976) summarize the many questions introduced by developmental screening aside from availability and efficacy of treatment:

> Although the number of instruments and techniques to serve this purpose [developmental assessment] are increasing, few, if any, have been suffi-ciently standardized on the kinds of populations for which they are to be used to make legitimate claims of validity and reliability. This has raised questions about possible cultural bias embedded in screening instruments and diagnostic procedures. Furthermore, identification of mental health problems involves naming or describing them in some fashion. . . . Could not this information or "labeling" of the child color a teacher's view of his capabilities, making the labels the basis of a self-fulfilling prophesy? Who then would be entitled to see the records? Where would they be main-tained? How would they be used? (p. 301)

Parents, professionals, and child advocates, sensitized to issues of test bias and labeling of minority children, expressed their objections. As state agencies grappled with the complexities of developmental screening, however, public policy changes in special education restruc-tured the field of early identification and intervention so radically as to remove EPSDT from the limelight. The responsibility and controver-sies associated with developmental screening shifted to another institu-tion: the public schools.

Education for Handicapped Children

Until the 1970s, the right to a free public education was still being denied to many members of one group: children with handicapping conditions. Two class actions suits resolved in 1972 signaled the end of this practice that had long been supported by state and local regulations. Parents were on the winning side in *Pennsylvania Association for Retarded Children v. Commonwealth of Pennsylvania* and in *Mills v. Board of Education of the District of Columbia,* both of which affirmed the right of every child to educational services regardless of the scope of their needs.

Many states with similar litigation pending followed suit and adopted similar policies. In 1972 Massachusetts adopted a state law insuring educational services for children with special needs, Chapter 766, that remains among the most progressive of its kind. (Chapter 766 largely served as a model for the federal law that followed.) Still, court cases and new state laws were insufficient to insure educational rights to all children on a nationwide basis, as indicated by congressional committee findings in 1975 that:

- Over 1.75 million children with handicaps in the United States were being excluded entirely from receiving a public education solely on the basis of their handicap.
- Over half of the estimated eight million handicapped children in this country were not receiving the appropriate educational services they needed and/or were entitled to.
- Many other children with handicaps were still being placed in appropriate educational settings because their handicaps were undetected or because of a violation of their individual rights.

(Abeson & Zettel, 1977, p. 121)

In response, Congress made universal access to public education the law of the land by approving the Education for All Handicapped Children Act, Public Law 94-142, on November 29, 1975.

P.L. 94-142 assigns the nation's public schools the responsibility of providing handicapped children with "a free appropriate public education which emphasizes special education and related services designed to meet their unique needs" (P.L. 94-142, Sec. 601c). Let us review point by point what is meant by the terms "handicapped children," "free appropriate public education," and "special education and related services."

P.L. 94-142 defines handicapped children as

mentally retarded, hard of hearing, deaf, speech impaired, visually handicapped, seriously emotionally disturbed, orthopedically impaired or other health impaired children, or children with specific learning disabilities who by reason thereof require special education and related services. (Sec. 602)

Weintraub (1977) describes this definition of handicapped as "two-pronged" because it involves, first, a classification by disability category and, second, determination of need for special services. This is an important distinction in an area that can become easily confused. Given a disability, e.g., color blindness, a child may or may not be handicapped in relation to learning at school under typical conditions. In other words, disability does not automatically imply need for special educational services. Handicap is defined by the relationship between a particular disability and the task demands of a particular situation. A disability, once identified, must then be determined to interfere with a child's educational progress under normal circumstances in order to warrant special services. Developmental disabilities in certain areas, e.g., language comprehension, are more relevant to school performance than other disabilities.

P.L. 94-142 defines "children" with considerably more precision: the law specifies that services are to be provided for handicapped children ages 3–21. The exception to this is when provision of services for the age ranges 3–5 or 18–21 conflict with a court order, or state law or practice. The Office of Special Education (1980) reported that 16 states mandate services for the full 3–5 age range, 22 offer services beginning at age 4 or 5, and 12 states initiate services at age 6. Some states go beyond the federal law by extending services to handicapped children as early as birth for particular handicapping conditions. As an example, Indiana provides special services for handicapped preschool children ages 3–5, except for hearing impaired children who are eligible for services from age 6 months.

A "free" public education means at no cost to the individual parent or guardian. It is free in the same sense that public education is always free, i.e., fully supported by taxes. Public schools do not have the option to deny access to a child who is too difficult or expensive to educate. Nor can the schools merely engage in a token effort to accommodate exceptional children: the educational program must be "appropriate."

An "appropriate" public education is more easily prescribed than defined. In providing services, schools are caught in a bind between providing insufficient special educational programming and providing too much. During the same years in the early 70s when parents of educationally underserved and unserved handicapped children became increasingly adamant in their demands for more services, Dunn's (1968)

plea to educate mildly handicapped children in "the mainstream" (i.e. , regular educational settings) to the greatest degree possible became increasingly heeded. Thus, while lack of services clearly interferes with the educational progress of a handicapped child, overly restrictive experiences are seen as limiting a child's self-expectations, reducing opportunities for social development, and perpetuating the stigma of negative labels. In response to these cross-currents of educational reform, the formulators of P.L. 94-142 tried to design a system to insure that children with handicapping conditions receive educational services that are appropriate both in terms of serving their educational needs and not assigning them to unnecessarily restrictive placements.

The primary feature of P.L. 94-142 for insuring appropriateness of services is the individualized education program (IEP). For each child deemed eligible for services, the local educational agency (i.e., school district) must devise an IEP, which consists of a written statement of educational objectives and the type of instruction that will meet the needs of the child. Furthermore, P.L. 94-142 requires that out of all the educational placements that might meet the needs of the child, the child must be placed in the "least restrictive alternative." For example, an integrated program combining both regular and special education class placement is less restrictive than a self-contained special class, which is less restrictive than a full-time residential center placement. The "least restrictive alternative" clause is often incorrectly equated with mainstreaming of children with special educational needs. Mainstreaming is not explicitly addressed by P.L. 94-142.

The extent of special education and related services that are to be incorporated into a child's IEP is broadly defined in the federal law. P.L. 94-142 defines special education as

> specially designed instruction . . . to meet the unique needs of a handicapped child, including classroom instruction, instruction in physical education, home instruction, and instruction in hospitals and institutions. (Sec. 602)

In addition to this comprehensive coverage of the child's educational needs, P.L. 94-142 mandates the provision of related services that extend far beyond the educational domain. Related services are defined as

> transportation, and such developmental, corrective, and other supportive services (including speech pathology and audiology, psychological services, physical and occupational therapy, recreation, and medical and counseling services, except that such medical services shall be for diagnostic and evaluation purposes only) as may be required to assist a handicapped child to benefit from special education, and includes the

early identification and assessment of handicapping conditions in children. (P.L. 94-142, Sec. 602)

With this definition, the schools are required to attend to all aspects of a handicapped child's development: social, emotional, physical, and sensory, in addition to educational.

Appropriateness of educational planning also hinges upon the evaluation process that leads to identification of the child and to writing the IEP. P.L. 94-142 stipulates that evaluation materials and tests are to be selected and administered so as not to be racially or culturally discriminatory, that the evaluation should be done in the child's native language or "mode of communication," and that no single procedure is to be used for determining educational placement. A parent who disagrees with the outcome of the evaluation may contest the decision by following a formally established appeals process. Other "procedural safeguards" mandated by P.L. 94-142 protect the rights of children and parents by requiring school districts to inform parents about all aspects of the process, to obtain parent consent for evaluation, to maintain confidentiality of information, to provide services within specified time periods, to include parents at IEP meetings, and to revise IEPs and reevaluate identified children at periodic intervals.

Overall, P.L. 94-142 mandates a comprehensive package of services that comprise a veritable Bill of Rights for children with handicapping conditions. In spite of the overwhelming support of P.L. 94-142 by Congress in 1975, President Ford expressed the following reservations——as he signed the law:

Unfortunately, this bill promises more than the Federal Government can deliver and its good intentions could be thwarted by the many unwise provisions it contains. Everyone can agree with the objectives stated in the title of this bill—educating all handicapped children in our nation. The key question is whether the bill will really accomplish that objective.

Few suspected just how prophetic this statement would prove to be. First of all, the mandated task of identifying all children with special needs in an accurate and non-discriminatory manner requires technology and professional expertise that is beyond the resources of many school systems, and perhaps beyond the state of the art. Errors in the assessment process introduce serious consequences that threaten to compromise the entire undertaking.

Second, monumental expenses are incurred by the comprehensive assessment and intervention services and by the extensive procedural and bureaucratic requirements mandated by P.L. 94-142. These costs were introduced at the same time when many school districts were beset by financial crisis due to declining enrollments and dramatically

curtailed support at local, state, and federal levels. In spite of the funding formulas enacted by Congress, the federal government has provided only a fraction of the appropriations originally designated to underwrite P.L. 94-142 (*without* adjusting for inflation). Schools have been faced with a difficult juggling act of making ends meet while serving children, meeting requirements, documenting eligibility for state and federal funds, and defending against charges of legal violations from parent and child advocates.* Furthermore, recent trends in federal government policies—cutting taxes, eliminating regulations, and reducing the education budget—suggest that funds allocated to carry out P.L. 94-142 are more likely to be reduced than increased.

Third, despite the extensive regulations designed to safeguard the rights of children and parents, P.L. 94-142 fails to adequately address the matter of assigning labels to children. Children are labeled as handicapped in the very title of the law. P.L. 94-142 requires school districts to classify children into various disability categories so that the handicapped can be counted and school districts can be reimbursed. A service delivery system does not have to operate in this manner, as demonstrated by the Chapter 766 plan in Massachusetts. Dispensing with conventional labels, the state of Massachusetts accounts for children and provides reimbursements to local districts on the basis of the services required by each child.

Shortcomings aside, P.L. 94-142 has ushered in an unprecedented era of special education services for children, and for the preschool age group in particular. By extending these services to children beginning at age 3, P.L. 94-142 brought about the creation of entire new identification and intervention programs for preschool children. P.L. 94-142 contains a clause authorizing "special incentive grants" (a maximum of $300, but actually closer to $100) to reimburse school districts above and beyond the standard per-child allotment for special education for each preschool child identified and served. Funding through P.L. 94-142 has become far and away the primary source of special services for preschool children; services which include preschool screening.

The Impact Upon Early Identification Today

What are the implications of these historical influences for identifying preschool children with special needs?

---

*In fact, one state (New Mexico) has opted to provide special educational services under its own system, thereby forfeiting federal funds, rather than be constrained by compliance with P.L. 94-142.

The early experiences/compensatory education movement has had a major, though indirect, impact upon early identification. Its contribution has been to promote (with great success) the practice of early intervention, and to demonstrate (with somewhat lesser success) its value. Identification of individual children is not a significant factor in this orientation. The early education movement emphasizes promotion of developmental growth for all children, rather than prevention of developmental problems for specifically identified children. There is no advance selection of individuals according to special needs or handicapping conditions. For compensatory education programs such as Head Start, the target population is comprised of children from low income families, regardless of level of functioning, since they are most prone to environmental deprivation and stand to benefit most from enrichment experiences.

Advocates for handicapped children have singled out as particularly important those intervention programs for preschool children with developmental problems (Cohen, Semmes, & Guralnick, 1979; Soeffing, 1974). The Bureau of Education for the Handicapped established as a major objective for the 70s the enrollment of nearly 1,000,000 preschool handicapped children in day care centers. Meanwhile various states implemented early childhood programs through the Handicapped Children's Early Education Act of 1968. Project Head Start, boosted by specially earmarked federal funds, increased the proportion of handicapped children in its programs to reach the target figure of 10 percent of the total Head Start enrollment (Ackerman & Moore, 1976). Most significant of all, inclusion of the preschool age group within P.L. 94-142 confirmed the nation's commitment to providing special services for young children.

Special services under P.L. 94-142 are targeted for children with educational handicaps. Consequently, identification is an essential component of the service delivery system. In order to actively identify children with special needs in the 3–6 age range, many school systems and other agencies involved in implementing P.L. 94-142 have adopted the screening approach. Screening programs established for this purpose have become so common that they basically define what is popularly known as preschool screening. The typical preschool screening program has the following characteristics:

1. The target population consists of children from age 3 or 4 to school entry.
2. The program is conducted or coordinated by a school district or analogous "local educational agency."
3. At least one occasion for mass screening is arranged prior to school entry.

4. While health and sensory, in addition to developmental, factors are assessed, the primary basis for identifying handicapped children is according to educational needs.

Interestingly, there is no mention of preschool screening in P.L. 94-142, even though the approach has been formally adopted in the implementation plans of some states (e.g., Minnesota). The federal law simply requires that all handicapped children "in need of special education and related services will be identified, located and evaluated." (Sec. 614a)

EPSDT has features in common with both the compensatory education and education for handicapped children movements, while approaching early identification from a rather different perspective. EPSDT serves a similar population as Head Start, with eligibility based upon family income. But services are provided only for children with identified problems, as with P.L. 94-142, and therefore EPSDT involves considerable emphasis upon individual assessment. The age range, 0–21, served by EPSDT is more inclusive than the other programs. But it is the model underlying EPSDT that makes it so distinct.

Identification of children through EPSDT is problem-oriented in accordance with the medical model, which assumes that problems in development can be detected in the same manner as childhood diseases and health problems. Central to the medical model is the notion that a clear distinction can be drawn between the presence and absence of a disease or of a problematic condition, and that this will be determined through the assessment process. Presumably, the resulting diagnosis indicates the kind of treatment that is required. The labeling of children is regarded not as a hazard, but as a necessary precondition to providing services.

The expansion of pediatric screening from health-related to psychological and educational concerns was initially hailed as an obvious improvement over narrowly defined health screening (Lessler, 1972). However, many of the assumptions of the medical model are incompatible with the nature of child development. A child's developmental status is continually changing over time. The developmental model of assessment focuses upon a child's functioning at a given time across a wide range of areas—upon strengths as well as weaknesses—rather than assuming a problem orientation. There is no clear discontinuity between levels of functioning that are problematic and not problematic; it is in relation to age expectations and to situational demands that a child's functioning may be judged to be advanced or delayed, adaptive or maladaptive.

Early identification and treatment of problems before they reach full expression is a model that applies to children's illnesses far better than it does to children's development. A young child's developmental functioning does not tend to progress from a presymptomatic to a symptomatic state as in the case of illness; spontaneous recovery from developmental problems is common among young children. As Kochanek (1980) points out,

> studies that have followed a "medical model" of disease, attempting to identify a linear relationship between cause and outcome [of developmental disabilities], have produced disappointing results. (p. 350)

Nor can we make clear distinctions between sick and well, as in the medical model:

> A condition or characteristic which may be adaptive for one person, in one set of circumstances, and at a given point in his life, may be problematic for another person at a different time, or in a different cultural milieu. (Lessler, 1972, p. 193)

Finally, tentative identification at the screening stage of a child being at risk for developmental problems cannot necessarily be confirmed or refuted by a subsequent diagnosis to determine the child's true status.

The shortcomings of applying the medical model to development are most apparent with regard to treatment issues. Once a medical problem is accurately diagnosed, the range of treatment options is typically well established and systematically prescribed. This is not the case for developmental problems, for which treatment implications of a given diagnosis are far from automatic. Developmental intervention options are widely variable in nature and cost, the most promising of which require considerable resources, and none of which guarantee results.

With its medical model focus, EPSDT legislation and guidelines concentrate on the "S" (screening) and the "D" (diagnosis) while virtually ignoring the "T" (treatment). EPSDT regulations have been spelled out in detail through successive revision and additions to the Federal Code of Regulations (Title 42, Chapter IV, part 441, Subpart B), but treatment is still described in the same general terms as the original mandate ("health care, treatment, and other measures to correct or ameliorate defects and chronic conditions") leaving the individual states to formulate policy on intervention for developmental problems.

Despite the drawbacks of assessing development using a medical model, the developmental screening approach advanced by EPSDT provided the blueprint for a new generation of early identification programs. The pediatric screening approach, which revolves around cost-effectiveness and decision-making, has been preserved virtually intact by the majority of preschool screening programs established to carry out P.L. 94-142. After all, the manner in which special services are to be delivered under P.L. 94-142 is similarly problem-oriented and follows from similar assumptions, i.e., that children can be accurately and meaningfully assigned to disability categories. School districts must make all-or-nothing decisions about whether or not children qualify for special education. It is almost as though children were being pronounced sick or well. The screening approach conceived in the medical tradition is consistent with the task of large-scale identification of problems required of school systems by P.L. 94-142. The consequence, however, is that the typical preschool screening program is plagued by the inconsistency of trying to operate under a developmental and medical model at the same time (a troublesome issue that will be taken up later in the book).

Further confusion is caused by differing conceptions as to the population to be identified and served by preschool programs. The movement to insure appropriate educational services for the handicapped initially addressed the plight of severely disabled children, the deaf, blind, mentally retarded, and autistic, who clearly require special services and educational programs. But inadequate educational programming is not limited to the extremely disabled, and more and more parents discovered that children who are floundering must be classified as exceptional in some way (if not learning disabled, then perhaps gifted) in order to receive an appropriate education. Largely due to political action by parents and other advocates, children with less pronounced needs (e.g., speech impairments and specific learning disabilities) were added to the ranks of the handicapped. This has led to major difficulties in determining whether a given child's disability is "serious enough" to qualify for special services. Although the intent of the law may have been to address the needs of the "truly handicapped," school administrators are hard pressed to draw the line when confronted by adamant parents and faced with prospects of a legal action. School systems are faced with the extraordinary task of trying to distinguish slow learners from the mentally retarded, underachievers from the learning disabled, and the maladjusted from the seriously emotionally disturbed.

Another factor affecting the character of the service population is that, for a school district, identified children translate into desperately-needed funds. While the seriously disabled often require services that cost far more than the reimbursements received, the opposite is true for the mildly disabled, which gives school districts an opportunity to break even. Pressures exist in some school districts to classify children rather liberally as eligible for services under P.L. 94-142.

Expansion of preschool services to include children with mild to moderate learning difficulties substantially changes the nature of identification programs. Preschool children with learning problems (i.e., who are delayed in such areas as language development and understanding of concepts) far outnumber preschoolers who are severely impaired by sensory deficits, physical impairments, and gross mental deficiency. Children with early learning problems are at risk for experiencing school problems sometime in the future, but this is a circumstance that may or may not come to pass. Thus, the decision to serve these children at the preschool level results in major increases in the size of the target population and introduces considerable complications in making assessment decisions.

When the focus is upon early and prospective learning problems rather than established handicapping conditions, the imperative to provide early educational services is less clear. The *school readiness model* introduces a very different perspective than the idea that early school difficulties necessitate special intervention. Proponents of the readiness model (Ilg & Ames, 1972; Moore & Moore, 1975) contend that instruction should not begin before the child is ready to learn, and that a child's cognitive and perceptual functioning must be allowed to mature before he or she is equipped to make progress in academic areas. They regard the delaying of school entry for the young child with mild learning problems as a powerful means of preventing school failure.

To summarize, the various historical influences are reflected in the current diversity of perspectives, and lack of consensus, about which children to serve and what services to provide. The early childhood education movement has stressed services for all children, or at least all children from deprived environments. Pediatric care providers focus on medically oriented services for children with developmental handicaps or neurological impairment. Special educators are mandated by P.L. 94-142 to provide a broad range of special educational and related services for handicapped children. There is least agreement of all about what to do for young children with mild or incipient learning problems—whether to place them in early intervention programs, monitor their school progress to see if problems develop, or delay their entry into the educational system.

ISSUES IN PRESCHOOL SCREENING

Is the concept of preschool screening reasonable and workable in practice? This has been seriously questioned by observers who have expressed various reservations about preschool screening. Their concerns may be summarized under four general categories: provision for follow-up services, accuracy of screening procedures, labeling and classification, and parents' rights and responsibilities.

Provision for Follow-up Services

In keeping with the objectives of early identification a screening program is obligated to provide follow-up assessment and intervention services as needed for children who are referred. Plans for providing these services must be intact before screening begins. Although a supplementary purpose of screening may be to determine prevalence of problematic conditions and the extent of services required, the capacity to do something about service shortages is an essential precondition for conducting a screening program. Gaps in service may occur unintentionally when unanticipated types of problems or numbers of problems are identified, however such gaps should be short-lived. Poor organization and insufficient funding are also factors that may lead to follow-up failures, which has been a particular problem with some early screening programs (Divoky, 1977b; Lessler, 1973). Implementation of a screening program that lacks the means to provide follow-up services constitutes irresponsible policy and practice.

Accuracy of Screening Procedures

Factors contributing to errors or to uncertainty in the early identification of developmental problems, e.g., elusiveness of definitions, unpredictability of developmental growth, short-term variability in functioning, and limitations of assessment procedures, apply to screening as well. Adequacy of assessment procedures is a particular concern at the screening level, since screening procedures are by definition less sophisticated and precise than other methods of identification. Screening procedures are administered in relatively little time, often by screening personnel with limited expertise and training. Many instruments currently available for developmental screening are relatively new and unproven, lacking in psychometric qualities, and devoid of research support (Barnes, 1982; Hobbs, 1975; Lichtenstein, 1979; Meisels, in press). Not surprisingly, critics have questioned the adequacy of existing screening procedures to carry out the functions required of them. Further controversy is introduced by questions about whether available screening procedures are equally applicable and valid for children of different geographic, socioeconomic, or cultural backgrounds (Rojcewicz & Aaronson, 1976).

Inaccurate screening procedures pose serious problems because they may lead to identification errors. Identification errors are of two types, and each has distinct consequences. The first type of error occurs when a child with problems is not identified and is therefore denied educational or related services from which he or she might benefit. The opposite type of error occurs when a child is referred erroneously for further assessment when there is no actual need for it. In addition to the cost of the unnecessary intervention, negative consequences associated with this type of error include inconvenience and possible anxiety for parents, and the prospect that the inappropriately referred child will also be inappropriately identified as handicapped.

Labeling and Classification

The typical screening program initiates a process that results in certain children being assigned labels—handicapped, mentally retarded, emotionally disturbed, hyperactive, learning disabled, etc. The potentially negative effects of labels have touched off serious objections to their institutionalized use (Adelman, 1978; Hobbs, 1975; Keogh & Becker, 1973; Mercer, 1973).

The stigma associated with being called handicapped or disabled may evoke feelings of inadequacy and shame in labeled children and their parents. Labeling may also engender maladaptive behaviors on the part of both labeled children and those who interact with them. As expressed by Adelman (1978),

> . . . it has been hypothesized that persons who are labeled and treated as different may be stigmatized, isolated and excluded from important experiences, and this may negatively affect their motivation and further hinder their full and healthy development. The hypothesis of the self-fulfilling prophecy suggests that attaching labels which connote disturbance and educational deficiency may just provide socializing agents with excuses for failure to relate to or teach a child. (p. 152)

Keogh and Becker (1973) warn that identifying children's problems at an early point in time may be particularly hazardous in that early identification may have a negative effect upon a child's course of development: hypothesizing that a child will develop problems may trigger anxieties and lower the expectations of teacher and parents.

Hobbs (1975), in his comprehensive report of the Project on Classification of Exceptional Children, reviews the rationale for and consequences of labeling. While acknowledging the above criticisms, he contends that classification of children's problems is necessary to guide public policy, to gauge the effectiveness of programs, to insure accountability for funds, and to guarantee services for individual children. Hobbs (1975) sees the need for some way of classifying children with problems, but takes serious exception to the collection of categories currently in use:

> For the purposes of programming at all levels, from the Congress to the classroom, the conventional categories and labels and procedures for arriving at them are inadequate. They are imprecise: they say too little, and they say too much. They suggest only vaguely the kind of help a child may need, and they tend to describe conditions in negative terms. Generally, negative labels affect the child's self-concept in a negative way, and probably do more harm than good. (p. 102)

> . . . to call a child retarded, disturbed, or delinquent reduces our attentiveness to changes in his development. To say that he is visually handicapped makes us unappreciative of how well he can see, and how he can be helped to see even better. Not only do subtle changes go unnoticed but even major transformations can be ignored or denied when those who would serve children become captive to categories. (p. 104)

Parents' Rights and Responsibilities

The expanding role assumed by school systems and agencies engaged in screening affects parents in several respects. One issue concerns the extent to which the family is displaced by public institutions in providing for a child's needs. The argument favoring delivery of early identification and intervention services by specialists is that parents lack the expertise to deal with significant developmental problems. The success of such programs is, however, highly dependent upon the cooperation of parents. The value of involving parents in screening, as well as in other components of early identification and intervention programs, is becoming increasingly recognized.

Parents may also be concerned about whether a screening program respects their rights and the rights of their children. Mass screening, by including all children in early identification programs, introduces issues regarding the rights of consent and confidentiality. Parental consent to screening and follow-up services for their children is a complex issue. Parents' resistance to outside interference may be due to valid concerns about the value of screening and follow-up services, but it may also be detrimental when families with pronounced needs shut out all forms of assistance. Perceived threats to their rights of privacy may be additional cause for caution on the part of parents. Screening and identification programs generally have policies designed to safeguard against improper use or release of information, as required by P.L. 94-142. Nevertheless, the sensitivity and respect for the rights of children and parents actually exercised by program personnel is the critical factor in determining whether or not this is a real cause for concern.

SUMMARY

To determine whether early identification is of value, its ultimate objective must be kept in mind: to provide effective help for those children with developmental, physical, or sensory problems that interfere with their learning and adjustment. The basic assumption that unremediated problems become more serious and more intractable over time is generally accepted. Given this assumption, the value of early identification hinges upon our ability to accurately identify children with these problems and to provide effective remedial services at an affordable cost. The evidence to date regarding the effectiveness of early educational intervention is not conclusive. Yet, there are compelling reasons as well as some encouraging evidence that lead professionals to endorse early identification and intervention, with the expectation that continuing efforts will generate more conclusive proof.

Professionals in the areas of early childhood education, pediatrics, and special education have long supported the delivery of special services for young children. Each of these movements has a unique history and a different perspective with regard to early identification and intervention. Because of the enormous impact of Public Law 94-142, the special education perspective is currently taking precedence and preschool screening programs with an educational emphasis have proliferated.

Preschool screening, which involves a multi-stage approach to large scale identification, is currently in such wide use that the term has become practically synonymous with early identification of preschool children. But the existence of a preschool screening program is no guarantee that the objectives of early identification will be met. The usefulness of preschool screening is related to several issues: availability of follow-up services, accuracy of screening procedures, effects of labeling children, and consideration for parents' rights and responsibilities. The situation has become more ambiguous in recent years as target populations are often expanded to include children with less severe and less obviously handicapping conditions. Some persons argue that it is foolhardy to extend special services to children on such a wide basis given the possible negative effects; others find it untenable to deprive children of potentially beneficial services, and note that this may result in greater long-term costs for educational and social service agencies.

What can be safely stated is that the manner in which a preschool screening program is organized and implemented will greatly affect the success with which it addresses the issues discussed thus far. And so we suspend the argument about the logic and value of preschool screening until later in the book, and address practical issues in implementation.

2

Practical Issues in Preschool Screening

The rationale for preschool screening is that some preschool children are at risk for school failure by virtue of certain characteristics of themselves or of their environments, and that these children can be identified through screening and can then be helped in a variety of ways that enhance their ability to learn in school. School systems and agencies that accepted these assumptions whole-heartedly early on established some of the first preschool screening programs; others have followed suit in response to Public Law 94-142. Preschool screening is now a fact of life in many school systems across the country. It may be instructive to first describe some of the ways it is being carried out in various locations across the country. Then we can look at the practical issues and specific questions that need to be addressed in setting up and running a preschool screening program: initial implementation, types and sources of screening information, areas of development to screen for, matters related to timing and personnel, and guidelines for testing young children.

SAMPLE SCREENING PROGRAMS

Bloomington, Minnesota

Bloomington is a suburban, predominately white community of about 80,000 in the greater Minneapolis-St. Paul area. Socioeconomically, as a group, parents are relatively well-educated and above the national average in income.

Children in Bloomington are screened at two age levels: 3–4 year olds are screened during the fall two years prior to kindergarten; 4½–5½ year olds are screened in the spring preceding kindergarten entry. Eligible children are identified through computerized census information.

The screening coordinator is a licensed school nurse. Nurses in each school contact the parents of eligible children by letter or telephone and invite them to participate. Screening is conducted at the neighborhood school.

Components of the Bloomington preschool screening include a health history questionnaire completed by the parents, immunization review, blood pressure, growth assessment, a developmental screening test, a parent report of the child's development, and vision and hearing assessment. For developmental screening of 3–4 year olds, the Developmental Indicators for the Assessment of Learning (DIAL) is used. The DIAL is administered by trained paraprofessionals except for the Communications area, which is administered by a speech and language clinician. In cases where screening with the DIAL is not possible because of the child's refusal or other reasons, the parent's in-depth report of the child's development is obtained by means of the Minnesota Child Development Inventory.

Procedures for prekindergarten developmental screening of 4½–5½ year olds depends upon whether the child was previously screened at age 3, and on the results of that screening. If the child was previously screened and passed the DIAL, the prekindergarten screening is based upon the parent's report of the child's development measured by the Minnesota Preschool Inventory. In addition to measuring development, the Minnesota Preschool Inventory provides the parent with an opportunity to report on the child's adjustment and symptoms, if any. For those children who were not previously screened or who failed the DIAL, both the DIAL and the Minnesota Preschool Inventory are obtained at the prekindergarten screening. It is important to note that the psychologist involved in screening has established Bloomington norms for the DIAL. Also, the Minnesota Child Development Inventory and the Minnesota Preschool Inventory were both originally normed in Bloomington.

For each child, there are three possible outcomes of the screening: (1) no physical problems or developmental delays are apparent, and the child passes the screening; (2) screening results are incomplete or questionable and rescreening is, therefore, indicated; (3) screening results suggest possible delays or problems, and further assessment by the child study team or other community resources is recommended.

The screening process also provides valuable information as to which students may benefit from delayed or early entrance to kindergarten.

A psychologist reviews results of the screening with parents before they leave the screening site. School social workers, speech clinicians, and nurses are also available for consultation.

Following the screening, results are discussed by the building child study team, which consists of the principal, nurse, psychologist, social worker, speech clinician, kindergarten teacher, and special education teachers.

Resource programs include a summer speech program, a parenting program sponsored by Community Education, a special education program for handicapped preschool children, and nursery school experiences.

Madison, Wisconsin

Madison is an urban community with a population of 170,000. It is the state capital and the site of the University of Wisconsin main campus. It is a predominately middle income, white collar community with nearly one-third of its labor force employed by the local, state, or federal government. The minority population is only 6 percent, and there is minimal ethnic and linguistic diversity.

The Madison Metropolitan School District has a child identification service for children from birth to age 21. The present description is limited to two programs: (1) the screening program for preschool children "who may be suspected of having a disability or handicapping condition" and (2) the kindergarten screening program. The school district operates an Early Childhood Program to serve children from birth to 6 years of age who are in need of special educational services, and efforts are made to find the eligible children as early as possible in the preschool years.

Preschool child identification is directed by a coordinator, who is a social worker, and a coordinating committee that includes the coordinator, an early childhood teacher, a speech and language clinician, and a psychologist. The coordinating committee meets monthly to review, discuss, plan, and coordinate early identification efforts within the school district.

The coordinator carries out a variety of public awareness activities. These outreach activities include media announcements, brochures, flyers, and film strips. Presentations are made to professional and parent groups on a continuous basis. A slide-tape program that describes the free services available to young developmentally delayed or high risk children has been created by an interagency coordinating committee. The school district screening staff works closely with Head Start and other preschool programs that, at any time during the school year, may refer children who are suspected of having disabilities and handicapping conditions.

For preschool children, referrals are processed throughout the year as they are received by the coordinator. The coordinator completes an intake form, schedules a screening appointment with appropriate staff persons, and sends a parent questionnaire (Minnesota Child Development Inventory) to parents for completion. Usually the initial screening contact involves a home visit by the Early Childhood Program support teacher and a speech and language clinician. A psychologist, social worker, occupational or physical therapist, or nurse may also be involved. Sometimes the intitial screening or an additional observation is scheduled in a day care center, nursery school/preschool, or hospital, depending upon the individual circumstances.

During the screening visit, the child is administered the Developmental Activities Screening Inventory, the Peabody Picture Vocabulary Test, and/or the Goldman Fristoe Articulation Test. The screening tests administered vary with the suspected delay areas and the age of the child. The screening staff explains the screening procedures to parents and responds to any questions they may have. The results of the evaluation, including the developmental questionnaire, are shared immediately following the testing. If a child demonstrates suspected delay, a referral is made for further assessment by a multidisciplinary team.

For children entering kindergarten, screening is done annually, either in the spring before or in the first month of kindergarten. This screening is intended to provide teachers with developmental information about all children, not only those at risk. As screening information it provides only an initial overview of the child's strengths and weaknesses.

The kindergarten screening instrument administered individually to each child was developed by the Madison Metropolitan School District by kindergarten teachers, psychologists, and speech and language clinicians. The items provide a sample of a child's emerging skills in academic readiness, cognitive development, speech and language development, and fine motor development. It is important to note that the screening instrument is not diagnostic, not a measure of school achievement, not to be used for excluding children from school, and not a tool for predicting who will fail. Administration and scoring can be completed in approximately 30 minutes.

Each school in the district screens its own kindergarten students using support staff and kindergarten teachers from the building. Release time is available for teachers to screen children in their class-rooms, compile screening results, consult with team members about meeting individual needs of students, and plan for various academic groups within the classroom. Districtwide support staff are also avail-able to assist teachers and the school team in compiling and interpret-ing screening data.

Usually it is the child's performance on the screening instrument that initially alerts the teacher to an area of suspected disability. The child who is suspected of having a disability or handicapping condition is referred for an evaluation by a multidisciplinary team. The teacher's observations of the child in the natural environment of the classroom contribute to this evaluation. If the child is identified by the multi-disciplinary team as having special educational needs, parents are then offered a placement for the child in an appropriate educational program.

A related program of interest is the Mini-Kindergarten evaluation. The Mini-Kindergarten is a program designed to assess children's readiness for kindergarten. Most participants are children with birth-dates in August, September, October, and November whose parents are considering delaying their school entry for a year. During the three days of Mini-Kindergarten, the children experience a typical kindergarten program, including free play, song and rhythm activities, directed art projects, snack, group discussions, stories, and recess. Two profes-sional staff members, a psychologist and a speech and language clini-cian, in addition to the teacher observe in each classroom. The observers watch for social, language, listening, and direction-following skills. Each child is also given the school district's screening instru-ment to assess individual skills.

At the end of each day, the classroom team discusses each of the children. On the third day, a decision is made regarding each child's readiness for kindergarten. Recommendations are shared with parents during a conference at the end of the week. If the recommendation is made for the child to wait a year, it is usually because of immaturity. If a child has special needs that a year of growth will not remedy, parents are encouraged to enter the child in school and get additional help within the school environment.

Holyoke, Massachusetts

Massachusetts has pioneered in the area of special education since 1972 when Chapter 766, the state's Comprehensive Special Education Law, was adopted with the purpose of providing for a flexible and uniform system of special education program opportunities for all children requiring special education. (Chapter 766, in large part, provided a model for federal policy mandated by Public Law 94-142.) Recognizing that 3 and 4 year olds have been underserved, Massachusetts also established the Early Childhood Project to encourage school systems to develop programs for young children in need and to create screening and outreach services in order to identify these children. One of the early identification/intervention systems that developed with this support is in Holyoke, Massachusetts.

Holyoke is a city of 45,000 located in the western part of the state in the Connecticut River Valley region. From 1880 to 1950, jobs in the textile and paper industries attracted various immigrant populations to the city, first the Irish, then the French Canadian, and finally the Polish. While this population has declined with the loss of industry, a new immigrant population, primarily Puerto Rican, has been drawn to the city since the mid-60s by the availability of inexpensive housing. The total school enrollment is expected to continue to increase through 1985, with minority pupils (Puerto Rican and black) accounting for over half of the elementary enrollment.

A substantial part of the Holyoke program revolves around the cooperative interagency effort orchestrated by the Holyoke Public Schools. At the E. N. White Early Childhood Center, the school system operates six special half-day classes for both "special needs" and "non-special needs" children ages 3–5; a Head Start classroom includes some special needs children (that is, not the entire class); and the Department of Mental Health runs an early intervention class for special needs infants and toddlers. The mainstreaming of several special education students is an incidental purpose of the classes as a special service. A resource room to provide additional support services to children ages 3–6 is also at the center. This arrangement allows children to be placed in any of several classes, or a combination of classes at the center. Under this model, the transition of students from one class to another is facilitated by communication between teachers and by consistency in support services. To further support the early childhood service program, the center had added a parent room and parent/professional library staffed by specially-trained parents.

Screening of 3–5 year olds is done at the request of parents. In May and September, the local newspaper publicizes that parents of children ages 3–5 who suspect that their child may have a speech, physical, emotional, or learning problem may have their child screened by the Holyoke Public Schools. The school system also conducts informational meetings for representatives of local social agencies (e.g., Children's Protective Services, Welfare, Office for Children, Head Start, Migrant Program Day Care Center) and for community professionals

who provide speech, hearing, and pediatric services. Services for preschool children are described to this group, the referral process is
explained, and questions about programs and services are answered.

Preschool children who are brought in to be screened are given a
physical exam, vision and hearing screening, an informal speech and
language assessment, and an individual screening test (the Cooperative
Preschool Inventory). If it is determined that they need to be referred
for further assessment, they are placed on a "diagnostic educational
plan" that runs for 8 weeks. During this time, the child spends five half-
day sessions per week in one of the preschool special needs classes,
and is both observed informally in the classroom and individually
tested by a team of specialists. As needed, this team might include the
classroom teacher, psychologist, speech therapist, occupational therapist, and physical therapist. Also, a guidance counselor, working together with the parent, does a developmental history of the child. At
the end of the diagnostic period, the team meets to determine which
classroom or what services would be most appropriate for the child,
and to devise an individualized educational plan.

A separate, but similar, identification process takes place upon
school entry. Kindergarten screening is conducted for both public and
private school children in September and October. The following elements are included:

1. Child's health and development history, obtained from parents.
2. Comprehensive health assessment, including physical examin-
    ation.
3. Vison and hearing screening.
4. Perceptual-motor functioning in practical tasks and activities.
5. Language functioning, by a speech therapist.
6. Developmental screening, using the Cooperative Preschool
    Inventory.

In January the screening program coordinators return to each school
and review the results with the kindergarten teachers and school
principals.

The kindergarten screening places much emphasis upon parent
involvement. Included among the data obtained from parents by questionnaire and interview are developmental milestones, results of previous evaluations, history of special services or treatments received,
and a current description of the child. Various steps are taken to insure
that parents are fully involved in and informed about the screening
program:

•   Parents are given advance information about the screening pro-
    gram. Special orientation sessions are also arranged for this
    purpose.

- Parents are told what a screening test consists of, its rationale, how it fits into the school system's overall program, who will perform the screening, how confidentiality will be respected, and how results will be communicated.
- Any screening or assessment may be waived if the parents arrange, at their expense, for the results of an equivalent screening or assessment to be presented to the school.
- The results of the screening are discussed with the child's parents and the kindergarten teacher and, in special cases, with the principal and guidance counselor as well. A feedback letter, to which parents may respond, is also sent.
- If the kindergarten teacher and parent both disagree with the screening results or otherwise believe that the child should not be referred for further assessment, the screening recommendation is suspended. Further screening information is then collected during a subsequent period in which the kindergarten teacher and parents observe the behavior in question.

The programs just described illustrate how school systems or agencies may vary in their approaches to screening and to providing preschool services. Programs differ in terms of the age ranges and populations they serve, and in the types of services they provide. Some are more precise and quantitative than others in the screening procedures they use. Program features such as outreach, location, time of year, and personnel may vary. Differences may also be noted in the scope and nature of the resource networks that programs have developed.

However, some common themes are evident among programs that have both a real commitment to early identification and the organizational maturity to carry it out. First and foremost, a preschool screening program needs to be integrated within an overall service network. The most effective preschool screening programs are products of cooperation between various professionals within a school system, collaboration among various agencies, and involvement of parents. Clear goals, careful planning, and commitment by the professionals involved are also prerequisites for a successful screening program.

STEPS IN IMPLEMENTATION

Putting together an effective preschool screening program requires thoughtful and systematic planning. A lot of grief and wasted effort can be avoided by following the steps outlined in Table 2-1.

The first step taken is the appointment of a coordinator. As sug-

Table 2-1
Steps in Implementation

Appointing a coordinator
Creating a planning group
General planning
  Purpose
  Population

Specific planning
  Outreach
  Coordination with other agencies, programs, professionals
  Content
  Screening procedures
  Time and place
  Personnel/training

Screening
  Collecting data
  Interpretation: making screening decisions
  Reporting results
  Follow-up

Evaluating screening program and procedures

gested in the preceding section, the individual's professional identification should not be an issue in selection. The first prerequisite is that the coordinator should have considerable knowledge about, and understanding of, young children and their parents. A second key qualification is the ability to function effectively within a larger system: to coordinate a new program that may not be initially understood or accepted by others in the system; to work effectively with colleagues, with parents, and with other agencies, and to welcome their input; and to be able to effect changes in the screening process while at the same time maintaining a stable and supportive structure.

The diversity of expertise required to implement a screening program calls for the formation of a planning group. Ideally, the planning group as a whole should have special knowledge in the following areas: (1) the community, community resources, and public communication network, (2) administrative operations within the school system or agency, (3) young children, child development, and developmental problems, (4) early child education and special education, (5) psychological and educational measurement and evaluation, and (6) communication with parents.

The next step involves clarification of general objectives, including specification of the purposes of screening and of the population to be served. These two items are intimately related; the purpose defines the population. School systems differ in their interpretations of federal and state mandates to identify preschool children with handicapping conditions, and some have chosen to provide services well beyond the minimum required. The purpose might be to identify those children with suspected serious handicaps at the earliest possible time, or to identify 3–5 year olds experiencing lesser development problems or environmental deprivation, or to provide all parents of 3–5 year olds with a summary of and recommendations regarding their child's developmental progress. Consequently, screening might be provided only to parents who suspect their children have serious problems, or to all parents and children in particular neighborhoods, or to all parents of children in a given age range.

Once the overall orientation of the program is established, many specific elements of the screening process must be planned. The first such element, outreach, was described in the previous chapter as a separate stage that is an essential prerequisite to screening. Outreach communication makes parents and professionals in the community aware of the screening program, its nature and content, and eligibility for services. Various means of disseminating this information may be used: brochures or letters sent by mail (a school census, if available, makes this more cost-effective), articles in local newspapers and newsletters, posters, radio and TV announcements, notices to other agencies (e.g., community health centers) and service programs (e.g., Head Start, preschools, and day care centers), and of course word of mouth. One economical and effective method is to send notices home with schoolchildren directed to both their parents and to their neighbors with no children yet in school. Zehrbach (1975) reported greater success in response to notices delivered by schoolchildren and to a direct telephone survey, while agency contacts yielded limited returns. Kurtz, Neisworth, and Laub (1977), in their review of the research, noted that outreach efforts involving direct and personal contact with parents are far more effective than mass media announcements. Clearly, the nature of outreach communications sets the context and atmosphere for screening. How parents construe the purpose and process of screening will ultimately determine the success or failure of outreach efforts.

Planning may involve coordination with other agencies or service programs. The school system or agency operating the screening program may need assistance to cover areas that go beyond developmental screening, e.g., hearing, vision, and medical screening. Furthermore, the intervention services to be offered must be as comprehensive as the screening program. Other agencies or service providers may be in the best position to deliver the intervention services required by children identified as having special needs. These collaborative arrangements should be established early in the planning process.

Other matters to be worked out by the planning group include the focus and content of screening procedures, sources of information, time and place of screening, and personnel selection and training. The many practical issues introduced by these matters are the subject of the remainder of this chapter. Special attention should also be devoted to planning the role of parents, which screening procedures to use, and how to interpret screening results to arrive at a screening decision. Parent involvement, characteristics of specific screening procedures, the decision-making process, and evaluation of screening results are covered at length in the four chapters that follow.

TYPES OF SCREENING INFORMATION

Decisions must be made about the types of screening information to be gathered. For example, screening can focus exclusively on the child's present functioning or it can include historical data regarding past functioning (e.g., medical history, developmental milestones). In addition, there are a wide variety of disabilities and handicapping conditions that may or may not be targets for identification. For example, some disabilities are more likely to affect the child in his or her everyday interactions with the environment (e.g., motoric problems), while others are more relevant to the child's functioning in the school setting (e.g., short attention span).

Three general types of information relevant to preschool screening are reviewed: physical and sensory functioning, environmental influences, and developmental functioning.

Physical and Sensory Functioning

Handicapping conditions of early childhood that are directly related to physical and sensory impairment (e.g., orthopedic impairment, cerebral palsy, spina bifida, epilepsy, hydrocephaly, hearing or vision loss, etc.) account for approximately 8 percent of the total number receiving services under Public Law 94-142; this is over 300,000 children (Office of Special Education, 1980). Typically, children with such problems are first identified as needing services by health care professionals. Physical and sensory impairments also tend to limit one's capacity to interact with the environment, and therefore these children are highly likely to be at an educational disadvantage. However, when a child has a physical or sensory impairment, it is not a certainty that educational intervention is warranted. A child who has adjusted well to using a hearing aid or wheelchair may be able to meet all the essential demands of a regular school setting. Thus, while physical or sensory impairment is meaningful in terms of the child being at risk, it constitutes an educationally handicapping condition only when functioning that is related to school performance is affected.

Past as well as current health factors may be included in assessment. Highly abnormal physical, neurological, or sensory conditions that affect a child at birth or early in life (e.g., viral infections, dietary deficiencies, birth trauma, metabolic disorders, severe childhood diseases) greatly increase the risk that a child will have subsequent developmental problems (Rubin & Balow, 1980; Denhoff, Hainsworth, & Hainsworth, 1972; Zinkus, & Gottlieb, 1980). There are also certain conditions of a less apparent nature that may disrupt a child's processing of information from the environment, thereby interfering with early sensory experiences essential for development and organization of mental functions. The most notable example of this is chronic otitis media, an infection of the middle ear. Gottlieb, Zinkus, and Thompson (1979) found that children with a history of chronic otitis media have a disproportionately high incidence of learning disabilities. Their study documents the detrimental effect of early hearing loss upon language development in particular, and shows this to be a function of auditory processing deficits.

Behavior patterns that are secondary to physical or sensory problems may also have a negative impact upon a child's development. A child whose auditory reception is repeatedly disrupted due to ear infections during the formative years may develop poor listening habits that continue even after the medical problem ceases. As another example, it is not uncommon for orthopedically handicapped children to "learn" not to look after their own needs because parents or other persons feel obligated to do so for them.

While a medical history is certainly an important part of a comprehensive developmental assessment, its value for preschool screening is not so clear. The statistically significant relationship demonstrated between historical information and school performance applies for entire groups of children, but as Rubin and Balow (1980) note, "the relationships are not strong enough to support individual predictions" (p. 341). The strength of this relationship is greatly limited by the tendency for infants and young children to spontaneously recover or shift in the direction of normalcy in the course of their development (McCall, 1981). Thus, for children identified as high risk due to early medical factors, the likelihood of later developmental problems may be increased, but generally not to the point where problematic outcomes are assured or even highly probable. For example, Rubin and Balow (1980) found that infants with clearly abnormal neurological exam results were well above the group average in their incidence of IQ scores in the retarded range (i.e., below 70) at age 7, yet this significantly high incidence rate for at risk infants was only 1 in 6. A ten year follow-up of a pregnancy study on the Hawaiian island of Kauai (Werner, Bierman, & French, 1971) revealed that children experiencing severe perinatal stress had school achievement problems at a rate of 58 percent, but the rate for children in this population with no perinatal stress was 44 percent.

While it has been traditional to obtain a medical history, often a lengthy one, in the course of preschool screening, this practice needs to be reconsidered. The presence of early trauma, severe illness, or physical problems in the child's medical history does not enable any conclusions to be drawn, although it does alert professionals to look carefully at the child and perhaps at particular areas of functioning. This suggests that medical history may be relevant as a pre-screening variable; that is, as a basis for defining a high risk population for selective screening. Otherwise, however, the time spent on obtaining a medical history might be better spent on an examination of the child's *current* physical and sensory status.

The extent to which examination of current health conditions should be incorporated into preschool screening introduces several issues. The rate at which a particular medical or physical problem exists undetected in the preschool population may be too low to warrant the expense of using procedures for direct screening. Difficult decisions arise in situations where enormous benefit may follow from early identification of children with a rare medical problem, but a thousand or perhaps ten thousand children must be screened to identify each case. Convincing arguments could be made to screen for one or two such conditions, but in actuality there are a multitude of such medical and physical problems, of which only a limited number can practically be included in a health screening program (such as EPSDT), and even fewer in a preschool screening program with a developmental focus.

Health-related screening tests can be justified for inclusion in the typical preschool screening program in order to identify conditions that (1) are relatively common in the screening population, (2) allow sufficient lead time between onset and obvious manifestation to make early identification worthwhile, (3) are relevant to school functioning, and (4) have implications for available treatment. The two health-related conditions that clearly fulfill these criteria are vision and hearing impairment. Screening for vision and hearing impairment is a natural accompaniment to developmental screening, first, because intact sensory perception is essential to a child's functioning in school and, second, because it is a necessary prerequisite to insure that direct testing of a child is valid.

Other health conditions may also fulfill the criteria above, depending upon the focus and resources of a given screening program. Even then, time and organizational constraints may make it unfeasible to incorporate all prospective tests and procedures into a single screening occasion. A second screening date may be needed if screening is to include comprehensive coverage of both health and developmental areas. Another alternative is for physical examinations to be done separately through existing medical or community health care resources.

Environmental Influences

Environmental influences upon the young child, particularly the care, attention, stimulation, and discipline provided in the home, exert a significant ongoing impact upon a child's functioning. The extent to which a child's home environment influences early at risk status was demonstrated by Werner, Bierman, and French (1971) in the book *Children of Kauai*. These researchers found that early ratings of home environment, which included socioeconomic status (SES), educational stimulation, and emotional support, were significantly related to learning and behavior problems at age 10. Interestingly, the relationship between SES and later learning and behavior problems was "not as pronounced as the association with the other environmental ratings— educational stimulation and emotional support in the home" (Werner et al., 1971, p. 69). Educational stimulation was the environmental factor most related to achievement problems, and emotional support was the factor most related to behavior problems. The study also revealed that environmental influences moderated the long-term effects of perinatal stress. Children exposed to perinatal stress who were from homes rated high in educational stimulation scored above the group mean on a measure of ability at age 10, while children with perinatal stress from educationally disadvantaged homes performed substantially below the mean. The implication of these findings is that two young children who appear to be functioning at a similar level but are in substantially different home environments should not be regarded similarly. The child from a deprived home environment is at greater risk than the children from an adequate home environment.

Recent research is beginning to elaborate upon the nature of environmental factors that affect cognitive and educational functioning. In particular, Caldwell and Bradley's work with the Home Observation for Measurement of the Environment (HOME) Inventory has greatly contributed to our understanding of these factors. The HOME Inventory (Caldwell & Bradley, in press) is an observation and interview procedure for evaluating a child's environment in the course of a home visit. There are two levels of the HOME Inventory, one for children from birth to age 3, and a preschool inventory for ages 3–6. The 6 subscales of the birth to 3 version are (1) Emotional and Verbal Responsivity of Mother, (2) Avoidance of Restriction and Punishment, (3) Organization of the Physical and Temporal Environment, (4) Provision of Appropriate Play Materials, (5) Maternal Involvement with the Child, and (6) Opportunities for Variety in Daily Stimulation. The preschool HOME Inventory consists of eight subscales: (1) Stimulation through Toys, Games, and Reading Materials, (2) Language Stimulation, (3) Physical Environment: Safe, Clean and Conducive to Development, (4) Pride, Affection, and Warmth, (5) Stimulation of Academic Behavior, (6) Modeling and Encouragement of Social Maturity, (7) Variety of Stimulation, and (8) Physical Punishment.

In a study by Bradley, Caldwell, and Elardo (1977), the HOME was administered at age 2 and the Stanford-Binet Intelligence Scale at age 3 to a racially mixed sample of 105 children. HOME Inventory variables were more predictive of IQ than were SES variables for the sample, particularly for the 68 black children in the sample, which led to the conclusion that "measures of specific environmental processes are more strongly associated with cognitive development than are measures of social status" (p. 699).

Another study (Bradley & Caldwell, 1979) with the HOME Inventory provided validity data for the preschool scale. This research goes beyond just making the case to intervene through the child's home environment, and begins to pinpoint the environmental aspects to be targeted. Of the HOME Inventory subscales, Stimulation through Toys, Games, and Reading Material had the highest correlation with both SES variables and Stanford-Binet IQ. Correlations between these subscales and IQ ranged from .47 to .55. High correlations with IQ at age 4½ were also obtained for Variety of Stimulation ($r = .51$), Stimulation of Academic Behavior ($r = .47$), and Language Stimulation ($r = .40$). These findings support the importance of early stimulation and enrichment experiences for cognitive development.

Clearly, there is much reason to consider information relating to family influences and the home environment as part of an assessment of a young child. Family-related factors are particularly important to assess when considering intervention that focuses upon the home environment. But it is another question as to when home environment data can and should be directly assessed at the screening level. Demographic variables (e.g., SES, race, social class, geographic data) that, because of their relationship to home environment factors, have some predictive value for early identification are more accessible than observations of or reports about the home environment. Given both the economic constraints upon making home visits and issues relating to privacy, obtaining demographic data may be a more feasible, although indirect, approach to estimating environmental factors for screening purposes. In fact, demographic data available at birth, such as race, SES, and the month at which prenatal care began, have been shown to be significantly related to educational status in first grade (Ramey, Stedman, Borders-Patterson, & Mengel, 1978). As indicated by Bradley, Caldwell, and Elardo (1977), however, demographic variables disregard a significant amount of within-group variation.

Common practice in current screening programs is to disregard both demographic and family-related factors. In addition to economic considerations, there are frequently concerns about possible misuse or misinterpretation of such data. School administrators typically elect not to collect such sensitive information, and parents may opt not to provide it when given the choice.

At least the economic constraints upon assessment of the home environment have been addressed by one recent screening instrument. The Home Screening Questionnaire (Coons, Gay, Fandal, Ker, & Frankenburg, 1981), a parent report measure adapted from the HOME Inventory, can be quickly completed by a parent at the screening site. Initial research (Coons, et. al., 1981) has shown a high correlation between results obtained with the Home Screening Questionnaire and the HOME Inventory. Subsequent findings should be of great interest.

Family factors play a significant role in a child's development; of this, there is no doubt. However, since we are particularly concerned with the resultant impact upon development, one might propose to simply measure a child's developmental functioning with the understanding that the findings are a product of both characteristics of the child and of his or her environment. To some extent this holds true, and information about developmental functioning may suffice by itself. However, this logic has its limitations. The influence of the home environment not only shapes the child's development through the present time, but can be expected to continue exerting a significant impact. The result, as shown by Werner et. al. (1971), is that assessment data concerning a child's developmental status may take on a different meaning when considered together with information about the home environment.

Developmental Functioning

Collecting information about the developmental functioning of the young child is central to the process of preschool screening. Whatever physical/sensory impairments or environmental obstacles a child may have to contend with, the child's capacity for developmental growth and learning is a major determinant of success or failure at school.

Development refers to a number of things. It can be used to describe the orderly sequence of behaviors, from simple to complex, that emerge and are displayed by most normal children over a period of time. At a more subtle level, it refers to the underlying, evolving mental processes including representation, memory, reasoning, judgment, and many others. At another level, it refers to the processes that contribute to, or interfere with, the emergence of the developmental functions. The developmental perspective views these processes longitudinally, in an effort to understand how these phenomena unfold over a period of time. Understanding these factors increases the chances that we can do something about them.

A developmental approach provides a systematic way of looking at the behavior and progress of young children. Developmental norms provide guidelines as to what should be expected of the "typical" child at different age levels. At any given age, some children are accelerated and others are delayed in their development. We characterize the level of a child's functioning by comparing his or her development with age expectations. A child whose language skills at age 5 are more characteristic of a 3–4 year old would be called developmentally delayed in this respect. Developmental instruments frequently express results in terms of functional level relative to age level. In fact, this was the original meaning of IQ: a quotient, or ratio, of mental age to chronological age.

Not only do children differ developmentally from one another, but an individual child's rate of development may proceed unevenly over time. McCall (1981), in describing this phenomenon, notes that individual differences are particularly unstable during the early months of life:

> The result is that infants who are advanced early in life may or may not be advanced a few months later; and by the same token, infants who are developmentally delayed early in life may or may not be delayed later. (p. 15)

The implication of this is that future development is not easily predicted from a child's status at an early age.

Development is multidimensional. This means that a child may be delayed with respect to motor development; at age level in cognitive and language functioning; and advanced in terms of social development. We speak of different dimensions, or areas, of development in order to characterize the various aspects of a child's development. A model outlining different areas of development is helpful not only for organizing our understanding of development, but for determining what to assess.

The content and structure of a developmental model depend on the age period under consideration. As an example: acquisition of psychomotor skills, a critical area of development during the first year of life, is overshadowed by language development in the immediately following years, which in turn becomes secondary in importance to symbolic and abstract thinking. In the following section, a set of developmental areas that are meaningful at preschool age level is outlined.

Before taking a closer look at developmental functions, an important and perhaps familiar point should be brought out. Environmental influences and developmental functions have been considered separately to this point, yet each by itself is insufficient to account for school problems. Handicapped or disability status depends upon the interaction between what the child brings to a situation and the nature and demands of that situation. A child may be fully functional in the home environment, but encounter problems in a classroom environment where unfamiliar skills and behavior patterns are required. Furthermore, different classroom environments make different demands upon a child in terms of cognitive skills, attention, motor control and inhibition (i.e., sitting still), independence, and social maturity. Thus, a child may be handicapped or disabled in one situation, but not in another. Given that there is no single environment in which all children will fare best, assessment of child-environment interactions has major implications for intervention. The assessment process, in addition to establishing whether a child is in need of special services, should determine what kind of educational services and educational environment matches his or her particular needs. For this reason, assessment of the child's behavior in various situations, and in a classroom situation in particular, is of great importance. (The fact that information about a preschool child's behavior in a classroom environment is not routinely available imposes a serious limitation upon preschool screening.)

AREAS OF DEVELOPMENT

There is no one ideal way to separate developmental abilities into distinct and non-overlapping categories. Many different sets of developmental categories have been devised, each similar in some respects and different in others. A fairly typical breakdown of developmental functioning at the preschool age level is presented in this section. While this taxonomy of seven broad areas is highly simplified and general, it provides a useful outline for describing various aspects of development and the relationships between them.

Cognitive

This area encompasses a wide range of mental abilities that are often subsumed under the rubric of "intelligence," which (to gloss over a venerable history of theorizing by cognitive psychologists) implies some sort of general mental efficiency or capacity. This is best represented by mental activities that involve reasoning (e.g., association, classification, seriation), judgment, memory, and understanding of concepts. Easily-tested tasks that reflect cognitive development at the preschool age level include sorting or matching by shape, color, and size; naming letters, numbers, and colors; identifying similarities and differences; repeating digits, words, or phrases from memory; defining words; and completing analogies (e.g., "Brother is a boy; sister is a ....").

The substantial verbal component of many of these tasks should be noted. Piaget emphasized the importance of language during the *preoperational* phase of cognitive development (from approximately 2–6 years of age), in that language enables the child to attach labels to objects and experiences and thus to begin to think in symbolic terms. To exclude verbal tasks from assessment of the cognitive area in order to get a "pure" measure of cognitive functioning (that is, apart from language) would be inappropriate, since cognitive functioning and language development are so closely associated. Accordingly, similar results are typically obtained when administering general cognitive and language measures to preschool children.

Language

Language is difficult to distinguish from the cognitive area, since a major part of cognitive functioning involves processing of verbal material and relies upon comprehension of language. While it is not possible to obtain a pure measure of language, certain tasks place greater emphasis upon language relative to other cognitive factors, e.g., sentence repetition, defining words, providing words to identify objects or to complete sentences, and following instructions.

Language functioning can be divided into two general components: *receptive* language, which involves decoding and comprehension of verbal material, and *expressive* language, the formulation and expression of thoughts in verbal form. The decoding aspect of receptive language may be regarded as encompassing perceptual processes such as auditory reception and discrimination, which are prerequisites for higher order processing of verbal information. Expressive language pertains to aspects of verbal output, such as syntax, grammar, and word use. Expressive language may be assessed by analyzing a child's speech for sentence length, complexity, and grammatical features. As a rule, a young child's expressive language capabilities lag far behind what he or she is able to comprehend.

Speech/Articulation

Speech is often classified as part of the same category as language. The connection seems quite natural, and is further reinforced by the fact that speech and language together constitute an area of specialization for a professional group (i.e., speech and language clinicians). However, speech and language are two rather distinct aspects of verbal communication. Speech involves the child's proficiency at producing desired speech patterns so as to be comprehensible to others. A sample of speech may represent highly sophisticated use of language, yet be delivered in a barely intelligible manner.

The primary component of speech is articulation, the accurate formation of sounds. Two other components of speech are voice (i.e., quality, pitch, and intensity of vocal production) and rhythm, which when highly irregular is known as stuttering. Specific components of articulation and speech production can be assessed in isolation. However, the primary concern is the general, nontechnical question, "How intelligible is the child?" As long as the young child is capable of communicating and of developing more mature speech over time, it could be argued that minor speech distortions are not of consequence. Kirk (1962) characterizes speech problems in such socially-mediated terms:

> . . . it is generally accepted that any speech which deviates from the average so far as to draw unfavorable attention to the speaker, whether through unpleasant sound, inappropriateness to the age level, or lack of intelligibility, may be classified as defective. (p. 294)

Fine Motor

Fine motor development primarily refers to a child's eye-hand coordination and control over fine muscles. The preschool child uses these skills in tasks such as drawing and coloring, building with blocks,

and cutting with scissors. However, fine motor is something of a mis-
nomer since the term is also applied to tasks such as copying shapes
and drawing human figures, which involve complex cognitive/percep-
tual processes in addition to motor output. (These processes are referred to by various names such as sensorimotor integration, motor
planning, visual-spatial ability, and visual-motor integration.) This constellation of skills and abilities is related to a child's readiness to
embark upon reading and writing activities.

Gross Motor

In the course of actively exploring the environment and exercising
new-found physical capabilities, children develop their large muscles
and gain increasing control over their bodies. From the age of 2, they
attempt increasingly complex movement patterns such as climbing,
running, throwing, hopping, and skipping. At the preschool age level, a
variety of tasks can be used as indicators of gross motor control and
coordination: walking backwards, up and down steps, and heel-to-toe;
hopping and balancing on one foot; and catching and throwing a ball. It
is not uncommon for gross motor skills to be uneven at preschool ages,
that is, for the child to have mastered certain feats and not others at a
comparable level of difficulty.

Self-help

Adaptive behaviors related to self-care and survival, e.g., feeding,
toilet training, washing, dressing and undressing, crossing the street,
handling money, avoiding safety hazards, come increasingly under the
child's control with gains in motoric and cognitive functioning. An
additional component that affects self-help skills is that of attitude: the
child must have not only the capacity, but the inclination to engage in
these activities. There is a natural tendency for children to want to be
independent and to exert their control over the environment. This,
combined with basic motoric and cognitive skills, enables most children to master a wide range of self-help skills by the time of school
entry. Self-help is one area of functioning that is of diminished importance beyond preschool age, since all but severely disabled children
master basic self-help skills by this time.

Social-Emotional

Evidence increasingly indicates that the foundation for healthy
adjustment begins to form during infancy, as the child develops a basic
sense of trust in others and security within the environment. The

ability to separate from parents is one indicator of social-emotional adjustment that is frequently associated with the quality of early attachments. Other socialization experiences throughout early childhood shape a child's behavior: a child learns to adhere to rules and expectations, develops a sense of right and wrong, and begins to relate to persons outside the family. Inate characteristics also account for individual differences in social-emotional functioning. Individual differences in such behaviors as social responsiveness, frustration level, reactivity, and activity level are apparent almost from birth.

Behaviors that are suggestive of social-emotional problems at the preschool level include frequent temper tantrums, excessively high activity level, passivity, withdrawal from interpersonal contact, extreme aggressiveness or disobedience, bizarre verbalizations, excessive worrying or crying, and persistent sad affect. The difficulties in identifying problematic social-emotional functioning should be apparent, given that instances of the above behaviors are displayed by all young children at one time or another. These behaviors become cause for concern when observed too frequently or, according to Bower's (1981) formulation of emotional disturbance, "to a marked degree over a period of time" (p. 115), but these subjective judgments may be difficult for professionals as well as parents to agree upon.

More detailed description of these developmental areas and guidelines for comprehensive assessment may be found in *The Psychoeducational Assessment of Preschool Children* (Paget & Bracken, 1982). In addition to cognitive abilities, language and communication, gross motor, perceptual-motor/fine motor, and social emotional development, this book also includes chapters on adaptive behavior, auditory and visual functioning, and neuropsychological assessment.

Two general categories, in addition to those described in this section, that are deserving of special attention are *perceptual and integrative processing* and *school readiness*. Since these categories cut across other areas of development, they are being discussed separately.

Perceptual and Integrative Processing

This category may best be described from a neurological perspective. Information received by the senses must be conveyed and integrated, without distortion, through complex brain circuitry before it is available for higher-order mental operations such as reading and writing. A child may see a shape or letter perfectly well, but be unable to distinquish it from similar ones. Or, a child with fully intact hearing may be unable to discriminate between two similar sounding words. These are skills that develop over time and with practice for most children, as a first grade teacher can testify; but not for all children, as teachers of children with specific learning disabilities can verify.

A child develops the capacity for increasingly complex perceptual and integrative processing over time. The typical preschool child will have difficulty distinguishing left and right, copying a complex design, blending isolated sounds to form a word, or distinguishing whether intricate designs are similar or different. Poor processing relative to age expectations might be due to developmental immaturity, to limited stimulation experiences, or may simply reflect individual differences in neurological functioning. In rare cases, severe processing deficits may be indicative of organic neurological problems that require medical attention.

Perceptual and integrative processes are difficult to clearly distinguish from other developmental areas because they are essential elements of, or prerequisites for, various developmental functions. In the breakdown of developmental areas just presented, these processes were included under the areas with which they are most closely associated: auditory processing was included under receptive language, visual-motor integration was subsumed under fine motor, visual discrimination of shapes and patterns was characterized as a part of cognitive functioning, etc.

School Readiness

Another category that is often distinguished in the assessment of preschool children is that of school readiness. Rather than a distinct area, school readiness subsumes a wide range of skills and behavior that are related to the demands of a school setting. Typically, school readiness tests include cognitive, language, and fine motor tasks: copying of shapes or figures; concepts such as same-different, size, and color; knowledge of numbers and letters, etc. Some also include tasks of perceptual processing (e.g., left-right orientation, auditory and visual discrimination), gross motor development, and general knowledge.

Another general dimension of school readiness concerns attentional, attitudinal, and interpersonal characteristics that determine how well a child will adapt to classroom demands such as complying with directions, working independently, paying attention, and cooperating in groups. The interaction between the child and situational demands is typically assessed through behavioral data. Readiness measures that rely upon reports of parents and of preschool and kindergarten teachers have been designed to assess such behaviors.

Three main distinctions may be made between school readiness measures and developmental instruments. First is the theoretical orientation of the user. Proponents of the school readiness model use readiness measures to assess whether a child has reached a level of functioning that is adequate for entering school or for beginning academic instruction (see Ilg & Ames, 1972). They might conclude that a low-scoring child needs more time to mature and recommend delaying of kindergarten entry. Another professional might administer a developmental measure—with nearly the identical content—but interpret the results to indicate that the child has developmental deficits that require special attention in an educational program.

A second distinction, also more theoretical than real in terms of actual instruments, is that school readiness measures do not purport to cover the full range of developmental functions, but only those most relevant to school performance. However, school relevance is subject to great differences in interpretation. While some associate readiness for school with measures of "current skill achievement and performance" (Meisels, 1978, p. 7), others see the focus as being on "academic and social characteristics . . . that are predictive of the future acquisition of reading and arithmetic skills" (Telegdy, 1974, p. 127). Given the wide diversity of content covered by various school readiness measures, efforts to make clear content distinctions between developmental and school readiness measures appear to be futile.

The third distinction, and the one of greatest practical significance, is that school readiness measures are designed for a relatively narrow skill level or difficulty range—one that corresponds to kindergarten or first grade level classroom demands. Also, the dividing point between being "ready" and "not ready" for school is at a higher level of functioning than the level distinguishing "at risk" and "not at risk" for developmental problems. Given these two points, school readiness measures focus on a range of functioning that is more advanced than much of the content of preschool developmental screening instruments.

What to Assess

Given the areas of development described, what developmental information is meaningful to collect and to emphasize? The first guideline is that primary importance should be given to those areas that are most relevant to a child's success or failure in school. Not only is educational attainment a critical factor in our society, but it has significant implications for the well-being of children during their school years. The areas that are most closely related to educational status at the preschool level are cognitive, language, and fine motor development. The gross motor, speech, self-help, and social-emotional areas may also be relevant given that problems in these areas may interfere with educational progress.

The focus of assessment for an early identification program also depends upon the intervention services to be provided. An early identification/intervention program might emphasize academic functioning and concentrate on the cognitive, language, and fine motor areas. Or, the program might include a personal-social or mental health component, and include screening and assessment of social-emotional development and related behavior. Similarly, screening would include the gross motor area if occupational therapy or adaptive physical education services were to be provided, and speech would be screened if speech therapy were available. A second guideline, therefore, is that the developmental areas to be screened are those most directly related to the intervention services to be provided. This guideline, however, has it limitations in that gaps and inconsistencies may exist within a service delivery system. Should children with special needs be disregarded if no appropriate intervention is available? The "assess-according-to-intervention" guideline then creates a "Catch-22" situation: areas are not assessed because services are not available, and the need for services is not established because areas are not assessed.

A third guideline follows from the basic rationale for early identification. An area should be assessed when early identification of problematic conditions in that area results in a net benefit for the child. This expands upon the second guideline in that intervention must be not only available, but effective for the problem or condition identified, and appropriate for the child's age or developmental level. This is not an easy rule to apply, however, and dramatic inconsistencies may result (indeed, have resulted) from each school system or agency drawing its own conclusions about whether effective intervention can be provided.

Public Law 94-142 has to a great degree foreclosed the controversy over what to assess by specifying what conditions are to be identified and what services are to be provided. According to regulations, those children to be identified include "mentally retarded, hard of hearing, deaf, speech impaired, visually handicapped, seriously emotionally disturbed, orthopedically impaired, or other health impaired children, or children with specific learning disabilities." Thus, according to P.L. 94-142, identification programs should assess all areas of development plus vision, hearing, and general health. Still, the degree of emphasis to be devoted to each area is open to interpretation, and areas regarded to be of least importance may be deemphasized accordingly. At a minimum, however, a preschool screening program must attend to the areas of cognitive, language, and fine motor development, which are highly related to successful academic functioning in a primary school setting.

There is room for disagreement as to which areas of development should be primary targets for early identification. A strong case could be made that a child's mental health is as important, if not more so, than academic status. However, several considerations dictate against this shift in emphasis: (1) social-emotional development is highly problematic to efficiently and accurately assess, (2) funding for mental health services is fairly limited, (3) a low social priority is currently allotted to mental health services—as reflected by the previous point, and (4) remediation of social-emotional problems can be difficult, expensive, and uncertain. Clearly, the focus of child services is not determined by absolute principles, but reflects the nature of our society and the status of our service-providing technology.

SOURCES OF INFORMATION

Once we decide what it is we want to know about a child, how do we go about obtaining this information? While screening program planners tend to devote most attention to the use of screening tests, tests alone are insufficient to screen for the full range of physical and sensory, environmental, and developmental factors relevant to early identification. Three methods for obtaining screening information about the preschool child include (1) parent reports, (2) screening tests, and (3) observations of the child in the course of screening. Together, these three sources can provide a comprehensive and stable array of information for making screening decisions.

Parent Reports

While screening tests are designed to obtain pertinent developmental data, they are intentionally brief and tap only a limited sample of the child's behavior on one occasion. Parents have observed their child's behavior in a wide range of situations over a long period of time. Their descriptions of what the child is doing can provide valuable information about the child's development and personal adjustment, and their interpretations and concerns about how well the child is doing also add an important perspective.

Although parents possess a wealth of information about their children, one critical question is whether it can be obtained in a manner that is useful for screening purposes. Parent reports are not uniformly dependable; some parents are better observers of their children than others. Also, parents may give biased responses due to their own personal needs.

The value and validity of parent information is a function of a number of factors, as discussed at length in the next chapter. These factors include (1) the parent's willingness to participate in screening, (2) the parent's ability to comprehend the request for information and to provide accurate data about the child, and (3) the professional's ability to create useful ways of obtaining information from parents. Three major approaches to obtaining screening information from parents involve the use of interviews, comprehensive questionnaires (which are not formally scored or interpreted), and standardized inventories.

Screening Tests

A standardized developmental screening test consists of carefully selected questions or tasks that are presented to individuals in order to make systematic inferences about particular skills, abilities, traits, or types of behavior. One major advantage of standardized tests is that, by having the child respond to purposefully selected stimuli, much relevant data can be obtained in a short time. A second major advantage is the standardization, which permits a child's functioning to be objectively measured. By assessing a child based upon performance under standardized (i.e., uniform) circumstances, results can be systematically interpreted in terms of comparisons with other children or with a particular level of competency.

However, young children may fail to "appreciate" the importance of the standardized administration procedures that are so essential to testing. Administration of screening tests may require unintended modifications, or may simply be unfeasible, due to the nature of young children. They may be shy, fearful, or hesitant to respond to an unfamiliar adult; they may be distracted or tired or silly; or they may lack the motivation or attention span required by the testing situation. All this is noted and, to whatever extent possible, circumvented by the skilled examiner. Given the need to be flexible, to devote individual attention to the child's needs, and to carefuly observe responses of all types, individually-administered tests are far more appropriate than group tests for assessing the preschool child.

The first, and still one of the best known examples of an individually-administered test, is the Stanford-Binet Intelligence Scale (Terman, 1916). The Stanford-Binet evolved from a test by Binet and his colleagues around the beginning of the century that was designed to differentiate between mentally retarded and normal children in the Paris schools. At the preschool age level, the current-day Stanford-Binet (Terman & Merrill, 1960) contains cognitive tasks such as matching geometric shapes, naming objects shown in pictures, sorting buttons by color, and remembering and following a set of spoken instructions. A child's performance is translated into a score that is interpreted through comparison to a national normative sample.

Gesell (1926) also assembled an impressive collection of age-graded standardized tasks to systematically assess the preschool child's development in four areas: motor, language, adaptive behavior, and personal-social. This framework was preserved essentially intact by the Denver Developmental Screening Test (Frankenburg & Dodds, 1967), the first test designed specifically for developmental screening. The content of many preschool screening tests in use today bears considerable resemblance to the measures developed by Binet and Gesell. Chapter 4 is largely devoted to description and comparison of preschool screening tests.

Observational Methods

All screening procedures are based upon observations of some kind: parent reports are based on informal everyday observations; a child's test responses are observed and recorded by an examiner in a testing situation. As used here, however, *observational methods* refers to observation of a child's behavior, other than test responses, in the course of screening. Since observational methods, unlike parent reports and screening tests, are not discussed at length in later parts of this book, the topic is covered more extensively than the other two at this point.

In the course of their interactions with the child, screening personnel may obtain information that is not readily available through other means, for example, information regarding the child's disposition, attentional pattern, personal-social skills, and emotional adjustment. Some behaviors that are worth noting when observed during preschool screening include negativistic behavior, inattentiveness, inability to separate from the parent, excessively high or low activity level, and fearfulness. Observations might also provide a source of screening data in areas that are typically assessed through testing, e.g., speech, motor skills, verbal comprehension, but there is little reason to rely upon this approach when standardized testing is more efficient.

Methods of observation vary along the dimension of degree of structure. At the unstructured end of the scale, observations may be recorded in open-ended narrative form, with screening personnel relying upon personal experience and judgment to determine which behaviors they happen to find noteworthy or unusual. This may be satisfactory for a professional, but it is generally not satisfactory prac-

BEHAVIOR CHECKLIST

Child's Name _____   Location _____
Examiner _____   Date _____

Focuses on task . . . . ____ . . . ____ . . . ____ Easily distracted
Cooperative . . . . ____ . . . ____ . . . ____ Uncooperative
Thinks before answering . . . . . ____ . . . ____ . . . ____ Responds without thinking
Relaxed, assured . . . . ____ . . . ____ . . . ____ Fearful, nervous
Persistent . . . . ____ . . . ____ . . . ____ Gives up easily
Separates easily from mother . ____ . . . ____ . . . ____ Unable to separate
Responds readily . . . . ____ . . . ____ . . . ____ Reluctant to respond
Eager to continue . . . . ____ . . . ____ . . . ____ Tires quickly
Sits quietly . . . . ____ . . . ____ . . . ____ Moves around constantly
Easy to understand . . . . ____ . . . ____ . . . ____ Hard to understand
Uses complete sentences . . . . . ____ . . . ____ . . . ____ Uses single words only

Fig. 2-1.   Sample behavior checklist for screening examiner.

tice for a paraprofessional or volunteer. A more systematic approach is
to use a behavior checklist such as the one shown in Figure 2-1. A
checklist of this sort could also be expanded into a measure that
describes behaviors in greater detail, thereby requiring less interpretation and judgment. This degree of structure is generally necessary for
nonprofessional examiners who are less knowledgeable about what to
expect of a preschool child, and may also be of value to the professional
as a reminder of what to attend to and record. However, while structured approaches may help to insure consistency and objectivity, one of
the advantages is then lost: the opportunity to take note of whatever
behavior (particularly idiosyncratic behavior) may be observed. A combination of open-ended and structured observational techniques may
prove optimal. Relatively inexperienced observers should be instructed
to record open-ended observations in concrete, behavioral terms.

Although on-the-spot observations may appear to be significant
and valuable, they must be regarded with considerable caution. First,
uncertainty is introduced by the subjective judgment of the observer.
Even among professionals, behavior that is seen as abnormal by one
observer may be regarded as within normal expectations by another.
After all, preschool children are supposed to be negativistic, troubled,
and inattentive at times. A second major limitation upon observations
during screening is that the sample of behavior is severely limited.
Screening offers a relatively short period of time from which to general-

ize, usually far less than the hour or more of observation that is advised in order to get a reliable sample of behavior (Hunter, 1977). It is also dangerous to generalize from behavior seen during screening, given the novel and unfamiliar nature of the screening situation. What better time for a preschooler to be distracted, uncooperative, or fearful? Thus, how can one assume that the child is typically this way from observations on this one occasion? (One means of verification is to ask the parent whether the behavior observed is characteristic of the child. While this input may be valuable in many cases, reliance upon the parent brings us back to the question of how impartial and accurate parents can be about their children.)

To this point, it has been assumed that observational data are incidentally collected by screening personnel as they carry out other functions, and that the information obtained is at best supplementary to the screening process. However, observational methods can be instituted for the express purpose of providing primary input into screening decisions. As a formal screening procedure, a professional might observe each child for a brief period in a nontest situation and, based upon his or her clinical judgment, make a screening recommendation. For example, a speech and language clinician might converse with the child to obtain a speech sample, or a psychologist might arrange a standard play situation to get a general impression of emotional adjustment and interpersonal skills. Given the measurement problems cited earlier, this approach may be effective in screening for children with severe problems, but could not by itself be counted upon to discriminate at less severe levels.

One study that evaluated a screening procedure of this sort was conducted by Lindemann, Rosenblith, Allinsmith, Budd, and Shapiro (1967). Clinical teams at a mental health agency screened children just prior to kindergarten for social and emotional problems. From a brief interview with the mother and a play session with the child, the child's school adjustment was predicted on a three-point scale. A follow-up measure of school adjustment, based on classroom behavior, was obtained for 74 children in the screening sample at primary grade levels. Predictions were highly accurate for children assigned to the superior adjustment category, but error rates were high for those children who were assigned to at-risk categories on the basis of behavior problems observed during the play session. The authors concluded that "it is by no means certain that . . . preschool screening ought to be extended in scope to cover all entering pupils" (Lindemann et. al., 1967, p. 41).

One way to increase the validity of observations as a measure of expected school performance or adjustment is to observe the child in a classroom-like environment that provides opportunities for the child to interact with peers and adults and to handle age-appropriate materials and tasks. After all, observational data are obtained in order to get some idea of how the child is likely to behave in this very type of situation. A preschool classroom designed specifically to assess children during a short-term placement is used in some early identification programs. Given the cost of this approach, however, it is generally reserved for further assessment rather than for screening. A drawback to this approach is that the child may not adjust that rapidly to an unfamiliar classroom situation. The period of several days to a week or two that is typically allotted for assessing children in a trial classroom placement is far shorter than the eight-week period advised by Feshbach, Adelman, and Fuller (1977) in order to obtain reliable data. Novack, Bonaventura, and Merenda (1973) similarly found the predictive validity of teacher ratings to significantly improve over a period of several months. No research results have yet been reported on the validity of observations obtained during a trial classroom placement.

The classroom observation approach is considerably easier if the child is already situated in a classroom environment (e.g., a nursery school or day care center) rather than having to introduce a short-term trial. In screening children who are enrolled in preschool programs, the teacher's observations may be tapped as a valuable source of information. Like parents, they have the advantage of observing children over a period of time, but also tend to be skilled (and relatively objective) observers who have particular knowledge about age-appropriate expectations. Their observations might be provided informally, through interviews or open-ended questionnaires, or more formally through checklists or standardized ratings scales.

The value of observational methods must be weighed in the context of the available alternatives. In screening for cognitive abilities and other developmental functions related to academic readiness, observational methods compare unfavorably to tests both in terms of validity and cost-effectiveness. With regard to behavioral and social-emotional data, observations that can be obtained during a single screening occasion are limited (particularly in comparison to what a parent can provide) and unreliable. Behavior observed during screening might be most valuable as sample material for parent interviews; for example, a parent might be asked how frequently a given behavior is observed and whether they regard it as problematic. Observations of children in classroom settings obtained over a period of time, on the other hand, have potentially great value of preschool screening. The drawback is that unless the child is already enrolled in a preschool program the approach is generally impractical for screening.

TIMING OF PRESCHOOL SCREENING

A guiding principle of early identification is that it must be early enough to permit early intervention. The younger the child and the further the child is from entering school, however, the lower the validity of screening measures for predicting school performance. At what point in time is a child's development far enough along to accurately identify incipient school problems, while still allowing time for preschool intervention? This introduces two related questions about the timing of preschool screening: (1) the age of the child, and (2) the time of year.

Age of the Child

The main factor determining the earliest practical age for screening is the stability over time of the traits and abilities that we wish to assess. The critical question is, "At what age level can we first obtain valid and stable measures of functions that are relevant to school performance?" There must be sufficient consistency over time between a child's functioning in early childhood and what is educationally significant for the child in later years in order for early identification to make sense. Otherwise, one could just as well assume that early developmental problems will be outgrown and require no special attention, as predict that problems will continue and the child therefore needs special help.*

Researchers (Bayley, 1949; McCall, Hogarty, & Hurlburt, 1972) have shown that there is little relationship between measures of ability or IQ during the first two years (which focus primarily on sensorimotor functioning), and mental measures in later childhood and adulthood. In fact, during the first 18 months socioeconomic factors are better predictors of later IQ and achievement than measures of developmental functioning (McCall et al., 1972; Rubin & Balow, 1979). However, there are significant exceptions to this trend that are relevant to early identification. Infants whose development is clearly delayed can be predicted to have later cognitive deficits with greater certainty than infants in

---

*Adelman and Feshbach (1975), among others, argue that assessment of learning problems should be limited to identification of current status rather than prediction of future status. However, we identify children with the intent to provide special services that will "prevent or minimize later complications" (Adelman & Feshbach, 1975). This involves an implicit prediction; that is, that certain children will not be able to make up deficits in development simply through exposure to a typical set of experiences, and that early intervention is therefore called for.

general (Ireton, Thwing, & Gravem, 1970; McCall et al., 1972). Further-more, among children showing significant delays at an early age, low SES children are far more likely than high SES children to have later developmental or educational problems (Rubin & Balow, 1979; Werner, Bierman, & French, 1971). Still, these patterns are not strong enough to allow the future development of individual children with early delays or abnormalities to be confidently predicted.

A different picture exists for the later preschool years, as children begin to display skills, abilities, and behavior that relate to school functioning. By age 4 or 5, developmental gains in verbal fluency, fine motor and perceptual skills, and symbolic/representational thinking enable assessment measures to correlate substantially with subsequent school age measures of cognitive ability and educational progress (Bishop & Butterworth, 1979; Bloom, 1964; Robb, Bernardoni, & Johnson, 1972).

Longitudinal research (Bayley, 1949; Ebert & Simmons, 1943; Honzik, 1938; Sontag, Baker, & Nelson, 1958) on the stability of mental ability bears this out. Bloom (1964) summarized the results obtained in major longitudinal studies and discovered remarkable consistency in the degree to which later functioning could be predicted from scores obtained at different age levels. As shown in Figure 2-2, Bloom (1964) found that mental tests administered prior to age 3 correlate to a low degree (below .40) with intelligence measured at age 10. Correlations rise sharply during the age period from 3–5, reaching figures near .70, and continue to increase gradually thereafter. Interestingly, the greatest variability among the studies occurs at ages 3 and 4, leaving us rather uncertain as to how predictable other samples may be at this critical age period.

The finding that assessment measures gradually become more valid and stable as the child gets older and as the prediction interval becomes shorter leaves us with a complex decision regarding when to screen. Waiting until predictions are highly accurate may leave no time in which to intervene. There is, however, one consideration that "re-solves" the matter of how early to screen: legislative and/or administrative policy. Funding patterns dictated by federal and state laws determine whether services for preschool children with handicapping conditions will be extended down to age 4, age 3, or even younger. Policies at the local level may also define the lower age limit. The comprehensiveness of outreach efforts and of intervention services offered by a school district or agency may vary over the effective age range. For example, even in a state where special services are mandated beginning at age 3, a local screening program may be more active in its search for children with special needs at 4 years of age than at age

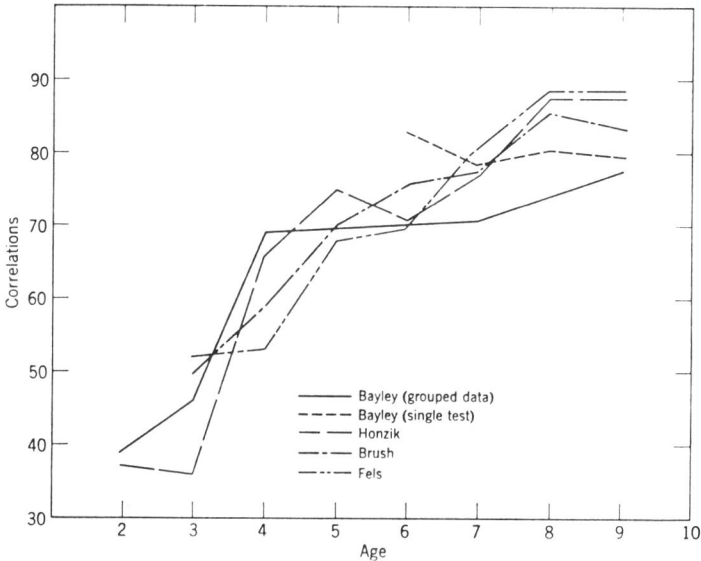

Fig. 2-2. Correlations between intelligence at each age and intelligence at age 10, corrected for differences in variability of samples. (From Bloom, 1964. Reprinted by permission.)

3, so that relatively few 3 year olds (presumably those with the most severe problems) are screened.

The lower age limit for large scale early identification efforts, as determined by legislative and administrative policies, typically falls in the range of 3–0 to 5–0. This age range, imprecise as it may be, is not inconsistent with the research. No precise lower age limit can be established, since this depends partly upon how much error can be tolerated in a given situation. However, evidence suggests that mass screening for educationally-related problems is impractical much before the age of 4. Early identification of developmental problems, more generally, might begin as early as age 2 or 3, but these efforts would best be limited to children with severely handicapping conditions.

Time of Year

To enumerate some of the most common arrangements for the scheduling of screening, a preschool screening program might arrange to screen each child (1) on a single occasion prior to kindergarten entry, usually either in the spring or the previous fall, (2) on more than one special (e.g., annual) occasion during the preschool years, (3) on a continuously or frequently available basis, or (4) on a single occasion just prior to, or soon after, the child has entered kindergarten. Let us address the last situation first, since it is philosophically the most troublesome.

The key question is whether a formal screening program at the beginning of kindergarten is justified in terms of moving up the point in time when early identification takes place. In the absence of a screening program, the most practical approach would be to rely upon referrals by kindergarten teachers to identify children who may have special needs. The use of systematic observation by kindergarten teachers to screen for school problems has been shown to be as effective as, and more economical than, formal testing (Bolig & Fletcher, 1973; Eaves, Kendall, & Crichton, 1974; Feshbach, Adelman, & Fuller, 1977; Novack, Bonaventura, & Merenda, 1973). Given that a teacher observation/referral system is not advised until several months into the school year (when a teacher's data base is sufficient to insure valid ratings), the savings in time that results from screening at the beginning of kindergarten is a few months at best, and often less, as in cases where children receive prompt attention due to an obvious handicap.

Formal screening at the beginning of kindergarten offers limited advantages. Screening as kindergarten begins does not allow for services to be provided during the preschool age range, as is generally the objective of preschool screening. Screening around the time of school entry may be more accurately referred to as kindergarten screening, and should not be regarded as a variation of, or substitute for, preschool screening. Once children enter school, observational methods are more practical than individual screening tests for early identification. Even when screening is instituted for children entering kindergarten, a trial placement in a regular kindergarten classroom may be a reasonable screening recommendation for all but the most disabled children. This is little different than the process that takes place using a teacher observation/referral system.

The practice of screening at the beginning of kindergarten is presently pursued in certain states because reimbursements for children receiving special education services are based on a "head count" conducted early in the school year. Thus, this questionable practice nets financial advantages for the local school system (i.e., funds would not be allocated for children identified later in the year through a teacher observation/referral system). It is clearly inappropriate for screening practices to be dictated by such arbitrary bureaucratic constraints. Hopefully, such policies will be reviewed and corrected.

Perhaps the best case that can be made for screening at the time of kindergarten entry is to determine a child's readiness for school; that is, in an educational system that subscribes to the school readiness model. The objective in this case is not to make a decision whether to provide services, but whether to delay formal education until the child is more mature. This decision is best made just as the child is scheduled to begin school. Of course, a decision to defer educational services would not be appropriate for handicapped children for whom special services are mandated through P.L. 94-142.

Let us next consider the other options for timing of preschool screening. To the guiding principle of identifying children early enough to provide preschool services, let us add a second: children should be screened at a point in time as near as possible to when intervention services are offered. Minimizing the screening-intervention time interval increases the validity of the screening procedure. The optimal situation is one in which children proceed quickly from screening to assessment to intervention. When this is not the case (for example, when children are screened in the spring but no services are offered until the fall), validity of screening results is unnecessarily reduced due to the passing of time. Thus, if special services are offered during the pre-kindergarten school year, the optimal time for screening (assuming prompt follow-up assessment) is early that fall. Screening during the spring before kindergarten is appropriate for a program that offers special services during the summer, but not so appropriate if services are not offered until the kindergarten years. The later is comparable to kindergarten screening, and less valid, given the time interval from screening to intervention.

Administrative considerations may lead to situations that are inconsistent with the guiding principle of minimizing the screening-intervention interval. Mass screening may introduce a bottleneck at the assessment stage. If mass screening takes place in September and the next six months are needed to assess those children who are referred, inappropriately long delays are introduced for many children. Or, children may be identified in the spring so that programs for fall can be planned with greater knowledge of expected numbers—the result of which may be well-run programs that serve the wrong children. Clearly, the timing of screening should be coordinated with both the follow-up assessment and intervention program schedules.

The approach of offering mass screening on a single occasion each year is currently in wide use. A time limited screening program can make use of volunteer or part-time personnel, use professional services cost-effectively, and enjoy other advantages of a large-scale operation. Furthermore, by identifying the majority of preschool children at one point in time, program slots can be accounted for and teaching positions filled in an administratively convenient manner. Mass screening at a single time of year is feasible when the follow-up assessment system can accommodate large numbers in a brief period or when numbers are small enough that this does not pose a problem. Otherwise, follow-up assessment should be staggered throughout the year and screening should be scheduled on multiple occasions.

The drawback to annual screening is that it will not suffice by itself. It is unacceptable to deny services to a child by telling the parent, "Sorry you missed it; wait until next year." Some children first become eligible for services upon turning 3 (or 4) soon after the annual screening date. Provisions must be made to accommodate those who miss the annual screening date, either by offering year-round screening on a small scale or by having several screening dates throughout the year. The optimal arrangement for many school districts may be to "mix and match"—i.e., to identify and initiate services for the majority of preschool children through an annual large-scale identification effort, and to screen at other times on a limited continuous basis.

Screening may be offered either as a one-shot affair (e.g., annually, for 4 year olds), or on a periodic basis (each year, or at regular intervals, throughout the preschool age range). Periodic screening offers clear advantages over one-shot screening in terms of its potential for identifying problems as they first appear. Still, there may be logical grounds for offering mass screening at a single point in time, as when preschool intervention programs first become available to children within a given service delivery system. However, this should not be the only opportunity for early identification to take place. Again, a combination of options, such as mass screening on a single occasion plus continuously available screening as needed for specially referred children, may make for a system that is both comprehensive and flexible.

SCREENING PERSONNEL

Above all else, screening should be done by qualified personnel. Also, since screening must be economical in order to be feasible, it should be done by qualified personnel in a cost-effective manner. The discussion of screening personnel that follows is simply an elaboration upon these two basic points.

Different roles in screening are associated with varying levels of expertise. Certain roles require the special skills and expertise of a professional. As discussed earlier, the screening program coordinator should have expertise in special education and early childhood as well as administrative skills. Additional professionals may be sought out to provide input into screening that involves other areas of specialization, e.g., speech and language, motoric functioning, vision, hearing, and health. The cardinal rule, however, is that the professionals involved in preschool screening should be knowledgeable about, and have experience in, working with young children.

Depending upon the types of screening procedures selected, professional participants in a screening program might be involved in directly observing and/or testing children; or, they might arrange for screening procedures to be carried out by others, in which case supervision and training would be among their major responsibilities.

Professional level experience and skill is required of those screening personnel who respond to parents' questions and concerns. This kind of interaction with parents is most likely to arise in the course of open-ended interviews and screening feedback sessions. It is highly desirable to offer such opportunities in screening (see Chapter 3). An appropriately trained professional should be available on site to answer questions about screening procedures, developmental expectations, significance of problematic behaviors, implications and consequences of screening outcomes, community resources, professional referrals, procedural safeguards, intervention services, etc.

Nonprofessionals can assist with screening in several non-specialized roles such as outreach and information services, scheduling, receptionist services, assisting parents with questionnaires, and escorting children to screening stations. These roles require interpersonal skills, but not the technical skills obtained through professional training. Still, these activities are clearly important to the success of a screening program. Special efforts should be made to insure that the screening personnel with whom parents first come in contact, e.g., those who make scheduling arrangements or who greet parents, perform these functions competently and sensitively.

What about the prospect of nonprofessionals or paraprofessionals serving in more specialized roles? The question is most frequently raised with regard to the role of screening examiner. Cost-effectiveness is the issue here. Administration of screening instruments is a time-demanding and, some would say, a wasteful use of professional services, services that may be in short supply or highly expensive. While the cost of operating a screening program may be reduced by using nonprofessional examiners, this savings may be offset by a loss in the value of the screening data obtained. Is it necessary for an expert to directly administer screening procedures, or are professionally-designed instruments in the hands of a well-trained paraprofessional or nonprofessional examiner suitable for this function?

There is no justification for concluding that only certified professionals can become competent screening examiners. A qualified examiner might be any individual who can master the screening measure used in a given situation. Practically speaking, the critical concern is not the examiner's professional or nonprofessional status, but whether the examiner has the necessary competencies to insure that valid screening information is obtained; specifically, the mechanical skills of administration and scoring, and the capacity to interact effectively with young children. Factors such as the screening procedures selected (some screening instruments are more difficult to master than others), the capabilities and attitude of the examiner, and the training provided, determine whether a nonprofessional will achieve the necessary level of competency. Thus, the prospects for using nonprofessional examiners effectively are maximized when screening instruments suitable for nonprofessionals are used, when examiners are carefully selected, and when sufficient training is provided.

A program implemented by community health agencies in Denver trained nonprofessionals from local low-income communities to serve as screening technicians administering the Denver Developmental Screening Test and other instruments (Frankenburg, Goldstein, Chabot, Camp, & Fitch, 1970). The job description stated that trainees should have the capacity (1) to read test manuals written at seventh grade level, (2) to administer tests proficiently, (3) to calculate children's exact ages, (4) to write results legibly, and (5) to have good rapport with clients and fellow workers. Dependability was also cited as a necessary characteristic. Few applicants were excluded on the basis of these standards. Short-term intensive training provided nonprofessionals in this program with the skills required of screening examiners. This report did not include outcome data regarding the proficiency of screening technicians.

Two studies provide evidence that adequately trained nonprofessionals can perform acceptably as screening examiners. The first was conducted by the coordinators of a preschool screening program in a suburban Minnesota school district. The screening program followed the not uncommon practice of having speech clinicians administer the language section of the screening test, while nonprofessionals administered the remaining sections. The study involved having both speech clinicians and trained volunteers administer the Communications area of the DIAL to the same group of children. The results obtained by speech clinicians and volunteers were highly similar, leading to the decision to have volunteers administer all parts of the DIAL in the future.

The second study (Lichtenstein, 1980b) assessed the reliability of the Minneapolis Preschool Screening Instrument (MPSI) when administered by nonprofessionals (mostly university undergraduates in education and related fields, and B.A. level educational paraprofessionals). The training procedures used, as outlined in the MPSI manual, consisted of a four hour training session, and a one hour follow-up session during the first day of testing. Reliability figures for this study (reported in Chapter 4) were at a level above that typically obtained by professionals.

These outcomes should not be construed to mean that nonprofessional examiners are as capable as professionals or that they will automatically obtain valid results, but they do mean that nonprofessionals can become accomplished screening examiners under the proper conditions. The best way to verify that the necessary skill level has been attained is to observe trained nonprofessionals administering a test in simulated, and subsequently in actual, screening situations. Occasional follow-up checks are also highly recommended to insure that acceptable standards are maintained.

Cost Considerations

The cost factor can be a deceptive one. To enlist the lowest-paid individuals who can capably function as screening examiners is not necessarily cost-effective. The paraprofessional or volunteer must be trained and supervised, sometimes at considerable effort and expense. A cost analysis for a given screening situation may reveal that professionals are actually more economical in the long run.

Let us take a hypothetical example in which a school district plans to screen 100 4 year olds. A school psychologist and speech clinician conduct two four-hour sessions training four volunteer screening examiners. In addition, the two professionals each spent four hours planning and preparing for the training. While the screening is taking place, one of the two professionals is always on hand to supervise. Finally, let us assume that an average of one-half hour is required to administer the battery of screening tests to each child.

To screen 100 children at one-half hour each takes 50 hours. With volunteer help, the total amount of professional time required is approximately 37 hours; 24 hours for training and 13 hours for supervision during screening (assuming the four volunteers do the 50 hours of screening simultaneously). This figure may be compared to the 50 hours that would be required if the professionals were to do the screening themselves. Other factors may chip away at the cost difference: volunteers must be located and interviewed; time demands upon the professionals may dramatically increase if volunteers are undependable, unprepared, or lacking in skills; or the screening program might use paid paraprofessionals rather than volunteers. In this example, the ultimate difference in cost between using professional and nonprofessional examiners would likely be negligible.

Use of nonprofessional examiners becomes more cost-effective as the size of the screening program increases. In the example above, the difference in the amount of professional time required with and without volunteer examiners is 37 vs. 50 hours in screening 100 children, but the difference would be 49 vs. 100 hours for 200 children, and 149 vs. 500 hours for 1000 children. (This assumes that the number of nonprofessional examiners remains constant at four.) The cost of training is increasingly compensated as more children are screened by each nonprofessional examiner.

Another cost variable is the availability of professional personnel. When there is a shortage of available professionals, their services may be put to best use by training others. A nearby college or university may provide a ready source of capable and motivated nonprofessional help. Community service organizations may also be a valuable resource.

Some school districts may find that teachers or teaching aides that are already employed by the district are available to serve as examiners. This may offer the added advantage that they have experience with young children (however, it should by no means be assumed that the need for training is substantially reduced). One possible drawback of this practice is that availability of teachers may be time-specific. For example, kindergarten teachers might be able to serve in this role only in the period immediately before school begins. As noted earlier, to adjust the screening schedule to conform with administrative convenience may be inappropriate and counterproductive.

In some instances, cost factors are manipulated in a highly inappropriate manner: the gains of using nonprofessional personnel are increased by minimizing the expense of training and supervision. It is not sufficient to have nonprofessionals read a test manual, receive a few general instructions, and begin screening preschool children. The end result of such practice is that screening personnel are not qualified, screening procedures are misused, and inaccurate screening decisions are made. A screening program operating in this manner could also result in legal repercussions for the school district or agency.

TESTING YOUNG CHILDREN

First and foremost, the examiner must have an understanding of, and respect for, the importance of standardized testing procedures. That is, the screening examiner must follow the exact instructions for administration and scoring in order to preserve the value of using standardized instruments. Inexperienced examiners often commit two types of "leniency" errors: (1) providing assistance to the child beyond that permitted by the instructions, and (2) giving the child "a break" on the scoring when the child "seems to know" an answer but cannot provide a creditable response. If examiners take liberties with administration and scoring procedures, the screening situation becomes different for each child and results are no longer comparable. Of particular concern is that leniency errors may result in the failure to refer children who are in need of special help.

To insure that standardized procedures are followed, much training must be devoted to learning the administration and scoring rules for the specific instrument or instruments used. Even though instructions to the child are to be read word for word, there are various aspects of test administration, i.e., arranging materials, performing demonstrations, applying scoring rules, etc., that must become second nature to the examiner.

While adhering to standardized testing procedures, the examiner must also ensure that the child's optimal performance is elicited. Recommended procedures concerning the examination process in general, and interacting with preschool children in particular, are provided in books by Goodenough (1949), Read (1976), and Sattler (1982). Some important considerations are discussed below.

Physical Environment

The testing room should be quiet, well-lit, and free from distractions (including parents, if at all possible). The chair and table provided for the child should be of appropriate height. All efforts should be made to insure that the child is comfortable, which may involve attending to the child's toilet needs or regulating the room temperature.

Establishing Rapport

Good rapport must be established before beginning, and maintained throughout testing. Some children are instantly responsive and attuned to the examiner. Others need time to feel at ease in the environment and with the examiner. To set the child at ease and to encourage cooperation, the examiner should be warm, supportive, friendly, and reassuring, but not overly playful or effusive. In most cases, rapport is established fairly quickly and test administration can begin soon after introductions and an explanation of the testing situation. If not, the examiner may want to give the child a chance to play with a toy or with familiar materials. The examiner may proceed when the child gives indications of readiness to respond—not before.

Manner of Presentation

In following standardized administration procedures, the novice examiner may feel so constricted that he or she functions in robot-like fashion: stiff, impersonal, and automatic. With preparation and practice, however, an examiner can administer a screening instrument in a more natural manner (e.g., by maintaining eye contact and varying the tone of voice). The child's interest and attention are effectively maintained by the well prepared examiner who presents tasks at a smooth, uninterrupted pace and handles materials skillfully. The examiner must also learn that certain extemporaneous examiner remarks and behaviors are not only acceptable, but advisable and perhaps necessary—as addressed by the next two points.

Praise

As a rule, young children are not intrinsically motivated to achieve in a testing situation, but do take great interest in the response they get from adults. To encourage optimal performance, the examiner should praise the child for his or her *efforts*. That is, praise should be offered for active cooperation and should not be contingent upon the child's success. Also, the manner in which praise is delivered greatly affects its impact; in particular, praise should be expressive rather than perfunctory.

Sensitivity to the Child

The examiner should be attentive to signs of boredom, fatigue, restlessness, or distress. While a good lively pace helps maintain the child's interest, the examiner cannot proceed when the child's attention drifts. Off-task remarks or requests to change activities by the child should not be ignored, but the examiner's objective is to quickly redirect the child back to the task at hand. The child's resistance may be transitory, as when a particular task is uninteresting or frustrating; or may become progressively worse, as in the case of fatigue. Flexibility and good judgment are needed in determining whether to plunge ahead, to introduce a break, or to terminate the session. At times, a balance must be struck between maintaining standardized administration procedures and responding to the child's needs.

Unless the child's cooperation is maintained by the examiner, a screening test will not yield a valid measure of performance. Goodenough (1949) notes that this will sometimes be the case "even under the best conditions and with the most skillful examiner," and proposes that "the safest procedure to follow is not to give any test at all, rather than to give a poor test" (p. 303). She suggests that the child return at a later occasion if cooperation is not obtained. For a screening program, this might entail either rescreening or a referral for further assessment.

SUMMARY

Preschool screening programs must deal with a number of issues in a systematic fashion if they are to be successful. The initial planning stage is critical. Screening program planners must be clear about the fundamental nature of the task, as defined by program objectives and the population to be served. These understandings in turn shape specific plans about outreach, scheduling, sources and types of screening information, personnel and training, decision-making, and evaluation of procedures.

Screening information concerning a child's physical and sensory functioning, home environment, and development may be obtained from several sources: standardized tests, parent reports, and observations by screening personnel or preschool teachers. The extent of screening information to be obtained depends upon how broadly the program is defined (e.g., as educational vs. health/developmental) and what follow-up services are to be provided for those children identified. The "generic" preschool screening program, at a minimum, assesses vision, hearing, and educationally-relevant developmental functions.

Preschool screening should be offered at a point in time early enough so that special services can be provided prior to school entry. However, the screening population must be old enough so that developmental functions that have significance for later school performance can be measured. Given this, the 3–5 age range is optimal for preschool screening, which coincides by and large with current legislative and administrative policies. Mass screening should be offered according to a schedule that allows children to proceed expeditiously from screening to follow-up assessment. Screening (or other means of early identification) should be available to young children on a periodic or continuous basis.

Both professionals and nonprofessionals may assume a significant role in screening. The cardinal rule is that screening should be conducted by qualified personnel, with cost-effectiveness being a second key consideration. Nonprofessionals may serve capably as screening examiners, but the feasibility of this practice depends upon the procedures used, the training provided, and characteristics of the individual. A competent screening examiner is one who conforms to the guidelines of standardized testing procedure and establishes sufficient rapport with preschool children to elicit their optimal cooperation and performance.

3

Involving Parents in Screening

> One of the great things about Public Law 94-142 is that it recognizes the importance of parents and brings them into the planning and programming every step of the way. Parents have to be recognized as special educators, the true experts on their children, and professional people—teachers, pediatricians, psychologists, and others—have to learn how to be consultants to parents. (Hobbs, 1978, p. 496)

The importance of involving parents in educational planning for their children, as articulated so well by Hobbs, is hardly a new idea. The value of parent input in providing special services for children, and particularly in identifying or assessing children's problems, has long been recognized. Yet, at the very first step of the process, preschool screening, parent participation remains an underutilized resource.

Almost 30 years ago, Gesell and Amatruda (1954) emphasized the importance of involving parents in diagnosing the developmental problems of young children. Even then the point must have seemed self-evident. There is little question that

> parents have the most information about the present functioning and past history of the child . . . the parent is the *first* and often *best* assessor of his/her child's functioning and problems. (Walker & Wiske, 1981, p. 32)

Information uniquely available to parents may help to compensate for the limitations of screening tests. Only certain kinds of behavior can be evaluated by testing. Information gained from a test may be inaccurate, and it is certain to be limited. A child's parent, having observed how the child actually behaves in many different situations, from the supermarket to the supper table to the backyard sandbox, can supply information that a test cannot provide.

Parents are therefore a source of critical information about their children. Information from parents may cover a wide range of material: medical history and current symptoms; the child's current developmental functioning and developmental history; personality and social-emotional adjustment, including behavioral/emotional problems; family information, including relevant stress factors such as loss of a parent through death or divorce; and other situational factors that might bear on the child's functioning.

Parent involvement should also be viewed in a broader context than simply for screening and diagnostic purposes. Parents are essential participants in the planning and implementation of interventions for children. As Walker and Wiske (1981) point out,

> The assessment process should offer parents a means through which they can communicate and collaborate with other persons and community agencies to understand their child's potential and difficulties and to obtain the best set of services for their child. (p. 32)

Parent input at the screening level is not only valuable in and of itself, but sets the tone for what comes after. Ideally, this kind of cooperation will begin with screening, be sustained throughout the assessment process, and have its big payoff with parents' involvement and support at the intervention stage. The objective is more than just keeping parents informed and occasionally tapping their knowledge to insure that they will be responsive to professional services. The ultimate benefit from active parent involvement is that the parent becomes better able to help his or her own child.

Direct parent involvement can have a significant effect upon the progress made by children in early intervention programs. Vopava and Royce (1978) reviewed outcome data from infant and preschool programs to determine what factors accounted for positive long-term effects. They found that programs that set goals for parents, used home visits by professionals, and trained parents to stimulate their children's development were most effective in preventing subsequent placement in special education programs. A survey of model projects and programs in special education reflects the trend towards increased reliance on parents (National Diffusion Network, 1980).

Despite increasing recognition that parents are the "true experts" about their children, this has not been easy to translate into preschool screening practice. Professionals continue to devote considerable effort to selecting or creating psychological tests to assess a child's developmental functioning, while paying relatively little attention to parent information. There appear to be two interrelated reasons for this. First, some professionals may not be oriented towards working with parents in a collaborative manner. Parents may be relegated to the role of passive observers while professionals exhibit their polished skills in diagnosing, teaching, or treating children. Professionals thus assume the role of being the child experts, both in their own eyes and in the eyes of parents.

Second, some professionals consider parents to be subjective, biased, and even defensive in providing information about their children. While this does occur, many professionals who routinely work with parents of children with developmental problems acquire great respect for parents' knowledge about and observations of their children. Perhaps the difference in attitudes is due to the fact that some professionals are far more effective than others in establishing rapport with and obtaining valid information from parents.

Is it possible to translate the best of clinical practice into standard operating procedure? The challenge is how to obtain the precious information possessed by parents in a manner that is not only valid and cost-effective, but also instrumental in the process of building positive working relationships with parents. These considerations are addressed in the following sections on methods for obtaining parent information and on working collaboratively with parents.

METHODS FOR OBTAINING PARENT INFORMATION

As part of the screening process, it is common practice to ask the parent to complete a comprehensive questionnaire that provides background information about the child and family. This questionnaire usually includes identifying information, family information, medical history, current physical or sensory symptoms, developmental milestones, current developmental behaviors, and social-emotional adjustment. At the beginning of screening, a brief interview may be conducted during which responses to the questionnaire are reviewed with the parent and the parent's questions and concerns, if any, are elicited. Also, less commonly, the parent may be asked to complete a more formal developmental inventory to describe the child's current functioning.

These options describe the three main methods of obtaining developmental and related information from the parent. The first makes use of a comprehensive questionnaire that encompasses both current status and historical data. This approach provides background information, but does not lend itself to consistent interpretation. The second approach is to conduct an interview with the parent early in the screening process. This interview may be highly structured, even to the point of being standardized, or relatively open-ended. A structured, standardized interview is similar to a psychological test in that it provides for standard administration and scoring, and makes use of norms for the interpretation of results. The third approach is to have the parent describe the child by completing a standardized developmental or personality inventory.

Parent Questionnaires

Questionnaires completed by the parent prior to or at the beginning of screening typically are comprehensive in the breadth of content they include, which ranges from health information to developmental information and also some family information. Usually both current status information and historical data are solicited. As a rule, these questionnaires do not provide norms or even guidelines for the interpretation of results.

Two multidimensional screening systems, the Comprehensive Identification Process (Zehrbach, 1975a) and the Preschool Screening System (Hainsworth & Hainsworth, 1980), include parent questionnaires covering health and developmental history and current behavior. The information provided by the parent adds to screening test results from direct testing of the child. However, guidelines for integrating this material for screening purposes are not clearly specified by these instruments.

The Denver Developmental Screening Test (DDST) (Frankenburg & Dodds, 1967), which is reviewed in Chapter 4, uses direct testing and parents' oral reports interchangeably; a child passes certain items either if the behavior is demonstrated in testing or if the parent reports they have observed the behavior. Almost half of the DDST items, and most of those in the Personal-Social area, can be passed on the basis of parent report.

The Denver Prescreening Developmental Questionnaire (PDQ) (Frankenburg, van Doorninck, Liddell, & Dick, 1976) is an adaptation of the DDST. The PDQ is a prescreening questionnaire that is completed by the parent. To develop the PDQ, 97 of the 105 DDST items were selected for modification into questions that could be answered "yes" or "no" by the parent. On some questions the parent is asked to present the child with a task before answering the question, in which case "refuse" or "no opportunity" could be the response. Please note that this establishes the parent as the examiner of the child as well as the observer. The parent is asked to answer only 10 age-appropriate items for their child. The results are intended to correspond with the outcomes that would be obtained from a standard administration of the DDST.

Also derived from another instrument is the Home Screening Questionnaire (HSQ) (Coons, Gay, Fandal, Ker, & Frankenburg, 1981), a parent questionnaire adapted from the Home Observations for Measurement of the Environment scale (Caldwell & Bradley, in press), which is discussed in Chapter 2. The HSQ consists of questionnaires for each of 2 different levels, ages 0–3 and 3–6. HSQ items, written at "third or fourth grade reading level," deal with materials, toys, and stimulation experiences provided for the child, and with parents' interactions with the child.

Parent Interviews

The interview with the parent(s) is a critical element in the screening process, both for creating a working relationship with the parent and for obtaining essential information. If the parent is the "first and often the best assessor of his/her child's functioning and problems," this may be the best time to offer them the opportunity. A screening interview, as with any interview, is designed so as to achieve a given purpose, in this case to provide an overview of what the child is doing and, especially, to determine whether the child is doing poorly in any respect. Screening needs to be keyed to the parent's expressed concerns and questions, if any, about the child. An interview with a parent who has reported their child's symptoms or problems on the background questionnaire would be conducted differently than an interview with the parent who has reported no problems for the child.

Unless problems or concerns have been reported in the questionnaire or volunteered at the outset of the interview, it is probably best for rapport and information-gathering to begin by asking the parent (usually the mother) to describe the child and the child's behavior. Subsequently, the parent should be asked for his or her interpretations about how well the child is doing, and specifically, concerns or anxiety about the child in various areas. Also, it is important to know what questions the parent might hope to have answered as a result of screening.

When interviewing parents, it is probably best to begin by asking them to describe their child briefly in their own words: "Tell me a little bit about your child." Most mothers like the opportunity to describe their child in their own way. This can then be given a developmental focus by asking them, "Please tell me what your child has been doing and learning lately." Depending on the parent's reply, more specific information can be asked about the child's motor skills, language development, etc. Moving beyond description, the parent can be asked for his or her interpretations, concerns, and questions regarding the child's development and adjustment: "How well do you think your child is doing? Are you concerned about your child's physical coordination, ability to run, climb, etc.? How well does your child seem to understand things that are said to him or her? Does he or she seem to understand things that are said to him or her? Does your child seem to be slow to catch on? Do you have any concerns about his or her behavior? What are your concerns? How easy or difficult is your child to deal with?"

As can be seen from the above questions, the focus of the interview moves from the descriptive to the interpretive, from the general to the specific. The screening interview constitutes a search procedure that allows the interviewer to determine areas of delayed development, poor adjustment, and/or of parental concern, anxiety, or outright distress.

Interview formats differ in the degree of structure they prescribe and the amount of latitude that is allowed the interviewer and interviewee. Even a so-called open-ended interview addresses a limited purpose and encompasses a finite amount of territory. Within these boundaries, the interviewer proceeds with certain fairly broad questions, and follows up with questions that are tailored in consideration of the preceding replies.

Since the selection, phrasing, and sequence of questions in an open-ended interview is up to the interviewer, no two interviews proceed exactly the same way. This is not the case for a structured interview. In a structured interview, the interviewer covers a predetermined set of questions, usually in the same order, and with the same wording. Some flexibility may be built into the structured interview with a branching procedure. For example, if the parent answers "yes" to a question about noticing unusual speech behavior, the interviewer might then follow up with a probe (e.g., "Tell me what seems to be unusual") or a series of questions (e.g., "Is the child intelligible? Does he or she speak in sentences?") according to some pre-established rule. A structured interview requires less interviewing expertise than an open-ended interview in which the professional is instantaneously interpreting data and deciding what to ask next.

A brief, structured parent interview for the purposes of screening might ask about the following:

- Questions or worries you have about the child's health?
- Vision and hearing?

- Ability to listen and to understand what is said to him or her?
- Ability to learn?
- Ability to get along with other people?
- Ability to take care of self (feeding, dressing, toileting)?
- Anything else about the child you wonder or worry about?
- Problems your child has, as far as you know?

Standardized Interviews

Standardized parent interviews provide not only a specified set of questions to be asked, but also standards for the scoring and interpretation of parent's responses. Standardized interviews can be locally developed, however, commercial instruments may offer the advantage of normative data to aid in interpretation. The Vineland Social Maturity Scale (VSMS) (Doll, 1935, 1965) is probably the best known measure of children's, and adults', adaptive behavior based upon the parent's or other caretaker's report. The Vineland measures adaptive behavior from birth to adulthood in six areas: Self-help, Locomotion, Occupation, Communication, Self-direction, and Socialization. The item sampling within each area across ages is rather inconsistent and the normative research was based on limited, inadequate samples. Although the Vineland is outdated and flawed from a systematic research perspective it has enjoyed wide usage because it taps critical information about the everyday functioning of both children and adults. A revised version is scheduled for publication in 1984.

Doll (1966) also developed the Preschool Attainment Record (PAR) as an extension of the Vineland for use with children from birth to age 7. The PAR measures functioning in eight areas: Ambulation, Manipulation, Rapport, Communication, Responsibility, Information, Ideation, and Creativity. Within each area, 14 items are arranged in developmental sequence, with 1 item at each half-year interval. The PAR was originally published as a "research edition." With the death of its author, apparently no further work has been done with the PAR.

The Developmental Profile II (DP II) (Alpern, Boll, & Shearer, 1980), which is reviewed in Chapter 4, is in the tradition of the Vineland. The DP II format and content provides for a structured interview with the parent or other caretaker, and may also be administered as a test with the child. The DP II measures adaptive functioning from birth to age 9 in five areas: Physical, Self-help, Socialization, Academic, and Communication. The authors of the DP II recommend its use for screening children, program placement, writing IEPs, assessing a child's progress, and program evaluation.

It should be noted that all of the above standardized parent interviews were initially developed for the purpose of assessment, not screening. None of them have been specifically adapted, or abbreviated, or most important, validated for screening purposes.

Standardized Inventories

Inventories are highly structured, self-administered questionnaires by means of which individuals may describe themselves or some other person (in this case, the parent describes his or her child). The inventory format includes specific statements (items) and limited response alternatives (Yes-No, Don't know; rating scale with limited number of points measuring frequency or intensity). Items are usually grouped to form scales measuring various areas or aspects of the individual's functioning. Results can be quantified (scored) and objectively interpreted in relation to established norms. The inventory format is cost-effective because inventories are self-administered, easily scored, and results can be summarized or profiled in a systematic, brief fashion that facilitates interpretation. In fact, the inventory format lends itself well to computerized administration, scoring and interpretation (Labeck, Ireton, & Leeper, in press).

The Minnesota Child Development Inventory (MCDI) (Ireton & Thwing, 1974) provides a standardized format for obtaining and interpreting mothers' reports of their young children's current development. The MCDI consists of a booklet listing 320 developmental behaviors of children in the first six years and an IBM answer sheet. The mother answers "yes" or "no" to each item to describe her child's current behavior. The results are summarized on a profile of eight scales: General Development, Gross Motor, Fine Motor, Expressive Language, Language Comprehension, Situation Comprehension, Self Help, and Personal-Social. Interpretations of delayed or normal range development are based upon norms from 796 white children, ages 6 months to 6 years, from Bloomington, Minnesota.

The Minnesota Preschool Inventory (MPI) (Ireton & Thwing, 1979), which is reviewed in Chapter 4, is an adaptation of the MCDI that was designed specifically for pre-kindergarten screening. The MPI contains 150 items that measure the development and readiness skills, adjustment, and symptoms of 4 and 5 year olds. The MPI has been validated for pre-kindergarten screening by comparing MPI results with teacher ratings of school performance at the end of kindergarten.

Two relatively recent instruments make use of parent reports to focus more on a child's personality and social maladjustment than on development. Their primary use is in clinical diagnosis of children who have already been identified as having behavioral and/or emotional problems.

The Personality Inventory for Children (PIC) (Wirt, Lachar, Klinedinst, & Seat, 1977) is standardized for 3–16 year old children. The 600 items of the PIC form 12 clinical scales: Somatic Concern, Depression, Family Relations, Delinquency, Withdrawal, Anxiety, Psychosis, Hyperactivity, Social Skills, Achievement, Intellectual Screening, and Development. In addition, three validity scales indicate the degree to which the parent has responded conscientiously and openly. Results are summarized on a profile and interpreted according to norms.

The Children's Behavior Checklist (CBL) (Achenbach & Edelbrock, 1981) is designed to assess the behavioral problems and social competencies of children ages 4 through 16. The CBL includes both a parent and a teacher form. The CBL consists of 118 behavior problem items and 20 social competence items, and can be completed in 15–20 minutes. Behavior problems are categorized into clinical scales, e.g., Depressed, Immature, Schizoid, Aggressive, Delinquent, and also summarized by two general dimensions, Internalizing and Externalizing. At the preschool level, the social competence items are broken down into two scales: Social and Activities.

RESEARCH ON PARENT REPORTS

The value of parental information in developmental screening depends upon the confidence that can be placed in the parent's report of the child's development and functioning. McShane (1973) identified four factors that affect the reliability and validity of parents' reports: nature of the information requested, the method of obtaining the information, characteristics of the parents, and characteristics of the child.

Nature of the Information

What kind of information is being obtained: Medical? Developmental? Social? Does the information pertain to historical events (e.g., pregnancy, labor and delivery, medical history, developmental milestones) or to current functioning (e.g., symptoms, developmental skills, personality, behavior problems, parent-child interaction)? Does the information requested concern the child's observable behavior, or does it involve interpretation and higher level inferences (e.g., judgments about the child's reasoning ability, or self-esteem)? Is information sought about subtle or complex behavior (e.g., the language of a 4 year old), or behavior that is easily characterized?

In general, the most reliable parent information consists of reports of current observable behavior that do not involve much inference (Graham & Rutter, 1968; Yarrow, 1963). Reports of historical events tend to be unreliable. Mothers' recall is generally poor for details relating to pregnancy and delivery, early illnesses, child rearing practices, and interpersonal relationships (see review by Wenar, 1963).

Method of Obtaining Information

Is the information obtained informally, in an open-ended fashion; or by means of structured interviews, questionnaires, or inventories?

The evidence demonstrates that structured interviews, questionnaires, and inventories yield more accurate and reliable parent information than do unstructured measures. Potential advantages of structured measures include clarity, consistency, and comprehensiveness. Graham and Rutter (1968) report that mothers are very inconsistent in their spontaneous reports of their children's symptoms. Novick (1966) found that in an unstructured intake interview, mothers fail to report many symptoms or problems of their children. A comprehensive survey procedure nearly quadrupled the number of problems reported. This finding is especially relevant to screening. Yarrow (1963) notes that parents are often asked to rate their children's behavior independent of any specific situation, or without reference to any particular comparison group. Ironically, parents' lack of objectivity may in part be the result of the professional's lack of clarity and specificity in the questions asked.

Another factor is length of parent report measures. As a general rule, the longer the instrument or interview, the more reliable and valid the results. More total material can be covered, and each item or question can be more specific. Not surprisingly, the most reliable and valid checklists and inventories tend to be over 100 items long, and some contain over 300 items. However, a point of diminishing returns is reached if an instrument is so lengthy that it adversely affects the parent's cooperation or concentration, or cannot be completed in the time available. A more practical view in screening is to consider both the value of parent reports and the valid response rate. Thus, an instrument must be long enough to insure comprehensiveness and accuracy yet short enough to be acceptable to the respondent.

Parent Characteristics

What accounts for the fact that certain parents provide more accurate information than others? Do parent characteristics such as socioeconomic status (SES) and level of education affect accuracy of report? Are mothers and fathers equally accurate observers?

Sturner, Funk, Thomas and Green (1982), using an abbreviated form of the Minnesota Child Development Inventory, found that lower SES parents were more likely than higher SES parents to produce questionnaires of questionable validity due to omitted items. Lichtenstein (in press) found the opposite pattern: preschool screening reports from low SES parents had equal or greater validity than reports from high SES parents in predicting teacher ratings of kindergarten performance. Other studies (Brekstad, 1966; Wenar & Coulter, 1962) have failed to show significant relationships between reliability of parent reports and SES. Pyles, Stolz, and Macfarlane (1935) reported a slight correlation between mothers' education and accuracy and comprehensiveness of recall. Similarly, Gottfried, Guerin, Spencer, and Meyer (in press) found that more educated mothers' Minnesota Child Development Inventory reports of their 3 year olds correlated more highly with scores on a general cognitive measure than did reports of mothers with less education. Differences between the two groups were consistent, although not dramatic. (It is important to note that SES and mother's level of education should not be equated; mother's educational level alone is a better indicator of the mother's ability to comprehend and comply with requests for information about her child.) Gottfried et al. (in press) also found that full-time mothers' MCDI reports correlated somewhat higher with test results than did MCDI reports of working mothers. Another finding in this study was that mothers who have had a course in child development produced slightly higher correlations with test results.

A related question has to do with the adequacy of the parent's observation base, i.e., how well does the parent who is providing the information know the child? Robbins (1963) found that fathers could recall less material than mothers. In research with the Minnesota Child Development Inventory, Ireton and Thwing have been accused of being sexist because it is based on the mother's report. However, clinical experience has shown that fathers' reports not uncommonly produce an understatement of the child's current functioning.

The research on parent characteristics, while much of it is more suggestive than conclusive, points to several factors that may affect the usefulness of parent information: (1) the parent's opportunity to observe the child, (2) the parent's inclination to note aspects of the child's development, (3) the parent's sophistication on the subject of child development, and (4) the parent's capacity to respond to requests for information (i.e., with regard to reading or communication skills).

Child Characteristics

Are parents more accurate in their reports as a function of the child's sex or age? Does birth order make a difference? (For example, parents may observe their first child's development more closely, or parents may be more sophisticated as they observe their subsequent children.)

There is some evidence (Wenar & Coulter, 1962), although not strong, that mothers of boys recall information more reliably than mothers of girls. While boys' behavior may be more memorable, however, researchers (Edelbrock, 1982; Stevenson, Parker, Wilkinson, Hegion, & Fish, 1976b) studying young children have found parent ratings of boys to have lower validity than ratings of girls. Also, a common finding is that parents' recollections about their children tend to be modified to conform to sex-linked stereotypes.

One study (Lichtenstein, in press), which investigated effects of population characteristics upon parent report validity, found that reports about first-born children were more predictive of school performance than were reports for later-born siblings. This study revealed the same pattern for screening test results, however, which suggests that the first-born children in this sample were more predictable in general. The study showed no sex differences in validity of parent reports. There was, however, a clear trend towards higher validity of parent reports for older preschool children.

To summarize, the most consistent findings regarding the type of parent information and methods of obtaining it are as follows: (1) reports of current status are more trustworthy than historical accounts, (2) descriptive reports of observable behavior are more reliable than those involving interpretation and inference by the parent, (3) structured methods of obtaining information that provide clear instructions and contain specific items produce the most meaningful data, and (4) measures must be of sufficient length to be reliable, but not so lengthy as to have a negative effect upon compliance and validity.

As for the effects of parent and child characteristics upon parent reports, the results are not clear-cut or consistent. One pattern regarding parent characteristics is that validity of parent reports correlates consistently (although to a low degree) with parent level of education, but inconsistently with SES. This suggests that the parent's ability to comprehend and carry out the information-providing task is the primary factor accounting for SES differences in those studies that yield this result.

Validity of Standardized Measures

Research for obtaining parent information with various standardized measures sheds further light on the value of alternative approaches. Two questions will be addressed here. The first is "How well does the parent's report of the child's behavior match up with the child's actual behavior?" This is typically evaluated by comparing the parent's report of the child's behavior and the child's behavior when tested. The second question, and the more relevant one for preschool screening, concerns the degree to which this information is predictive of the child's subsequent school performance, that is: "Can parent reports be used to predict those children who will have problems learning and/or adjusting to school?"

Research on the match between parent reports and independent testing of the same or similar behaviors has been conducted with both diagnostic parent report measures (Developmental Profile, Minnesota Child Development Inventory) and screening instruments (Denver Prescreening Developmental Questionnaire, Denver Articulation Screening Exam, Home Screening Questionnaire). These studies reveal fair to good agreement between parent information and a concurrent assessment of the child, with the strength of this relationship depending in large part upon the sophistication of the parent measure.

Boll and Alpern (1975) conducted a validity study in which 100 children ages 3 months to 12 years were both rated by mothers and tested on those items from the Developmental Profile (Alpern & Boll, 1972) that could be administered to children in test form. They reported that "the child's performance coincided with the parent's estimate of their ability to perform or not perform an item in 84 percent of the cases" (Boll & Alpern, 1975, p. 26). This percentage was fairly consistent across the five areas of the Developmental Profile, ranging from 81 percent agreement on the Communication scale to 87 percent on the Academic scale. As Boll and Alpern (1975) acknowledge, however, these results were obtained in a research situation in which mothers had little cause to distort their responses. In an actual screening situation, a parent might be more inclined to "shade" responses in either a consistently favorable or consistently unfavorable direction.

The correspondence between mothers' reports and psychological test data was investigated by Ireton, Thwing, and Currier (1977). This clinical study evaluated the validity of the Minnesota Child Development Inventory (Ireton & Thwing, 1974) by comparing mothers' MCDI reports with the results of psychological evaluations. The subjects were 109 preschool children who were evaluated for a variety of developmental problems at the Child Psychology Clinic at the University of Min-

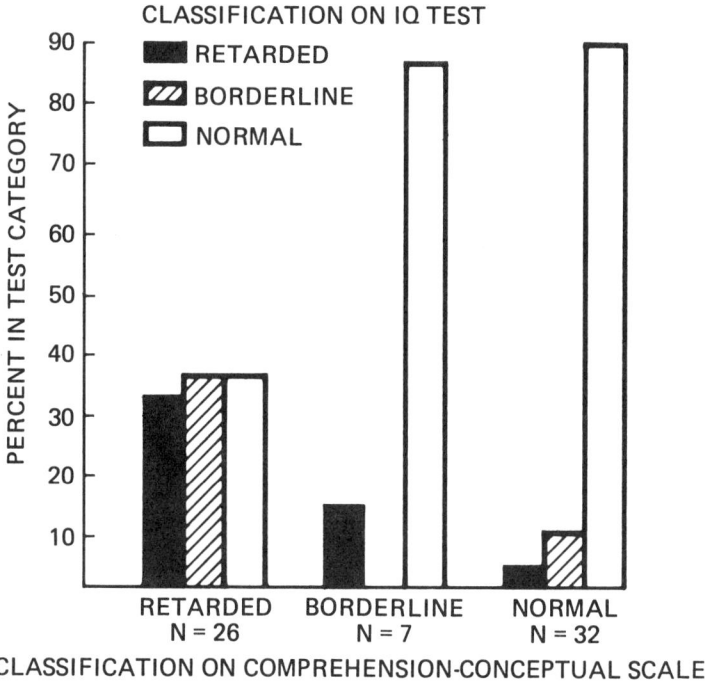

Fig. 3-1. Incidence of IQ deviation as a function
of comprehension-conceptual scale evaluation. (From
Ireton, Thwing, & Currier, 1977 with permission.)

nesota Health Sciences Center. Mothers' level of education ranged
from 11 to 20 years; 99 percent of the mothers were at least high school
graduates and 17 percent were college graduates. Mothers completed
the MCDI at the time of the psychological evaluation. Children were
classified according to the MCDI scales as normal, borderline, or
retarded on each scale. Psychological test results, including intelligence testing and fine motor and expressive language ratings, were
classified in a fashion similar to that used for the MCDI scales. Figure
3-1 shows the relationship between the MCDI Comprehension-Conceptual scale and intelligence test results. For those children classified as
retarded on the Comprehension-Conceptual scale of the MCDI, two-
thirds scored in the retarded or borderline range on intelligence testing; for those classified as normal on the Comprehension-Conceptual
scale, 90 percent had normal range IQ's and only one child had an IQ in
the retarded range.

The Denver Prescreening Developmental Questionnaire (PDQ),
designed to serve as an initial and additional step in the assessment

sequence, is based upon the assumption that parent reports will correspond closely with actual administration of the Denver Developmental Screening Test (DDST). From the results of a validity study comparing PDQ and DDST results for 1141 children, Frankenburg, van Doorninck, Liddell, and Dick (1976) concluded that the PDQ, used as a first-stage screening procedure, "decreased the need for DDST screening by almost 69 percent" (p. 752). This result was obtained by using a cutoff score of eight or fewer passes (out of a possible ten) on the PDQ as a basis for referring children for further screening. However, following this rule, the PDQ would have failed to identify 53 of the 136 children in this study who were classified as questionable or abnormal by the DDST. This discrepancy is understandable; the PDQ items given to the parent cover only part of the set of DDST items that would be administered, and a scale of only ten items can be expected to have limited reliability and validity.

Dopheide and Dallinger (1976) tried a somewhat different approach: they had parents test their children's articulation with a standardized screening test, and then compared the outcome with the same test administered by a speech and hearing clinician or aide at kindergarten screening. The instrument used in this study was the Denver Articulation Screening Exam (DASE) (Drumwright, 1971), an imitative test of 30 words. Two sets of DASE results were obtained for 73 children who were tested by parents approximately one week prior to kindergarten screening. High agreement was found primarily among those children whom parents reported to have no articulation problems. Of the 46 children whose parents reported no DASE errors, 38 were also scored as making no errors by the clinician or screening aide, and 45 were scored as making 3 errors or less. However, for the remaining 27 children there was little agreement and no consistent pattern of differences between parents' and screeners' DASE results. Dopheide and Dallinger (1976) concluded that "parent reports of errors made by their children on the DASE lack accuracy to the extent that the results cannot be accepted for children from four to six years of age" (p. 126), but noted the effectiveness of parents results when "no-error reports" are provided. (One wonders whether children with error-free articulation could be identified by parents equally well by report as by testing.)

Validity research with the Home Screening Questionnaire (HSQ) (Coons, Gay, Fandal, Ker, & Frankenburg, 1981) provided a comparison between the brief questionnaire format of the HSQ and the home interview/observation method of Caldwell and Bradley's (in press) HOME Inventory from which it was adapted. Since the HSQ is designed to quickly and economically approximate the results that would be obtained on the HOME Inventory, a validity study comparing the briefer measure with the "model" was a key part of the instrument development research. As part of the HSQ standardization study, parents from low-income areas of Denver provided data about their children with the HSQ and, two to four weeks later, in a HOME Inventory interview. The sample included 294 children in the 3–6 year age range, mostly white and Hispanic. The HSQ, in referring 66 percent of the children in this sample, identified 86 percent of the children whose HOME Inventory scores were in the bottom half of the sample. However, a heavy cost was incurred in the form of over-referrals: 21 percent of the children in the sample were referred by the HSQ yet scored in the top half of the sample on the HOME Inventory. These results suggest that the HSQ can introduce some economies in screening the home environment. But for this sample (i.e., families in the standardization population), two-thirds of the group was referred by the screening measure. Given this referral rate, it may be more practical to assess the home environment more directly (i.e., with the HOME Inventory) in all cases. Such a high referral rate for the HSQ may be expected as a matter of course. The instrument was standardized on a low income population and is not recommended for use with middle to upper SES populations or "in cultures which differ substantially from the population on which it was standardized" (Coons et al., 1981, p. 7).

Two validity studies addressed the matter of predicting a child's school performance from preschool screening reports by parents. The first (Lichtenstein, in press) provided a direct comparison between parent questionnaire and screening test results in predicting school performance. A developmental inventory that consisted of 29 items in the areas of social, self-help, and language functioning was completed by parents. The Minneapolis Preschool Screening Instrument (MPSI) (Lichtenstein, 1980b) was also administered as part of the screening battery. Screening test and parent report data on 391 urban children from a wide SES range were obtained throughout the year prior to kindergarten entry and validated against teacher ratings of school performance at the end of kindergarten. The developmental inventory total score correlated moderately with overall teacher ratings ($r = .49$), however, the correlation between the MPSI and overall teacher ratings was substantially higher ($r = .74$). This may be attributed to the nature of the criterion measure: the behaviors rated by teachers (e.g., learning habits, reading readiness, fine motor/perceptual motor, language development) were more closely related to the content of the screening test than to that of the parent inventory. Yet, the parent inventory language scale was remarkably successful in predicting school performance. The four-item scale had higher validity rates than the overall parent inventory in predicting school problems. Using a cutoff score that would refer 16 percent of the sample, the language scale identified 76 percent of the children who were later rated as having moderate or severe school problems.

In a second study (Ireton, Lun, & Kampen, 1981), validation research on the Minnesota Preschool Inventory (Ireton & Thwing, 1979) compared mothers' reports of their children obtained in the spring prior to kindergarten entry with children's performance in kindergarten. Kindergarten performance for a sample of 287 children was measured by teacher ratings obtained at the end of the school year. The Self-Help, Fine Motor, and Expressive Language scales of the MPI were not predictive of kindergarten performance, while the Comprehension, Memory, Letter Recognition, and Number Comprehension scales were predictive. Of 21 children with delayed performance on 1 or more of these 4 scales, 12 were rated as poor performers (bottom 5 percent) in kindergarten. This constituted 60 percent (12 of 20) of the children in the low kindergarten performance group.

As a whole, the research to date on parent report measures is fairly promising. In particular, instruments that focus on current observable behavior and that have been subjected to extensive test construction procedures have provided positive research findings. However, there is no evidence to suggest that the validity of parent reports is sufficient to justify their use in place of direct testing.

More research needs to be done on a wide range of relevant topics, such as (1) the effects of parents' level of education and their knowledge of child development on the validity of their reports, (2) the effect of extent of parents' opportunity to observe their child on validity of reports, (3) the relative efficiency of parent reports versus screening tests and other types of screening information, and (4) the optimal manner of combining parent reports and other sources of information in making screening decisions. Finally, we need to know when to utilize standardized inventory and interview formats in screening, and when to abandon these in favor of more informal or individualized strategies for dealing with certain groups or with certain parents.

Regardless of the validity rates demonstrated for parent reports in screening, they have one function of enormous importance and value: establishing a pattern of parent involvement.

THE PARENT-PROFESSIONAL PARTNERSHIP

Parents place their egos on the line when they submit their children to preschool screening. Much as they want the best for their children, they are also fearful that their children will be found deficient in some way. To their minds, this might imply that they are bad parents, that they have deprived their children, that they have bad genes, or any number of negative conclusions. By and large, parents do not want to be made to feel that they are responsible for, but they do want to take responsibility for, their children's problems. Parents have positive feelings about themselves as parents when they are active participants in the care and education of their children.

Screening professionals, recognizing the natural vulnerability of parents, must create a climate and a system of collaboration in working with parents. Actively involving parents in obtaining needed screening information conveys the message that their knowledge of, and concerns about, their children are of paramount importance. Professionals must convey to parents that "you can provide important information about your child's development and functioning," that "your concerns and questions will be heard and addressed," and that "your ideas and opinions about what is needed are valuable."

What may happen instead is that professionals, in demonstrating their expert skills in diagnosing and treating children, pronounce their verdicts about children with great assurance and excessive jargon. The professional rarely admits to uncertainty or acknowledges the limits of his or her expertise. Parents are made to feel stupid and incompetent by comparison. This trend can be reversed by programs with a genuine commitment to a collaborative model, as Litman, Barston & Nabin (1982) illustrated by some comments of parents participating in one early childhood program:

> It took me a long time to realize that I know more about my child than anyone else. Sometimes professionals try to make you think they know all the answers. They sometimes make you feel like you don't know anything. I spend 24 hours a day with my son and I know more about him. However, I've found that professionals really can help me and my son, because they have many techniques and skills which really work.

> I used to feel so stupid when I didn't understand what professionals were talking about. Now I'm able to stop them and ask them to explain what they're talking about in language I understand. I've realized I'm not stupid. I'm just not familiar with the words they use.

A basic starting point for establishing productive relationships with parents is at the communication level. The professional must establish rapport with parents by making them feel expected and welcome, addressing them personally, listening to them, encouraging their input, accepting their feelings, supporting their parenting efforts, and speaking to them in plain language without "talking down."

An essential element in screening is that parents need to be provided with clear, straightforward explanations of (1) the purposes of screening, (2) the procedures that are involved, and (3) the parents' role in the process. Yet, even when clear explanations have been provided in advance, misunderstandings and misconceptions are quite common. The following points bear repeating or clarifying with parents at the time of screening:

1. How much time the screening will involve.
2. What kind of participation will be requested of the parent.
3. What is the nature of screening procedures that involve direct assessment of the child.
4. What kind of information will and will not be provided consequent to screening (that is, screening will yield decisions regarding need for further assessment, not a diagnostic summary of developmental functioning).
5. What educational rights and procedural safeguards are guaranteed by state and federal laws.

It may be helpful to think of the parents' prospective role in terms of a continuum of involvement, ranging from passive recipient of a service on the one end to active participant and collaborator in the process on the other end. The parent-professional partnership can be put into effect at every step of the process: (1) collection of screening information, (2) integration or synthesis of the overall information, and (3) determination of the implications of this information, i.e., "what needs to be done?"

At the data collection stage, parents can contribute their observations and perceptions of the child. (Involvement of both parents in two-parents families is desirable, but typically not the case.) Parents may also raise questions or concerns about the child's development or behavior. The screening process is then shaped to some degree by the nature of the questions and concerns introduced by parents.

Integration of screening results should include all of the information obtained: parent report information, test results, and observations of the child in the screening situation. All of these sources are subject to possible invalidity. Discrepancies between parent reports and test results should not be treated as automatic evidence of invalidity of the parent's report, but should be resolved with the parent.

If test results reveal possible development problems while none are reported by the parent, further discussion may enable the professional to determine the reason for this difference in perceptions. This might involve situations such as the following:

• The child demonstrates a higher level of functioning in the home than that observed in screening because of the child's discomfort in a strange setting and/or lack of familiarity with the examiner. Rescreening at a later date might be proposed.

- Familial or environmental factors have shaped parent expectations of normal behavior for the child, expectations that are inconsistent with those introduced by screening procedures. These differences might be resolved by an explanation of age expectations and how they relate to school performance, something that a skillful professional can deal with on the individual level. Or, they may be indicative of cultural bias in the screening process, which is cause for examining the nature of the entire process.

- The parent is defensive about the possibility that the child may have a problem. When this occurs, considerable professional skill is required to maintain rapport and to handle the situation in such a way that the child will have access to the services needed. This is a matter of professional sensitivity and expertise that is beyond any simple recommendation for management. Maintaining the focus on ways to help the child rather than insisting that the parent acknowledge the potential problem is more likely to lead to a productive resolution of this situation. The immediate goal is to secure the parent's cooperation in proceeding with needed follow-up assessment.

Or, the opposite situation might apply: the parent may report problems that are unsubstantiated by screening. The parent's concern may involve behaviors or functions that could not be adequately assessed or were not assessed by direct screening procedures, e.g., telling bizarre stories, self-mutilation, bedwetting, or left-right confusion. In this case, the information from the parent would complement the direct screening results. The parent's added input may be cause to refer the child for further assessment (as in the case of self-mutilation), or may be something that the professional would explain to be typical for preschoolers and no reason to be concerned (e.g., left-right confusion). The child may also demonstrate competencies during screening that are more advanced than those reported by the parent. The professional might advise the parent to look for (or pull for) particular behaviors, and to return for rescreening if these are not observed.

Even when there is not a fundamental difference between the parent's and professional's perceptions, the professional's role in the feedback discussion demands great sensitivity. While the discussion focus is on the basic screening outcome, the professional should also address the issues initially raised by the parent—perceptions of the child, questions, concerns, etc. Some recommendations on conducting a feedback interview are as follows:

1. Even though the amount of time available to meet with each parent may be relatively brief, the professional must make every effort to establish a relaxed environment and to give the parent his or her undivided attention. To insure that time is used efficiently, the professional might preview the matters to be discussed and indicate how much time is available. If this is insufficient to adequately address relevant matters, a follow-up interview or phone contact might be arranged.

2. The discussion should take place in a room or area that affords adequate privacy. Otherwise, parents may be disconcerted, even upset, to be publicly discussing their child's screening results and may be reluctant to make frank disclosures. Lack of space is not an acceptable excuse; this is a consideration that should be addressed at the planning stage of the screening program.

3. The feedback interview should progress from the level of description (what the child is and is not doing), toward interpretation (what these findings mean), towards recommendations (what may be helpful for the child at this stage of development). This applies equally if the child is developing within normal expectations. The parent should not just be told that the child has passed, but how it was determined and what can be concluded from this outcome. Does a "no referral" outcome mean that the child has no developmental problems or special needs, that the child is assured of success in school, that there are no marked indicators of handicapping conditions, or what?

4. It is usually best to begin by acknowledging the child's strengths and most mature areas of development before raising questions about areas of development that are less mature.

5. If the parent reports significantly delayed development and is concerned about the child's functioning, the professional can integrate this with screening results to form the basis of a discussion about the child's possible problems and needs. This may lead to a referral for further assessment or to other relevant resources (e.g., a social service agency, an optometrist, a community health care center). Alternatively, if the professional is uncertain that the child is truly at risk, the professional may suggest activities that can enhance the child's development and schedule a return visit in the coming months.

6. If the parent has no particular concerns about the child's development and screening results indicate development within the expected range, brief guidance, encouragement, and general parenting resource materials can be provided.

The underlying objective that guides the professional in the interview, as throughout the screening process, is to promote the healthy development of the child. A key factor in this is to establish a cooperative relationship with the parent, which the professional fosters by supporting the parent's self-esteem and parenting skills in the course of their interactions.

As parents contribute to the assessment of their children, the stage is set for ongoing collaboration. Boll and Alpern (1975) observed this phenomenon in the course of interviewing parents with the Developmental Profile:

> Parents who have been interviewed about their child's developmental competence . . . have, in many instances, spontaneously suggested remedial action or shown increased acceptance of recommendations for remediation. They recognize that the data generating the recommendations have come from them rather than from an assessment in which they have no part. (p. 27)

Programs That Empower Parents

Some programs have been designed to enhance the development of children while enabling parents to assert their parent roles more confidently and effectively. They are based on the assumptions that learning begins at birth and that parents are the primary and most influential teachers of young children. By providing support, information, and education in parenting, these programs directly involve parents in the education of their children.

The Bloomington (Minnesota) Early Childhood and Family Education Program is one such program. The program provides support and information to parents to help them foster the physical, mental, social-emotional, and intellectual growth of infants and preschool children. Parents receive guidance in responding to the child's changing developmental needs, coping with the child's behavior and concerns, and developing positive parenting skills through weekly support/discussion groups.

While parents are in discussion groups with a parent educator/facilitator, the children are in the "Learn and Play" classroom conducted by a certified early childhood teacher and trained aides. During this time, the children engage in all kinds of free and structured play activities with same-age peers. As a source of material for the support/discussion groups, parents are encouraged to observe their children in various situations: (1) in the classroom (through an observation window), (2) when they join their child during the parent-child interaction portion of class, and (3) at home with the help of take-home observation sheets.

Following this first segment of class in which parents and children meet separately, the early childhood teacher joins the parents' group and shares his or her observations about what the children did during this period. The parents are then given an explanation of the activities that they will be doing with their children during the next portion of class. Activities center around a different theme each week. Along with explaining what the activities will be, the early childhood teacher tells the parents what developmental skills the activities are designed to teach and how the parent can assist as a teacher/observer. Ideas are shared as to how activities can be carried out at home.

During the 30–45 minute parent-child interaction portion of class that follows, the early childhood teacher guides the parents and children in large group, small group, and one-to-one parent-child learning activities. In addition to enhancing the young child's development, the aim of these sessions is to build parental and child self-esteem and encourage a joy of learning. Through these "hands on" experiences as participants in the child's learning, parents and teachers have opportunities to observe and assess how well each child is doing and can pinpoint specific developmental needs to work on in class or at home.

The Early Childhood and Family Education Program operates in conjunction with other school district programs and local agencies that provide educational, social, or health services to families with young children. For instance, the program may refer parents to professionals in the school system, i.e., nurses, psychologists, social workers, speech clinicians, or to the local health department, social service, community agencies, private professionals, etc. The program also receives many referrals from a variety of community professionals who feel that the program would benefit parents and/or children they are seeing.

SUMMARY

The importance of involving parents in meeting the educational needs of their children has long been recognized. The challenge of finding ways of working with parents in the early identification and remediation of their children's developmental and educational problems has only been partly met. At both screening and assessment levels, useful methods for obtaining developmental information from parents do exist. However, professionals' skepticism regarding parent's ability to be objective about their children have limited the use of this information source.

The reliability and validity of parental reports is a complex function of the characteristics of the parent, the type of information requested, and the nature of the method used to obtain the information. Research suggests that parents are most likely to provide trustworthy information when the method employed is structured, includes clear instructions and specific items, and the information requested pertains to the child's current observable behavior. Parent comprehension of the request for information is also a factor. It does appear that parents have been given less credit than they deserve for providing valuable information regarding their children's development.

Collaboration at the screening level sets the stage for collaboration when assessment is indicated and when intervention is planned and provided for the child. Parent involvement in screening begins by providing the parent with an opportunity to report on the child's development and to raise concerns or questions, if any. Screening data based both upon parent information and on direct observation and testing of the child then provide a sound basis for recognition and for discussion of the child's apparent problems. A positive, informative relationship with parents at screening (and thereafter) will be helpful to the parents as well as the child. A preschool screening program with these elements optimizes the prospects for making appropriate decisions, and lays the groundwork for effective parent-school relationships.

4

Selecting Screening Instruments

A critical link in the chain of planning a screening program is the selection of appropriate screening measures. A systematic approach to instrument selection involves (1) clarifying the needs and constraints of the particular screening situation, (2) gathering information on prospective measures, and (3) evaluating alternative choices on the basis of meaningful selection criteria. The early part of this chapter elaborates upon the process and principles of screening instrument selection. This is followed by an overview of currently available preschool screening instruments and comprehensive reviews of selected instruments.

FRAMING THE SELECTION TASK

The uncertainty and confusion that may arise in the selection of preschool screening procedures is often a consequence of the way the task is approached. The program planner typically follows a train of thought that goes something like this: (a) To do screening, we need a screening test, and (b) we want to use the best screening test, so what we need to know is (c) which is the best screening test? (The authors of this book can attest to the fact that this is far and away the most frequently asked question by planners of screening programs.)

Resolving the matter of "the best screening test" may result in a terminal case of exasperation, mainly because the question limits our thinking on the matter. Assumptions that inappropriately define the task are made by this question. The first assumption is that tests are the optimal and exclusive method for obtaining the kind of information needed. Other methods may also prove valuable, such as parental reports about the child and observation of the child by screening personnel. Second, the assumption that there is one "best" test (or procedure) implies that all preschool screening programs are the same and require the same kind of measures. Actually, each screening program is unique in terms of the population served and the resources available for screening, follow-up assessment, and intervention. The task should not be conceived of as identifying the best test, but as designing the most appropriate screening process for the situation.

A more productive question to begin with is, "What kind of information about the child is most useful and practical to obtain in this particular situation?" Before jumping to any conclusions about the methods to be used, it is important to establish how the screening process will be shaped by characteristics and constraints of the particular situation. Following are the considerations that must be taken into account.

Screening Program Objectives

The primary defining characteristics of a screening program—who is to be identified for what purpose—determine the nature and the extent of the information needed. In general, for preschool screening, the "who" is educationally handicapped children ages 3–5, and the purpose is to provide early intervention services that facilitate educational progress. Screening data on physical and sensory functioning, environmental influences, and developmental functioning may all be relevant to this task; a more precise statement of program objectives should indicate the relative emphasis to be placed upon each of these components. Furthermore, specifics regarding the nature of follow-up services to be provided may clarify what particular areas of development should be the focus of screening. Once the intended content of screening information is clear, the method of data collection can be purposefully chosen. Certain types of information are most effectively obtained through direct testing, others through third person reports.

Resources

A screening program's resources often pose limits upon the choice of procedures to be used. The cost of materials or the time required for administration may rule out certain procedures. Cost factors may require the use of paraprofessional or volunteer examiners, for whom some procedures would be inappropriate. Even if sufficient funds are available, professional personnel with the requisite expertise might not be. Also, when screening procedures are to be administered by nonprofessionals, the resources (i.e., money and personnel) for training and supervision that are required by a given procedure must be taken into account.

Nature of the Community

Community and parent characteristics may affect what sources of information are most readily available and will be regarded as acceptable. For example, it may be convenient and productive to obtain information about preschoolers from sophisticated, concerned parents who are eager to contribute. On the other hand, there may be situations where it is easier to arrange for direct testing of children than to obtain questionnaire or interview data from parents; for example, in a community with a high proportion of working parents whose children are enrolled in day care centers or preschool programs. Characteristics of the screening population—socioeconomic, cultural/racial, environmental, and geographic—may also determine the type and content of procedures that are appropriate and acceptable.

After assessing situational characteristics and constraints to determine the kind of information that will be most useful and practical, the next question to ask is "What instruments or measures will best provide this information?" In reviewing alternative instruments, the prospective user must, first, identify those measures that are compatible with the needs of the particular screening program and, second, determine the relative value of those instruments that are suitable.

The logical starting point is to review commercially available tests and inventories before giving any thought to constructing "homemade" measures. Instrument development is unnecessary if an acceptable existing measure can be found. Constructing a high-quality, standardized test or inventory is demanding, time-consuming, and expensive (that is, assuming the task is conscientiously done). In many instances, screening program planners seeking a simple and useful screening measure find no existing instrument to be fully acceptable, and proceed to construct a new test that is "acceptable" only to the program or agency for which it was devised.

Other procedures such as direct observation of the child by a professional or open-ended parent interviews may be considered. As discussed in previous chapters, each of these has its limitations and would most likely be used as a supplement to standardized instruments. Although the focus of this chapter is on screening instruments (i.e., tests and parent and teacher reports), the guidelines for evaluating screening measures presented in this chapter are applicable to other procedures as well.

REFERENCE SOURCES

As a first step toward identifying instruments that fit screening program needs, the user might consult sources that provide information on specific tests and measures. The references described below are particularly valuable sources of information. Some are general in their coverage; others specialize in measures for screening or for young children. All provide basic descriptive data (e.g., author, copyright date, publisher and address, cost, age range, administration time), and some include critical evaluation of instruments as well.

Barnes, K. E. *Preschool screening: The measurement and prediction of children at-risk.* Springfield, Ill.: Charles C. Thomas, 1982.

Exclusively devoted to preschool screening, this book is evenly divided between (1) measurement theory and guidelines that relate to screening procedures and (2) reviews of selected preschool screening measures. The coverage of measurement issues, such as construction, standardization, norms, reliability, validity, and utility is the most comprehensive to be found on the specific topic of screening, although rather technical in parts. With regard to the reviews, the author cautions that this is "not a comprehensive handbook or directory"; reviews are limited to those instruments that are suitable in design for screening and that have been the subject of some research. Instrument reviews are fairly long, with particular emphasis given to description and critique of research findings. As organized by chapters, the book includes eight reviews of hearing and vision measures (four each), three reviews of speech and language measures (all of articulation), three measures of general development, six of academic readiness, and nine "measures at the experimental-research stage."

Buros, O. K. (Ed.). *The eighth mental measurements yearbook.* Highland Park, N.J.: Gryphon Press, 1978.

This monumental work (two volumes, 2182 pages) is the definitive reference book for educational and psychological measures in general. In addition to basic descriptive data and an exhaustive reference list, critical reviews by testing and measurement experts are provided for many entries. Since the current edition is the eighth in a series, it is necessary to refer back to *The seventh mental measurements yearbook* (Buros, 1972) or earlier editions for reviews of older instruments. Instruments are arranged by subject but, with no category for screening or for preschool assessment, preschool screening instruments are scattered over the two volumes under various subject headings, such as intelligence, school readiness, speech and hearing, etc. Publication of *The ninth mental measurements yearbook* is planned for 1986.

Davidson, J. B., Lichtenstein, R., Canter, A., & Cronin, P. *Directory of developmental screening instruments.* Minneapolis: Minneapolis Public Schools, 1977. (Available as ERIC Document No. ED 172 466.)

A large proportion of the 137 entries in this collection are instruments for screening of preschool children. Entries are arranged alphabetically, with information presented in a standard format that includes publication data, age range, purpose, content areas, types of scores provided, examiner or rater characteristics, administration time, etc. Technical data and critiques from the research literature and from other reference sources are briefly summarized and cited.

Frankenburg, W. K., & Camp, B. W. (Eds.). *Pediatric screening tests.* Springfield, Ill.: Charles C. Thomas, 1975.

Although medical screening is the primary emphasis, this book contains chapters on developmental screening, speech and language, and school readiness and achievement. Each chapter opens with a discussion of the area, which is followed by reviews of selected tests by experts in the respective area. Most of the instruments reviewed in the developmental screening and the speech and language sections (with 10 and 11 entries, respectively) and about half of those in the school readiness section (16 total entries) are applicable for preschool age children.

Goodwin, W. L., & Driscoll, L. A. *Handbook for measurement and evaluation in early childhood education.* San Francisco: Jossey-Bass, 1980.

This encylopedic work devotes comprehensive coverage to the topics of individual evaluation of young children and evaluation of programs in early childhood education. Various chapters address the "nature and status" of observational measurement, intelligence tests, developmental and handicapped screening surveys, language and bilingual tests, creativity tests, psychomotor measures, and affective measures. However, reviews of specific instruments are limited to a selected set of "illustrative measures" in each area, 43 in all. These reviews provide descriptive and technical information as well as critical commentary on screening and assessment measures.

Johnson, H. W. *Preschool test descriptions: Test matrix and correlated test descriptors.* Springfield, Ill.: Charles C. Thomas, 1979.

Primarily descriptive information is presented on 130 preschool screening and assessment instruments. A standard format is used for test entries, which breaks down into general categories of identifying information, administration, examinee appropriateness, interpretation, and technical aspects. Much of this information, plus a checklist of content areas covered by each measure, is additionally compiled in matrix form. Caution is advised in using this as a sole reference; descriptions are brief and often incomplete.

Johnson, O. G. *Tests and measurements in child development: Handbook II.* San Francisco: Jossey-Bass, 1976.

This work in two volumes provides information and references on approximately 900 unpublished measures, those not to be found in Buros' *Mental measurements yearbook* series. *Handbook II* contains measures that appeared in the literature during the years 1966 through 1974. (*Handbook I* covered the previous decade.) Descriptions of measures are fairly complete and accompanied by examples of test items. Technical data are concisely reported and a bibliography is provided for each measure. (Unfortunately, the reader is left to guess which reference in the bibliography is the source of which research described in the review.) Given that this is a specialized reference (i.e., of unpublished measures) and that neither preschool nor screening instruments are grouped as a set, this reference is more useful for investigating specific instruments than for a blind initial search.

Southworth, L. E., Burr, R. L., & Cox, A. E. *Screening and evaluating the young child: A handbook of instruments to use from infancy to six years.* Springfield, Ill.: Charles C. Thomas, 1981.

This specialized reference book is the single most complete source of descriptive information on preschool screening instruments. The book is oriented towards the early childhood educator, and does not include instruments designed for administration by professional examiners. Individually administered screening and assessment instruments are arranged under eight categories: cognitive (with 17 entries), comprehensive (54 entries), language/bilingual (25), motor skills (3), readiness (23), socioemotional (21), speech/hearing/vision (7), and visual motor/visual perceptual (11). Group administered instruments are listed in a separate section. In addition to basic descriptive data, a one or two paragraph description of each instrument that summarizes the content of the measure and usually includes sample items is provided. Instruments are not evaluated in any way, and the only reference made to technical data is whether or not such information is to be found in the instrument manual.

Stangler, S. R., Huber, C. J., & Routh, D. K. *Screening growth and development of preschool children: A guide for test selection.* New York: McGraw-Hill, 1980.

This book by two nursing professionals and a psychologist has a clear pediatric emphasis and is best described as an update of Frankenburg and Camp's (1975) *Pediatric screening tests.* Overview chapters on early development, early identification, and test selection criteria are followed by five chapters devoted to separate content areas: growth measures, tests of general development, hearing tests, speech and language tests, and vision tests. The chapters on development and on speech and language include reviews of nine and four measures, respectively. The reviews contain descriptive and technical information, plus critical commentary.

Strully, C. F. *Test analyses: Screening and verification instruments for preschool children. Volume I.* Harrisburg, Pa.: Pennsylvania State Department of Education, 1977. (Available as ERIC Document No. ED 135 856.)

This is the first of three volumes produced by Project CONNECT, a technical assistance project specially funded through the Pennsylvania Department of Education's Lancaster-Lebanon unit, consisting of data on specific instruments for educational screening and assessment. In Volume I, 68 preschool level instruments are covered according to a comprehensive and standard outline. The general headings, which are in turn broken down into specific categories, are bibliographic (i.e., publication) information, descriptive information, examinee appropriateness, administrative considerations, scoring and interpretation, implications for programming, normative data, technical aspects, and references. While the *Test analyses* set was distributed on a limited statewide basis and is now out of print, Volume I can be accessed through ERIC (see Appendix for address).

In addition to this list, other sources should be noted that are now somewhat outdated but may be of occasional value. Johnson and Bommarito's (1971) *Tests and measurements in child development: Handbook I,* as indicated above, is not an earlier version of *Handbook II* but a completely distinct collection covering a previous time period. Another ambitious project, conducted at UCLA's Center for the Study of Evaluation and Early Childhood Research Center, undertook the perilous task of evaluating tests on the basis of objective criteria. These researchers (Hoepfner, Stern, & Nummedal, 1971), in compiling *CSE-ECRC preschool/kindergarten test evaluations,* assigned quantitative ratings to approximately 150 published tests in each of 25 specific rating categories, which in turn yielded composite ratings in four areas: measurement validity, examinee appropriateness, administrative usability, and "normed technical excellence." Walker's (1973) *Socioemotional measures for preschool and kindergarten children* contains reviews of instruments for assessing social-emotional development (self-concept, emotional adjustment, social skills, interests and preferences, behavior traits, etc.) of children ages 3–6.

Another significant reference is the *Tests in print* series, which serves as "a comprehensive bibliography of all known tests published as separates for use with English-speaking subjects" (Buros, 1974, p. xxi) as well as a master index to supplement the *Mental measurements yearbooks.* The most recent in the set, *Tests in print II* (Buros, 1974), is now rather dated (the late Oscar Buros' desire to have this collection updated every two years has been far from realized), but the publication of *Tests in print III* (Mitchell, in press) should coincide closely with that of this book. *Tests in print III* will contain nearly 2700 entries, listed alphabetically and indexed by subject heading, and will follow the same format as its predecessors, which includes publication information, test population characteristics, scores produced, references to reviews in *Mental measurements yearbooks,* and an exhaustive reference list for each entry.

An additional resource to help users identify prospective screening instruments is the set of tables appearing later in this chapter. Among the information included in these tables are reference sources in which each instrument is described.

CHARACTERISTICS OF A USEFUL SCREENING PROCEDURE

In selecting among screening procedures, the conscientious instrument user must assume a consumer's perspective. In many ways, choosing among alternative screening measures is like buying a new car. First, the auto consumer identifies the general class of automobiles from which to choose based upon particular needs and driving circum-stances: the long-distance commuter may look at high mileage com-pacts, while a station wagon may be the vehicle of choice for a large family. By analogy, selection of screening instruments is shaped by program objectives, resources, and community characteristics. The auto buyer typically has a price range as a limiting factor, a limitation that may rule out luxury cars . . . just as the screening instrument user may rule out procedures that require a professional examiner.

Next, the consumer is faced with the task of comparing the good and bad features among those alternatives that meet the initial specifi-cations. Foremost is the matter of how well a given car will carry out its basic function of transportation. A car should perform well in terms of acceleration, shifting, high-speed cruising, and braking; and it should start reliably and perform consistently. These considerations may be compared to the essential features, or *psychometric characteristics,* of measuring devices. A screening instrument should demonstrate high performance, i.e., *validity,* in carrying out its basic function of identify-ing individuals with special needs. And it should do so with high *reliability.*

In addition, the auto buyer needs to be assured that a given car will be virtually identical to others of the same model, and that the specifi-cations and instructions in the owner's manual (as well as spare parts) will match the car he or she might receive. This may be compared to *standardization* of a screening instrument.

Auto manufacturers provide all kinds of technical and testimonial evidence to support their claims that a car can be counted on for high performance and reliability—and more. The discerning consumer is well aware of the need to consider these claims carefully, and places greater weight upon independent reviews (such as from *Consumer Re-ports*) and comments of present car owners. Likewise, the instrument user must critically evaluate an author's or publisher's claims that a measure is reliable, valid, and appropriately standardized for various populations. The knowledgeable user, in analyzing the evidence, knows which technical data to focus on and which to disregard, and knows what are acceptable levels and standards for psychometric characteristics.

The new car buyer also cares about features that are secondary to the car's main function, such as attractive styling, a comfortable and quiet ride, a good radio, and ample storage space. Similarly, *qualitative characteristics* of a screening instrument's manual, administration and scoring procedures, materials, content, and acceptability to program participants may contribute to its value.

The final and critical factor for the auto buyer is cost, of which the sticker price is only one factor. Cars also vary in terms of operating costs, which are determined by gas mileage, repairs, maintenance requirements, and life of the car. Similarly, the operating costs of a screening program are affected by variables associated with the choice of screening instruments, e.g., consumable materials, personnel requirements, and administration time.

The consumer tries to arrive at the best decision based upon an estimate of "how much car can be bought for the money." The screening instrument user seeks to maximize cost-effectiveness as well. The overall value of an instrument is determined by weighing together all relevant factors, especially validity and cost.

Validity

Validity concerns the crucial question, "How well does a measure do what it is intended to do?" One would conclude that a college entrance test is valid if individuals with high scores subsequently graduate from college with honors, while those with low scores flunk out. In this way, a test may prove to be related to the "real-life" circumstances that test performance is designed to simulate. In the case of screening measures, the objective is to identify those individuals who prove to be in need of special services due to some problem or condition. A screening instrument is valid to the extent that it differentiates between those individuals who have the problem or condition in question and those who do not, or between those who are at risk for a given problem (e.g., school failure) and those who are not at risk.

Evidence of a screening measure's validity may be of several types. The first type, *content validity,* pertains to evidence that a test or instrument contains the "right stuff." That is, the instrument's content should be consistent with the domain of skills, abilities, or behaviors that the instrument purports to measure. Ideally, the material chosen should comprise a representative cross-section of the area or areas, of concern. For example, a self-help measure might include aspects of eating habits, dressing, personal hygiene, and mobility, although none of these categories by itself would suffice. The prospective user should not only take note of the areas represented, and the specific content within these areas, but also the difficulty level of the items. A screening instrument should be designed to discriminate between the majority of children who function within age expectations and the few who are notably below. Items that are easy for most children at a given age—passed by, say 75–95 percent of an age group—tend to be most effective for this purpose. Item difficulty figures, when provided, are useful for determining the appropriateness of instrument content at particular age levels.

Content validity is usually demonstrated (or claimed) by the author of an instrument by describing how the measure was constructed. Content validity is built into a measure by systematically defining the set of behaviors that should be assessed, and then matching the content to this set. For example, in order to construct a school readiness test with high content validity, a researcher might observe kindergarten and first grade classrooms or might interview teachers to determine what is actually required of students.

While content validity generally serves as an initial check on an instrument's appropriateness, the acid test is whether the measure works as intended in actual practice. In the case of a preschool screening instrument, this involves investigating whether the instrument refers those children, and only those children, with the particular problem, condition, or special needs that it is designed to identify. To test this out, the results yielded by a screening instrument are compared to some *criterion measure* that is a meaningful indicator of the target condition or problem. Commonly used as criterion measures for validating preschool screening instruments are (1) standardized measures of a child's skill or ability level (e.g., achievement or intelligence tests) and (2) teacher ratings of a child's classroom performance. The comparison of screening instrument and criterion measure results for a given sample provides an indication of *criterion-related validity*.

There are two types of criterion-related validity, which are distinguished by the temporal relationship between administration of the screening measure and the criterion measure. *Concurrent validity* refers to the situation where a screening instrument is administered at approximately the same time as the criterion measure. This is used to determine an instrument's value for describing a child's current status, skills, or behaviors. The second type, *predictive validity,* refers to the situation where the criterion measure is obtained some time after the screening instrument is administered, typically six months or longer. This would be used to assess a measure's capacity for predicting a child's status or performance at some future point. For example, a screening measure that is intended to predict those children who will have difficulty in school might be administered to children prior to school entry, and then validated against measures of school performance at the end of first grade.

The degree of correspondence between assessment measures and criterion measures is frequently expressed by Pearson correlation coefficients, also known as simply *correlations.* Correlations indicate the strength of the relationship between two measures. Or, put another way, correlations reflect the accuracy with which one measure can be used to predict a second measure. Correlation coefficient values range from minus 1 to plus 1. Positive values indicate a direct relationship, that is, an individual with a high score on one measure tends to have a high score on the other, and low scores similarly go together. Negative correlations indicate an inverse relationship—an individual with a high score on one measure tends to have a low score on the other. Zero or near-zero correlations indicate random correspondence, or independence, of scores of the two measures.

Correlations between various measures of development or of ability tend to correlate positively, although the exact magnitude may vary widely. Correlations of under .30 are rather low and would not be regarded as supportive of a measure's validity. Correlations in the range of .40–.50 reflect a moderate relationship between two measures; correlations near .60 may be described as moderately high; and correlations over .75 are distinctly high. In presenting validity data, researchers may state that a correlation is "statistically significant" or simply "significant." This is a technical term meaning that the probability that the measures are related is better than chance, and should not be equated with practical significance or meaningfulness. Such a statement may be trivial and misleading when the analysis is actually intended to demonstrate a substantial, rather than a "better than chance," relationship between measures. Significance levels are affected by the size of the sample used to derive the correlation. With a sufficiently large sample, correlations as low as .10 may be statistically significant.

Although criterion-related validity is often reported in correlational terms, correlations provide only an approximation, at best, of a screening measure's accuracy in assigning individuals to categories (Lichtenstein, 1981; Rubin, Balow, Dorle, & Rosen, 1978). A far more appropriate method for presenting validity of screening procedures is in terms of *classificational* outcomes. Using the classificational method, validity is measured by comparing the screening decision, i.e., whether or not to refer a child, with the child's "actual" status as determined by some criterion measure. As an example, Figure 4-1 shows the relationship between classificational outcomes on the Minneapolis Preschool Screening Instrument prior to school entry and on the Metropolitan Readiness Test in first grade. A favorable ratio of corresponding outcomes (represented by the upper-left and lower-right cells in Figure 4-1) to noncorresponding outcomes (the upper-right and lower-left cells) is indicative of high validity. The classificational, or *hit rate,* approach to presenting validity data provides a direct indication of a measure's suitability for the decision-making function of screening, whereas correlations provide only a hint as to how well a screening measure will perform its intended task.

Criterion-related validity studies are conducted in order to obtain an estimate of a measure's validity. It may seem self-evident that any

Metropolitan Readiness Test

		Low performance*	Satisfactory performance
MPSI	Refer	25	19
	Pass	17	235

*Low performance defined as more than one standard deviation below the mean (0-16th percentile).

Fig. 4-1. Classificational presentation of screening measure validity.

given study will yield unique results and provide only an estimate of validity, yet there is a tendency to regard the results of a study as revealing *the* validity of a measure. One factor that may vary from study to study is the criterion measure. A criterion measure that is itself an invalid instrument or that measures something quite different from the screening instrument will yield a poor estimate of validity. Furthermore, characteristics of the study sample affect the results obtained. For example, validity figures tend to increase with the range of abilities present in the sample. Thus, the validity of a screening instrument will be overestimated if derived from a sample that includes both extremely low and high functioning children. It should be stressed that the results of a criterion-related validity study are indicative of how an instrument may be expected to perform when used with a population that resembles the sample studies.

Reliability

A screening measure must yield consistent results. If contradictory results are obtained for a child when the same test is administered on different occasions or by different examiners, the information is meaningless as a basis for making decisions. Of course, measurement of a child's developmental functioning will not be as consistent as the measurement of height and weight. Still, a good screening procedure is one that is reliable enough to consistently yield results within a relatively narrow range. The more reliable the measure, the smaller this range will be; that is, the more confidence one has that the score or result obtained is close to the mark. (The term *confidence interval* refers to the range in which the true score may be expected to fall.)

Lack of reliability in a preschool screening measure may be due to any of the following factors:

1. Variability within the child.

    Some degree of performance variation from one occasion to another is present in any measure of human functioning. Just as a high jumper may clear six feet one day and not the next, a preschool child may draw a good likeness of a square on Tuesday and on Friday, but not on Thursday. A child's functioning also varies due to fluctuations in mood, alertness, and motivation. A preschooler may be alert and talkative on a given day and earn high scores on a screening test, or may be tired and uncomfortable on another day and perform relatively poorly.

2. Variability across situations.

    The circumstances under which screening information is obtained may affect reliability. For example, a young child, finding a testing situation to be unfamiliar and threatening, may respond cautiously, negatively, or not at all to test demands and thereby fail to demonstrate competencies typically shown at home. One testing environment may differ from another in terms of comfort, background noise, or visual distractions. Parent reports may also be affected by the nature of the situation. Circumstances may be such that a parent feels the need to present the child in a positively exaggerated light.

3. Variability among examiners or raters.

    To some degree, the outcome of a screening procedure depends upon the judgment of the person doing the scoring. Generally, the more judgment an examiner or rater must use in deciding whether to give credit for a particular response, the less reliable the procedure. For example, in scoring responses to a screening test, it may be unclear without precise scoring rules and samples whether a child has "copied a square", or whether a child can "walk backwards" without guidelines as to how far he or she must walk and how many attempts may be allowed. Examiner error in recording responses or computing a child's age also has an adverse effect upon the reliability of a measure. In the case of a rating scale or observation checklist, more precise definitions of behaviors or skills lead to higher reliability. For example, the item "Communicates well" is harder to rate objectively than "Uses sentences or four or more words." Each examiner or rater would operate according to a different (i.e., personal) set of guidelines with the former, but use more consistent criteria with the latter.

There is no one single method for determining the reliability of a measure, since various methods of estimating reliability reflect the impact of one, or another, or more than one of these factors described.

Test-retest reliability involves a comparison between results obtained on two separate occasions, typically a week or two apart. Differences in the results of a screening test from one occasion to another may be due to all three types of variability described: within the child, across testing situations, and between examiners. While test-retest reliability is highly applicable to screening tests, it is less appropriate for parent or teacher reports. That is because, due to the effects of memory, a rater may be even more "reliable" than the child's behavior warrants. A parent may remember the responses he or she provided earlier and answer the same way on a second occasion, even if inaccurate.

Certain types of screening procedures are more subject to short-term variability than others. For example, the social behavior of young children is so prone to day-to-day fluctuation that it is misleading to place great confidence in observations made on a single occasion (e.g., during screening). This lack of dependability would be reflected by low test-retest reliability.

Test-retest reliability rates should be considerably higher than for validity rates, since they reflect the relationship between a given measure and itself (that is, under different circumstances) rather than between two different measures. When correlations are used to express test-retest reliability, a figure of at least .90 is generally recommended for instruments used in making placement decisions, while a more lenient figure, perhaps as low as .80, may be acceptable for screening procedures.

Consistency over longer periods of time is known as *stability,* a special case of test-retest reliability. Particularly at young ages, a child's scores on a developmental measure may change considerably over a period of just a few months. However, if a child maintains the same relative standing within a group, an instrument will yield high stability correlations. This is a desirable characteristic of measures used in early identification, since a high likelihood that developmental delay will still be evident at some later point is justification to provide remedial services. Still, it should be noted that a measure's lack of stability is not necessarily due to measurement error associated with the instrument, the situation, or the examiner or rater. It is possible for a measure to accurately reflect developmental changes over time, but for stability to be low because the degree of change is highly variable for different children in the sample.

Inter-rater reliability addresses the question of whether two raters making independent judgments about a child, or two examiners observing and scoring the same set of test responses, will arrive at the same results. For tests, inter-rater reliability is estimated by comparing judgments made by different examiners as they independently score the same administration. This may be arranged by having one examiner observe as another administers a measure, or by having two or more examiners independently score a videotaped administration. Since the examiners observe the identical set of responses, variability in examiner judgment and recording is the only source of error reflected in this measure of reliability. Scoring agreements can be computed on an item-by-item basis to pinpoint the sources of scoring disagreements. Inter-rater reliability of a screening test is influenced both by the preciseness of its scoring rules and by how carefully the examiners adhere to these rules.

For third person reports, inter-rater reliability is estimated by comparing the responses provided by two individuals (e.g., parents or preschool teachers) who have had ample opportunity to observe the child. Independent raters not only apply different standards in making judgments, but have a different set of observations available to them upon which to base their ratings. These factors make reliability of observational data a particular concern. Greatest reliability may be expected when reports are based upon a large observational base, and are requested in specific, objective terms that leave little latitude for personal judgment and interpretation.

As with validity, an estimate of reliability is a function of the particular sample of children or of the examiners/raters from which data are obtained. Different findings may result when a screening test is administered to inner-city 4 year olds as opposed to suburban 5 year olds, or when a parent report measure is completed by homemakers rather than by working mothers or fathers.

Reliability and validity are related. Although a reliable screening instrument is not guaranteed to be valid, an acceptable level of reliability is necessary to insure that a measure may be valid. Without evidence of consistency, screening results may simply be products of chance.

Other types of reliability and validity have been devised, but are not addressed here because they are less relevant to screening. The reader is referred to texts on educational and psychological measurement (e.g., Anatasi, 1976; Salvia & Ysseldyke, 1981; Stanley & Hopkins, 1972) for more general and complete discussions of reliability and validity. Also, general guidelines for test development and research are specified in *Standards for educational and psychological tests* (American Psychological Association, American Educational Research Association, & National Council on Measurement in Education, 1974).

Standardization and Norms

Standardization is that which guarantees that the administration, scoring, and interpretation of a measurement procedure will be the same from situation to situation. This uniformity is the key to insuring that screening data obtained in different situations and by different examiners or respondents are comparable. There would otherwise be no basis for making systematic comparisons between screening results for different children. As an example, one examiner might consider it an act of generosity to give a child a few hints and an extra try after failing a test item, while another examiner may give credit only for letter-perfect responses. The result of this would be that the same score for two different children would not reflect a similar level of functioning, and that resulting decisions regarding the children may be inconsistent. To prevent such inconsistency, highly defined administration and scoring procedures are devised for a standardized instrument. In order to insure uniformity from one situation to the next, an examiner must follow the precise specifications provided in the instrument manual for giving instructions to the child (or parent), for providing assistance when required, and for scoring responses. Standardized administration and scoring procedures constitute one aspect of standardization, an aspect that is highly related to an instrument's reliability.

The second essential aspect of standardization involves the establishment of *norms*. Norms provide a basis for evaluating an individual's performance on a measure relative to a comparison group of other individuals. An instrument's norms describe the distribution of scores obtained by the *normative sample*. This may be expressed in terms of percentiles, age-equivalent scores, standard scores, stanines, or other norming methods. (See Anastasi, 1976, or Salvia & Ysseldyke, 1981 for explanations of these.) Norms introduce an objective standard for determining that a child's functioning is poor, above average, delayed, age-appropriate, at risk, etc. For screening instruments that yield classificational outcomes, norms provide a basis for establishing cutoff points.

Naturally, the characteristics of those individuals in the normative sample are of great consequence. When the normative sample is inappropriate or not clearly described, interpretation of screening results is subject to great uncertainty. The normative sample should be similar to the population with which the instrument is to be used with respect to important demographic characteristics, e.g., geographic, socio-economic, and cultural/racial factors. The fact that minority children are not always adequately represented in normative samples has been the source of a great deal of attention in the controversy over discriminatory assessment.

Qualitative Characteristics

In addition to technical considerations, there are characteristics of a qualitative nature that influence a user's evaluation of a screening instrument. For some characteristics, it is a matter of personal preference as to whether or not they are regarded as favorable. Certain features are universally regarded as desirable, however, and these warrant special attention in this section. It is often the case that these generally agreed upon desirable characteristics also have a positive effect upon reliability, validity, and/or standardization.

Instrument Manual

In addition to presenting the actual content of an instrument, the manual should serve to communicate the purpose of the instrument and guidelines for its use. A screening instrument manual should be fairly selective in terms of importance to the reader, but should address all of the following points: (1) the extent and limitations of its proposed uses, (2) the target areas or problems that the instrument is intended to assess, (3) the age range and populations for which it is designed, (4) qualifications and training required of examiners, (5) guidelines and instructions for administration and scoring, (6) procedures followed in the construction of the instrument, (7) research data, and (8) specific information pertinent to the interpretation of results. Explanations of purpose and intended use should include the role of the instrument in the identification process and, if applicable, should caution against improper diagnostic use of a measure designed exclusively for screening. The normative sample should be adequately described, and the manner in which cutoff scores were derived should be clearly explained. Validity and reliability data should be presented without undue confusion or "opportunistic selectivity."

Administration and Scoring Procedures

A screening instrument should involve brief, simple procedures that are quickly and easily administered. Instructions to the examiner should be sufficiently clear, precise, and complete to insure that the instrument can be administered and scored in a highly standardized manner. The complexity of demands made upon examiners should not be unrealistic, or inconsistent with the level of expertise and training that the instrument is said to require. For example, it takes a highly skilled examiner to administer test items that involve complicated demonstrations, or that require subtle scoring distinctions. Scoring that requires some degree of judgment is greatly facilitated by critical scoring samples that show how borderline responses are to be scored. The language used in giving verbal instructions should be appropriate for the child's age level. Highly stilted language is undesirable, as it encourages examiners to violate standardization by changing the wording to something that sounds more natural. Also, stilted language is likely to be less familiar and understandable to the child.

Materials

Materials for preschool measures should be appropriate for young children with regard to size and manageability, attractiveness, durability, and safety. Stimulus pictures (e.g., for vocabulary or speech articulation tests) should be simple and clear. (Confusing pictures are a common flaw of instruments designed for young children.) Materials should also be designed for easy handling by the examiner.

Interpretation

Several types of information contribute to the interpretability of screening measure results. The user should verify that a screening instrument can be used for the purposes recommended (e.g., screening, program placement, instructional planning) by reviewing the development and research procedures followed. Validity studies reported should be based on use of scores or results in a manner that is similar to the way they are to be used in screening. All too frequently, multiple regression or discriminant function analyses that are meaningless to the screening user are presented as evidence of validity. Also, the composition of the research sample and the nature of the criterion measure used should be noted to determine how applicable the results may be for the user's situation. Most important for interpretation, however, is information that allows the user to understand the meaning of particular scores or results. Instrument norms allow the user to relate a given score to a particular level of standing in the normative sample. Normative guides to interpretation are, of course, dependent upon the composition of the normative sample, which should be carefully noted in terms of characteristics such as age, demographic characteristics, and the basis for selection or exclusion of individuals. If cutoff scores are provided, it is important to note what percentage of the normative sample falls below these cutoffs. An instrument may contain various claims as to the meaning of scores at given levels, but unless supported in some way these claims should be cautiously re-garded as subjective observations offered by the author and/or "cos-metic" features designed to enhance the saleability of the instrument.

Culture Fairness

The content of a screening procedure should be consistent with the background experiences of the population with which it is to be used. A procedure will be unacceptable if it is inappropriate for any group of children in the intended population with regard to ethnic background, native language or dialect, type of residence (i.e., urban, suburban, rural, institutional), SES, or sex. For example, a measure that penalizes black children for their use of nonstandard English would clearly be questionable, as would questionnaire items asking inner city parents if their preschool children can cross streets and play outside unattended. While it is inevitable that some items may favor particular groups to some degree, these advantages should be minimal and should balance out for different groups over an entire instrument. Most important, a screening procedure should be fair to all children in the population in terms of the screening decisions it yields, a matter that concerns criterion-related validity. The implications of nondiscriminatory as-sessment for screening procedures are addressed at length in Chapter 5.

Acceptability to Participants

Screening procedures should be designed and presented so as to provide a generally positive experience for participants—children and parents. The child's experience depends upon several factors: interest level of instrument content (manipulative materials are usually well received), nature of personal interactions with screening personnel, and appropriateness of time and performance demands.

Demands made upon parents should also be reasonable. In the case of a parent report inventory, there is the need to find a suitable balance between comprehensiveness and reasonable demands upon the parent's time and attention. The educational level of the parent may be a consideration. In general, questionnaires or inventories should be written at no higher than a sixth grade reading level. Assistance for parents who are unable to read should be readily and diplomatically offered. When part of the screening population is non-English speak-ing, it is advisable to have bilingual forms and/or bilingual screening personnel available.

To maximize acceptability, parents should be well informed of the nature and purpose of the screening instruments used. Screening in-struments that involve the parent as a source of information about the child may get higher marks from parents.

Many of these considerations concerning acceptability actually apply more to the screening process as a whole than to specific instruments. A consumer-oriented screening instrument will recognize the importance of acceptability to participants and will recommend appropriate screening practices in the manual.

Cost

Cost factors are of critical importance in assessing the value of screening procedures. After all, screening has its origin as a cost-effective means of large scale identification. The primary characteristics of an instrument that affect screening costs are materials, personnel, and administration time.

Materials

The most apparent cost is the initial investment in the screening instrument. The cost of required equipment that is not provided with the instrument should also be considered. Another cost factor related to materials is the cost per child to administer the instrument due to the use of scoring sheets, recording forms, and other consumables.

Personnel

The professional expertise and experience of screening personnel translate fairly directly into salary costs. (Or, if professionals are already on salary, the cost is in terms of the loss of their services in other areas.) However, the savings realized from using nonprofessional examiners must be weighed against the cost of additional training required for such personnel. Of course, if neither price is paid, the consequence is a reduction in the validity of the screening procedure.

Administration Time

Administration time translates directly into operating expenses, first, in terms of the cost of maintaining paid personnel and, second, in overhead costs (if any) for the use of physical facilities.

Utility

The decision to use one screening procedure as opposed to another follows from the user's estimation of the overall value of each option for meeting the needs of the given situation. The notion of overall value, or *utility,* applies to any choice among alternatives, from selection of construction bids to classroom computers. To choose simply on the basis of quality without regard for cost and fit, which is analogous to selecting a screening instrument only on the dimension of validity, is impractical. The difference in cost may not justify the apparent differences in validity. Or, the situation may not enable the potential validity of the screening procedure to be realized; for instance, because of limitations on the professional personnel or screening time available. Other factors such as norms, reliability, acceptability to participants, and culture fairness each add to or detract from the utility of a measure. The weighting associated with each factor may vary not only with the situation, but with the person evaluating the various costs and benefits involved. It is for these reasons that two screening programs with similar goals might carefully consider the same options, but settle on different screening procedures.

While there are many factors to consider in judging the relative value of different screening procedures, the two key factors are validity and cost. Consider the case of two instruments that are appropriate and acceptable for a given situation in terms of qualitative characteristics, and appear to be equally valid. If one of the two proves to be more cost-effective, this instrument may be said to have greater utility, and would be the logical choice. Conversely, if two instruments are comparable in terms of cost, the one that is expected to have higher validity in the given situation would be selected.

Matters become more complicated when one screening instrument is both more valid and more costly than another. The trade-off between these two factors would then need to be evaluated within the context of the particular screening program. The prospective user would estimate the magnitude of the difference in validity and of the difference in cost, and weight these by the relative importance of each factor. In doing so, an administrator concerned with balancing the budget may come to one conclusion, while a screening practitioner concerned with accuracy of screening decisions may arrive at a different conclusion about which has greater utility. This clearly illustrates the point that attempts to identify "the best screening instrument" are misguided.

AN OVERVIEW OF
PRESCHOOL SCREENING INSTRUMENTS

Screening has only recently become a widespread practice, but screening instruments developed during the past ten years number in the hundreds. Unfortunately, the quality of most screening measures is rather poor, and concerns about the adequacy of existing instruments had led observers to question the viability of early identification (Adelman, 1978; Hobbs, 1975; Koegh & Becker, 1973). In reviewing the state of the art, Adelman (1978) concluded that the evidence *does not* support the efficacy of currently available predictive and identification procedures, especially those already being used for massive screening of preschoolers and kindergarteners. (p. 154)

Conspicuous flaws in choice of items, design of materials, phrasing of instructions, and scoring procedures suggest that the press to publish often supersedes the necessity to painstakingly develop and pilot test new instruments. A vivid, though perhaps extreme, example of such misguided efforts is provided in Divoky's (1977a) account of the construction and marketing of the Automated Graphogestalt Test and SCREEN battery in her article entitled, "Is this screening test worth $1,319,638.50?"

Developers of many screening instruments have also been negligent in conducting research to support claims made about these measures. A survey of screening instruments conducted in the late 70s found that a small proportion of measures were accompanied by validity data, and only two screening instruments were accompanied by validity data presented in terms of classificational outcomes (Lichtenstein, 1979). Meisels (in press) found only five preschool instruments that met the criteria of being (1) multidimensional, (2) developmental, (3) for screening purposes, and (4) accompanied by classificational reliability and validity data.

Despite the multitude of available measures, the prospective user can quickly narrow down the alternatives to a manageable few by applying the selection criteria of (1) suitability for the particular screening situation and (2) instrument quality. The basic information on screening instruments compiled in this section is designed to serve as an initial guide in this process.

Several criteria were applied in determining what measures to include in the listing of preschool screening instruments that follows. First, only those instruments with a standardization range that encompasses all or part of the 3–0 to 5–0 age range were considered to be applicable for preschool children. While some children in the 5–0 to 6–0 range are still preschoolers, instruments with a lower age limit at or above 5–0 are primarily designed for a school age population. Second, only those instruments designed for individual administration were included. Group tests are developmentally inappropriate for assessing children at the preschool level, as noted in Chapter 2.

The distinction between instruments for screening and those for diagnosis or more comprehensive assessment presented some difficulty. Many so-called screening instruments are simply brief versions of comprehensive assessment measures that are designed in a manner more suited to providing diagnostic information than to yielding a

screening outcome. These complications were circumvented by making
screening vs. comprehensive assessment distinctions simply on the
basis of administration time. Instruments that require more than 40
minutes, being impractical to administer to preschool children in a
single screening session, were excluded. For instruments that cover
only a single content area, a limit of 20 minutes was set.

Some instruments were excluded on the basis of their standardization population or purpose. Since screening is a process for selecting
out high risk individuals from an apparently normal population, instruments designed for an already identified group (e.g., hearing impaired,
mentally retarded) were excluded. Also, instruments designed for the
sole purpose of assessing a child's performance or progress in an
educational program (that is, rather than contributing to identification
decisions) were rejected as inappropriate for screening.

The final criterion was availability. Publishers and/or authors of
the instruments in this collection were contacted to verify that the
instrument is currently available. For those interested in contacting
authors/publishers for materials or information, addresses are provided
in the appendix.

Most of the information presented in the tables that follow is self-
explanatory: age range, administration time, instrument type (test or
parent report), requirement of a professional examiner, author(s), and
date of publication. An asterisk before the instrument name indicates
that the measure is reviewed at length in the final section of this
chapter.

The references column lists sources, by code letter, in which entries for the instrument may be found. The following letter codes are
used to refer to references sources described earlier in this chapter:

B   *Preschool screening: The measurement and prediction of children at-
    risk* (Barnes, 1982).
C   *Test analyses: Screening and verification instruments for preschool
    children. Volume I* (Strully/Project CONNECT, 1977).
D   *Directory of developmental screening instruments* (Davidson, Li-
    chtenstein, Canter, & Cronin, 1977).
F   *Pediatric screening tests* (Frankenburg & Camp, 1975).
G   *Handbook for measurement and evaluation in early childhood educa-
    tion* (Goodwin & Driscoll, 1980).
J   *Tests and measurements in child development: Handbook II* (Johnson,
    1976).
M   *The eighth mental measurement yearbook* (Buros, 1978).
S   *Screening and evaluating the young child: A handbook of instruments
    to use from infancy to six years* (Southworth, Burr, & Cox, 1981).

References to Buros' (1978) *Eighth mental measurements yearbook* are simply coded "M", however, a number follows the "M" if the instrument was last reviewed in an earlier edition. For example, "M7" refers to the *Seventh mental measurements yearbook* (Buros, 1972). There are some instances where references cited for an instrument pertain to an earlier version of the instrument. When this is the case, the reference source code letter appears in parentheses. If the earlier version of the instrument carried a different name than the present one, the former name is added in parentheses in the first column.

In the final column, pluses and minuses indicate whether or not the instruments' authors have assembled reliability, validity, and normative data on the measure. This is intended to reflect neither the adequacy of the research nor the nature of the results, but only that such data exist and that certain specifications are met. An instrument is indicated as having reliability data if any test-retest or inter-rater reliability figures are provided in the documentation that accompanies the instrument. To be regarded as having validity data, results of a criterion-related validity study must be reported.* An instrument is indicated as having normative data if norms or decision rules are based on a sample of at least 100 normal children in the preschool age range. Again, the existence of data does not imply a positive evaluation; the interested reader is strongly advised to review the data firsthand.

In grouping preschool screening instruments by content area, *multidimensional instruments* (that is, instruments covering multiple areas of functioning, although not necessarily yielding multiple scores) constitute the largest single category. Included among the multidimensional instruments compiled in Table 4-1 are the five screening tests singled out by Meisels (in press) as meeting essential criteria for developmental screening: the Denver Developmental Screening Test, the Developmental Indicators for the Assessment of Learning (DIAL), the Early Screening Inventory, the McCarthy Screening Test, and the Minneapolis Preschool Screening Instrument. The Denver Developmental Screening Test and the DIAL are the best known and currently most widely used developmental screening instruments. The latter three, being relatively recent, have yet to appear in most of the reference sources cited. All five are the subject of extensive reviews in the section that follows. Parent report measures may also be mutldimensio-

---

*Evidence of significant differences between mean scores for identified groups was not regarded as an indication of criterion-related validity, as such patterns are invariably found and contribute little information about the measure. Also, an instrument's correlation with chronological age was not considered evidence of criterion-related validity.

Table 4-1
Multidimensional Screening Instruments

Name of Instrument	Age Range	Admin. Time	Examiner (T = Test, P = Parent Report, E = Professional)	Cognitive	Language	Speech	Fine Motor	Gross Motor	Self-help	Social-emotional	Author(s), Date	Reference Sources	Reliability Data	Validity Data	Normative Data
ABC Inventory	3–6 to 6–6	10 min.	T	X			X				Adair & Blesch, 1965	D,F,M7,S	–	+	+
*Comprehensive Identification Process	2–6 to 5–6	30 min.	T P	X	X	X	X	X		X	Zehrbach, 1975	C,D,G,M,S	–	–	–
Cooperative Preschool Inventory, Revised Edition	3–0 to 6–0	15–20 min.	T	X	X		X				Caldwell, 1970	B,D,G,M7,S	+	+	+
Daberon: A Screening Devise for School Readiness	4–0 to 6–0	20–40 min.	T	X	X		X	X			Danzer, Lyons, & Gerber, 1972, 1982	(C,S)	+	+	+
Dallas Preschool Screening Test	3–0 to 6–0	15 min.	T	X	X	X	X	X			Percival & Poxon, 1972	C,S	+	+	+
*Denver Developmental Screening Test	0–1 to 6–0	15–20 min.	T P	X	X		X	X	X	X	Frankenburg & Dodds, 1967	B,C,D,F,G, M7,S	+	+	+
Denver Prescreening Developmental Questionnaire	0–3 to 6–0	5 min.	P	X	X		X	X	X	X	Frankenburg, van Doorninck, Liddell, & Dick, 1975	C,D,S	–	+	+
Developmental Activities Screening Inventory	0–6 to 5–0	25 min.	T	X			X				Fewell & Langley, 1977	S	–	+	–

126

Test	Age range	Time	T/P		Author, year	Code			
*Developmental Indicators for the Assessment of Learning (DIAL)	2–6 to 5–6	25–30 min.	T	X X X X X X	Mardell & Goldenberg, 1975	B,C,D,G,M,S	+	+	+
*Developmental Profile II (Developmental Profile)	0–0 to 9–0	30–40 min.	P	X X X X X X	Alpern, Boll, & Shearer, 1980	(D,M,S)	+	+	+
Developmental Tasks for Kindergarten Readiness	4–6 to 6–2	20–30 min.	T	X X X X	Lesiak, 1978	S	+	+	+
Early Detection Inventory	3–6 to 7–6	15–30 min.	T P	X X X X X X	McGahan & McGahan, 1975	C,(D),S	–	+	+
*Early Screening Inventory (Eliot-Pearson Screening Inventory)	4–0 to 6–0	15 min.	T	X X X X X	Meisels & Wiske, 1981	(D)	+	+	+
Hannah-Gardner Test of Verbal and Nonverbal Language Functioning	3–6 to 5–6	25–35 min.	T	X X X	Hannah & Gardner, 1978	J,S	+	+	+
Inventory of Readiness Skills	3–0 to 7–0	20 min.	T	X X X	Shelquist, Breeze, & Jacquot, 1973	D,J,S	–	–	–
Kaufman Developmental Scale	0–0 to 9–0	30–45 min.	T P	X X X X X X	Kaufman, 1974		–	+	–
Kaufman Infant and Preschool Scale	0–1 to 4–0	25–30 min.	T P	X X	Kaufman, 1979		–	–	+

(continued)

Table 4-1 (continued)

Name of Instrument	Age Range	Admin. Time	T = Test / P = Parent Report / E = Professional Examiner	Cognitive	Language	Speech	Fine Motor	Gross Motor	Self-help	Social-emotional	Author(s), Date	Reference Sources	Reliability Data	Validity Data	Normative Data
Kindergarten Questionnaire	4-0 to 6-0	20–30 min.	T P	X	X			X		X	Berger & Perlman, 1976	S	–	+	–
Lexington Developmental Scale, Short Form	0–3 to 6-0	30–45 min.	T	X	X			X		X	United Cerebral Palsy of the Bluegrass Inc.	D,J,S	+	+	–
*McCarthy Screening Test	4-0 to 6-5	20 min.	T	X	X		X	X			McCarthy, 1978	S	+	+	+
*Minneapolis Preschool Screening Instrument	3–7 to 5-4	10–15 min.	T	X	X		X	X			Lichtenstein, 1980	B	+	+	+
*Minnesota Preschool Inventory	4–8 to 5–7	15 min.	P	X	X	X	X	X	X	X	Ireton & Thwing, 1979	B	–	+	+
Pennsylvania Preschool Inventory	3–0 to 6-0	15 min.	T	X	X						Dusewicz, ?	C	+	+	+
Preschool Attainment Record, Research Edition	0–6 to 7-0	20–30 min.	P E	X	X		X	X	X	X	Doll, 1966	B7,C,D,F, M7,S	–	–	–

128

Instrument	Age range	Time			Author, year		Rating
Preschool Screening Instrument	4–0 to 5–0	5–10 min.	T P	X X X X X X X X X X	Cohen, 1979	S	+ + –
*Preschool Screening System (PSS Field Trial Edition)	2–6 to 5–9	15–20 min.	T P	X X X X X X X X X X	Hainsworth & Hainsworth, 1980	(D,S)	+ + +
Riley Preschool Developmental Screening Inventory	3–0 to 6–0	5–10 min.	T	X X	Riley, 1969	C,D,S	– +
School Entrance Checklist	4–0 to 5–0	15 min.	P	X X X	McLeod, 1969	D	– –
School Readiness Checklist—Ready or Not?	4–0 to 7–0	10–15 min.	P	X X X X X X	Austin & Lafferty, 1963, 1979	D,F,M7,S	– + +
School Readiness Survey	4–0 to 6–0	25–35 min.	T P	X X	Jordan & Massey, 1967, 1975	D,(M7),S	+ + +
Slosson Intelligence Test	0–1 to adult	10–20 min.	T	X X	Slosson, 1963, 1981	F,M7,S	– + +
Vineland Social Maturity Scale	birth to adult	20–30 min.	P E	X X X X X	Doll, 1947, 1965	C,D,G,M4,S	+ + +

*Reviewed in this chapter

129

nal. Two such examples, the Developmental Profile and the Minnesota Preschool Inventory, are also reviewed.

A multidimensional screening instrument is a logical choice for a developmental screening program of a comprehensive nature. Still, some are broader in their range of coverage than others, and the user should not assume that a multidimensional instrument is (or ought to be) a complete screening battery by itself. Educationally oriented measures (usually, tests) focus on developmental areas most highly related to school achievement, i.e., cognitive, language, fine motor, and perceptual processing. Instruments for obtaining parent reports and those designed for younger children tend to assume a broader developmental focus, and may include motor skills, adaptive behavior (i.e., self-help), and social-emotional functioning in addition to academically oriented areas. Some instruments incorporate both direct testing and parent reports to obtain a broad array of information. Convenience is the apparent advantage of using inclusive developmental screening instruments. However, greater flexibility is possible through the strategy of supplementing an educationally oriented measure with selected single-area measures, thereby creating a screening battery tailored to the needs of the particular situation.

Two entries in Table 4-1, the Comprehensive Identification Process and the Preschool Screening System, are not simply or strictly instruments, but entire systems that include guidelines for conducting a screening program in addition to specific screening instruments. The logic of providing an overall screening system is sound, since the context in which screening procedures are employed largely determines whether they are effectively and appropriately used. The success of these two systems in "packaging" both the screening process and screening procedures is addressed in the reviews that follow.

Instruments that are limited to coverage of a specific area are compiled in Tables 4-2 to 4-6. A screening program planner may choose to round out a screening battery or give greater emphasis to one area by including a screening instrument with a single area focus. Also, a screening program of a specialized nature may rely strictly upon one or several specific area instruments.

Table 4-2 contains instruments for screening of language development. Those that evaluate a child's language production are classified as *expressive,* while those that require nonverbal responses to demonstrate language comprehension (e.g., following directions, pointing to pictures) are classified as *receptive.* Speech articulation measures are listed separately from language measures in Table 4-3. (The rationale for this is discussed in Chapter 2, "Areas of Development.")

Table 4-4 breaks down screening instruments for assessing motoric and perceptual functions into four categories: fine motor, gross motor, auditory perception, and visual perception. Table 4-5 lists instruments for screening social-emotional development, which is broadly defined to include self-concept, self-help and social skills, emotional adjustment, and behavior.

Since only one screening instrument falls under the category of assessing the child's home environment, the following paragraph is provided instead of a table. The Home Screening Questionnaire (HSQ) (Coons, Gay, Fandal, Ker, & Frankenburg, 1981), which has separate forms for ages 0–3 and 3–6, consists of items relating to mother/child and father/child interactions, the emotional climate of the home, the physical environment, and discipline techniques. A parent can complete the questionnaire in 15–20 minutes. The HSQ was standardized on a primarily "Anglo" and Spanish low SES population in Denver. It is not recommended for use with middle to upper SES populations, or "in cultures which differ substantially from the population on which it was standardized" (Coons et al., 1981, p. 7). Data from reliability and validity studies are reported in the manual. Research on the HSQ is reviewed by Barnes (1982). Also, see Chapter 3 of this book for the discussion of the validity study comparing the HOME Inventory (from which the HSQ was derived) and the HSQ.

Instruments designed for teachers to rate behaviors or competencies observed in the classroom (e.g., nursery school, preschool center) are listed in Table 4-6. These are of a specialized nature, since they may be used only with that subset of the preschool population enrolled in early childhood programs. Although inappropriate for mass screening, they provide a cost-effective source of valuable data for that select subset. For general descriptions of these instruments, the best reference by far is the handbook by Southworth, Burr, and Cox (1980) described earlier in this chapter.

Hopefully, this compilation of preschool screening instruments will help the prospective user in the initial review phase. Of course, the user will want to obtain specimen sets or test kits in order to critically evaluate those instruments under final consideration. (See Appendix for addresses of sources.) Also of value in this process are reviews such as those provided in some of the reference sources cited and in the following section.

Table 4-2
Language and Vocabulary Measures

Name of Instrument	Age Range	Admin. Time	T = Test / P = Parent Report / E = Professional Examiner		Expressive	Receptive	Author(s), Date	Reference Sources	Reliability Data	Validity Data	Normative Data
Assessment of Children's Language Comprehension	3–0 to 6–6	10–20 min.	T	E		X	Foster, Giddan & Stark, 1969, 1973	M,S	–	–	+
Bankson Language Screening Test	4–1 to 8–0	25* min.	T		X	X	Bankson, 1977	D	+	+	+
Del Rio Language Screening Test	3–0 to 6–11		T		X	X	Toronto et al., 1975	C,D,M,S	–	–	+
Expressive One-Word Picture Vocabulary Test	2–0 to 11–11	10–15 min.	T		X		Gardner, 1979	S	–	+	+
Northwestern Syntax Screening Test	3–0 to 8–0	15–20 min.	T	E	X	X	Lee, 1969, 1971	C,D,F,M	–	–	+
Peabody Picture Vocabulary Test—Revised	2–6 to adult	10–20 min.		E		X	Dunn & Dunn, 1981	(G,M6)	+	+	+

Test	Age Range	Time				Reference		
Pictorial Test of Bilingualism and Language Development	4–0 to 8–0	15 min.	T		X	Nelson, Fellner, & Norrell, 1975	G	+ + –
Preschool Language Assessment Instrument	3–0 to 6–0	20 min.	T		X X	Blank, Rose, & Berlin, 1978	G	+ – +
Screening Test for Auditory Comprehension of Language	3–0 to 6–0	5–10 min.	T	E	X	Carrow-Woolfolk, 1973	B,C,D,J,M,S	+ – +
Test of Early Language Development	3–0 to 7–11	15–20 min.	T		X X	Hresko, Reid, & Hammill, 1983		+ + +
Vane Evaluation of Language Scale	2–6 to 6–0	10 min.	T		X X	Vane, 1975	S	– – +
Verbal Language Development Scale	0–1 to 16–0		P	E	X X	Mecham, 1952, 1971	D,F,M7,S	+ + –

*Subset of 38 items may be administered for brief screening.

Table 4-3
Speech Articulation Measures

Name of Instrument	Age Range	Administration Time	T = Test, P = Parent Report, E = Professional Examiner	Author(s), Date	Reference Sources	Reliability Data	Validity Data	Normative Data
Denver Articulation Screening Exam	2–6 to 7–0	5 min.	T	Drumwright, 1971	B,D,F,M,S	+	+	+
Photo Articulation Test	3–0 to 12–0	5 min.	T E	Pendergast, Dickey, Selmar, & Soder, 1969	C,D,F,M	+	+	+
Screening Speech Articulation Test	2–6 to 8–6		T E	Mecham, Jones, & Jex, 1970	C	–	–	–
Templin-Darley Screening Test of Articulation	3–0 to 8–0	10 min.	T E	Templin & Darley,	B,D,F,M7	+	–	–

Table 4-4
Perceptual and Motoric Measures

Name of Instrument	Age Range	Administration Time	T = Test, P = Parent Report, E = Professional Examiner	Auditory perception	Visual perception	Fine motor	Gross motor	Author(s), Date	Reference Sources	Reliability Data	Validity Data	Normative Data
Developmental Test of Visual-Motor Integration	2–0 to 15–0	5–10 min.	T		X	X		Beery & Buktenica, 1967	D,G,M,S	+	+	+
Motor Free Visual Perception Test	4–0 to 8–0	10 min.	T		X			Colarusso & Hammill, 1972	C,D,S	+	+	+
Riley Motor Problems Inventory	4–0 to 9–0	10 min.	T	E		X	X	Riley, 1976	C,D	+	+	–
Tree/Bee Test of Auditory Discrimination	3–0 to adult	10–15 min.	T	X				Fudala, 1978	S	+	+	+

135

Table 4-5
Social-Emotional Measures

Name of Instrument	Age Range	Administration Time	T = Test / P = Parent Report / E = Professional Examiner	Author(s), Date	Reference Sources	Reliability Data	Validity Data	Normative Data
Burks' Behavior Rating Scales: Preschool and Kindergarten	3–0 to 6–11	10 min.	P E	Burks, 1977	(D),S	+	–	–
Child Behavior Rating Scale	4–0 to 9–0	10 min.	P	Cassel, 1962	D,G,M7,S	+	+	+
Children's Self-Social Construct Tests: Preschool Form	3–6 to 10–0	10–15 min.	T	Long, Henderson, & Ziller, 1964	D,G,S	–	–	–
Joseph Preschool and Primary Self Concept Screening Test	3–6 to 9–11	5–7 min.	T	Joseph, 1979	S	+	+	+

136

REVIEWS OF SELECTED SCREENING INSTRUMENTS

The nine preschool screening instruments reviewed at length in this section were selected on the basis of frequency of use, extent of research efforts, and quality of construction and standardization. The instruments are both described and critically evaluated, with emphasis given to the criteria identified earlier in this chapter, i.e., validity, reliability, standardization and norms, qualitative characteristics, and cost. The two screening systems, the Comprehensive Identification Process and the Preschool Screening System, are reviewed first. These are followed by traditional screening instruments: four screening tests (Denver Developmental Screening Test, DIAL, Early Screening Inventory, and McCarthy Screening Test) and a parent report measure (Developmental Profile II). The section concludes with reviews of the Minneapolis Preschool Screening Instrument (Lichtenstein, 1980b) and the Minnesota Preschool Inventory (Ireton & Thwing, 1979), which are more descriptive than critical in nature so that "reviewer bias" is not an issue.

Comprehensive Identification Process

The Comprehensive Identification Process (CIP) (Zehrbach, 1975a) was designed to provide a system for locating, screening, and evaluating preschool children ages 2½–5½ who may be educationally handicapped. The CIP is designed to yield several types of data that lead to alternative recommendations, such as a vision or hearing examination, a complete medical checkup, or a total evaluation of the child. The CIP is not designed to yield a numerical score. The rationale for this approach includes the desire to (1) prevent labeling a child before he or she is fully evaluated, (2) prevent comparison of children by paraprofessionals on the basis of numerical scores, and (3) permit consideration of a constellation of behaviors rather than one or two specific scores.

The CIP provides a system, i.e., an organized set of steps and methods, for conducting the screening and early identification process. The system includes specific measures for developmental testing and for obtaining parents' reports. The CIP involves a station approach with a screening team typically composed of a team leader, three to five child interviewers, one parent interviewer, and two hearing and vision screeners (preferably specialists). Parent interviewers and child examiners may be paraprofessionals who have been trained according to specified guidelines. Screening covers eight areas: fine motor, cognitive-verbal, gross motor, speech and expressive language, social-affec-

Table 4-6
Observational Instruments for Classroom Use

Name of Instrument	Age Range	Administration Time	Areas assessed	Author(s), Date	Reference Sources	Reliability Data	Validity Data	Normative Data
Basic School Skills Inventory—Screen	4-0 to 6-11	5–10 min.	multidimensional	Hammill & Leigh, 1983	(B,C,D,M,S)	+	+	+
California Pre-School Social Competency Scale	2-6 to 5-6	10 min.	self-help, social-emotional	Levine, Elzey, & Lewis, 1969	C,G,M,S	+	–	+
Classroom Behavior Inventory, Preschool Form	2-0 to 6-0	10–15 min.	cognitive, social-emotional	Schaefer & Edgerton, 1978	S	–	+	–

Test	Age range	Administration time	Area	Reference	Type			
Florida KEY: A Scale to Infer Learner Self-Concept	2–0 to 13–0	10–15 min.	social-emotional	Purkey, Cage, & Graves, 1973	J,S	–	+	–
Inventory of Language Abilities	4–0 to 7–0	10 min.	language, perceptual processing	Minskoff, Wideman, & Minskoff, 1972	D,S	–	–	–
Movement Skills Survey	3–0 to 7–0		gross motor	Orpet & Heustis, 1971	D,S	–	–	–
Preschool and Kindergarten Performance Profile	4–0 to 7–0	10 min.	multidimensional	DiNola, Kaminsky, & Sternfeld, 1970	C,S	–	–	–
Preschool Behavior Rating Scale	3–0 to 5–11	5–10 min.	multidimensional	Barker & Doeff, 1980	B	+	+	+
Primary Self-Concept Inventory	4–0 to 10–0	20 min.	social-emotional	Muller & Leonetti, 1973	J,M,S	+	–	+
Pupil Behavior Inventory	3–0 to 5–0	5–10 min.	social-emotional	Sarri & Radin, 1973	J,S	–	–	–
School Behavior Checklist, Form A1	4–0 to 6–0	8–10 min.	social-emotional	Miller, 1977, 1981	S	+	+	–

139

tive, hearing, vision, and medical history. Total screening time is 30–45 minutes.

The screening materials include an administrator's manual, an interviewer's manual, a symbol booklet, a screening booklet, a record form, a parent interview form, an observation of behavior form, a speech and expressive language form, test objects such as blocks and beads, and a record folder. The CIP record folder provides a convenient means for storing the various forms accumulated during screening and, more important, the inside of the folder provides a systematic means of recording findings, comments, and recommendations.

The screening administrator's manual deals with issues from rationale and preparation, to training of team members, to conducting the screening itself, to indications for referral. The interviewer's manual covers the parent interview, developmental testing, and observation of the child, speech and language, vision and hearing screening, and data summarization.

The parent interview form includes identifying information, family information, medical history, developmental milestones, signs of difficulty regarding vision and hearing, current developmental behaviors, social-emotional adjustment, and assets or special talents of the child. Some of the items are focused on developmental achievements, e.g., "walks up and down stairs alone"; others have a symptomatic focus, e.g., "acts without reason, on the spur of the moment."

The CIP screening booklet contains the developmental test items. Subtests are organized in six-month age intervals, beginning at the oldest level (60–65 months) and proceeding to the youngest (30–35 months). For each age interval, five tasks are included under each scale heading: Fine Motor, Cognitive-Verbal, and Gross Motor. The test items have been adapted from other tests, particularly from the Stanford-Binet. Figure 4-2 displays the format and items from the 48–53 month interval.

Scores and Interpretation

A classification of P (pass), R (refer or rescreen), or E (evaluate) is assigned to a child's behavior in each of a number of developmental areas. The *pattern* of these ratings is then reviewed by a professional or team of professionals, and a decision is made to pass the child, to refer the child to an agency, to gather additional data through rescreening, or to provide the child with a complete evaluation.

For the developmental screening test, results are interpreted according to a "minimal-acceptable-behavior" approach. This approach involves selecting as test items behaviors that reflect the minimum expected behaviors for a given age interval. Children who cannot demonstrate those behaviors fall below the minimal level and require re-screening or formal evaluation. In each of the three developmental areas the child is required to perform the five minimal acceptable behaviors (tasks) at his or her age level. If the child fails one to three items he or she is administered the tasks at the next higher level. Passes at the higher level are credited against failures at the lower level. The child passes if the number of failures in an area is 0 or 1; with a score of 2–3 failures, he or she is marked for rescreening; if the score is 4 or higher, the child is rated as needing evaluation.

The speech and language assessment is by far the most elaborate part of the screening. The speech and expressive language record form contains items measuring articulation, voice, fluency, and expressive language.

The observation of behavior form includes items pertaining to hearing/comprehension problems, vision, motor incoordination, speech/language problems, social behavior, and affective behavior.

Research Data

No norms or reliability and validity data for the CIP are presented. Instead, construct validity and face validity are claimed for the items, but not elaborated upon.

Cost

Approximate cost is $75 for the screening kit, which includes manuals, test administration materials, and record forms for 35 screenings. Cost for additional sets of record forms is approximately $1 per child.

Critique

The CIP needs to be critiqued at two levels: first, as a comprehensive screening process or system for early identification and, second, for its developmental screening instruments. The CIP follows a broad-based clinical approach to screening. Preschool screeners will probably, and with good reason, welcome the CIP format and materials because they provide a relatively clear framework for the process of screening.

Turning to the elements and instruments for the screening itself, we are left with some serious reservations. For the developmental screening test, the logic of minimal acceptable behavior for each age level appears sound. However, no specific rationale is provided regarding the assignment of items to age levels, and there are no data regarding how this approach works in practice. From a psychometric point of view, this is a glaring weakness.

48-53 Months

FINE MOTOR⁻

1. Cuts paper with scissors
2. Copies cross (+) from Symbol Booklet
3. Touches thumb to four fingers on the same hand
4. Builds bridge using three blocks

5. Builds tower of ten blocks

COGNITIVE-VERBAL

1. "Give me the longer stick." (Understands "longer")
2. "How many circles have I drawn?" (Two; understands concept of "two")
3. "Show me your knee." "Show me your tongue." "Where is your arm?" (3 of 3)
4. Sorts five black and five white buttons (No errors)
5. "Why do you take a bath?"

GROSS MOTOR

1. Hops forward on one foot for two hops
2. Walks forward heel-to-toe for five steps
3. Stands on one foot for four seconds
4. Jumps down from eighteen-inch height with both feet together
5. Walks downstairs one foot per tread, using rail or other support (P.F.)

MONTHS	FINE MOTOR							COGNITIVE-VERBAL							GROSS MOTOR						
48-53	1	2	3	4	5	T		1	2	3	4	5	T		1	2	3	4	5	T

142

Fig. 4-2. Developmental test items from CIP at 48–53 month level. (Copyright © 1975 by R. Reid Zehrbach, Ph.D. Reprinted by permission of Scholastic Testing Service, Inc. from CIP Screening Booklet.)

The speech and expressive language section is by far the most elaborate part of the evaluation. Since the instrument may be administered by paraprofessionals as well as by trained speech and language clinicians, the lack of objective criteria for scoring this section is a serious problem. Screening criteria for vision and hearing are presented clearly.

Professionals involved in preschool screening could benefit by making use of the systematic approach and data organizing materials of the CIP. The framework for preschool screening, including parent involvement from the beginning, is well founded. However, the CIP is not particularly clear at the level of administration, scoring, and interpretation of results. Standards for acceptable performance on each and every task are not consistently provided. It is best advised to use a developmental screening test and a speech and language review method that are better defined in terms of administration and scoring, and better supported with research on their validity for screening. The CIP is a good example of a screening device that is sound in terms of providing screeners with an organizational structure and encouraging them to operate within a developmental perspective, but weak from a psychometric point of view.

Preschool Screening System

As implied by the name Preschool Screening System, Hainsworth and Hainsworth (1980) have developed not only a screening test but a complete screening program "package." The Preschool Screening System includes a screening test of "body awareness, visual-perceptual-motor, and language skills," a parent developmental questionnaire, and a step-by-step guide to screening program development and implementation. This is all contained within the 230-page spiral-bound book that doubles as test manual and screener's handbook.

Both the package as a whole and the component instruments are reviewed here in turn. The authors make no clear distinction between the overall screening system and the screening test that is the central component of the system, referring to both as the Preschool Screening System. To reduce confusion, the screening test is abbreviated as PSS, while Preschool Screening System is written out in referring to the overall system.

The System

The authors devote most of the introductory section of the Pre-school Screening System manual to an overview of how a screening program should be organized. Six "stages" are addressed in turn: (1) Involving all relevant personnel in preplanning, (2) Getting ready to train personnel and screen, (3) Training staff in administration and interpretation, (4) Conducting an efficient and comfortable screening day, (5) Using screening results to meet children's needs, and (6) Evaluating screening and follow-up services.

The remainder of the manual is divided into three parts of approximately equal length. The PSS screening test is the primary focus of Part A. Part A contains administration and scoring guidelines, test instructions, and stimulus cards for administering the PSS, with the remainder devoted to use and scoring of the Parent Developmental Questionnaire. (These screening instruments are discussed at length later in this review.)

Part B, on interpretation of screening test results, elaborates upon the three purposes to which PSS scores may be put, each in a separate and lengthy section. The first of these purposes is "to find children who require further observation or testing to determine need for assistance" (p. 101). In this section, norm tables are presented and explained, and the diverse options for scores and cutoff points are reviewed. The second stated purpose is "to further observe or test children to determine their needs for special assistance" (p. 123). This section describes the "follow-up analysis and observation" procedures that are recommended for further assessment of children at risk. The authors promote an approach that involves placing children who are identified by the PSS in a special classroom. Teachers then evaluate referred children while remediating areas of apparent need. The third purpose of PSS scores is to assess child progress through pre and post evaluation, a rather atypical function for a screening test. Provided for this purpose are tables for converting PSS raw scores to "Developmental Age Equivalents" so that gain scores (in months) can be computed for the period of time that a child is placed in a special program.

Part C of the manual, entitled "Program Supports," is a collection of three assorted sections. The first consists of an expanded discussion of the program development and implementation guidelines introduced at the beginning of the manual. Practical "nuts-and-bolts" level suggestions are offered from the authors' personal experiences, for example,

> At the screening session, warm greetings, an explanation of what will happen and why, availability of someone to handle questions or emergencies, and a relaxed purposeful environment are important. Most schools

provide coffee and a place for parents to talk informally or meet the principal, social worker or guidance counselor (p. 186).

The second section of Part C describes the manner in which PSS results can be used diagnostically within a psychological or psycho-educational assessment battery. The final section describes construction of the PSS and presents psychometric data on the measure.

The Screening Instruments

The centerpiece of the Preschool Screening System, the PSS screening test, is designed for children aged 2-6 to 5-9 and can be administered in 15-20 minutes. The PSS consists of 15 subtests of 3 to 11 items. The test is subdivided into three areas of four subtests each: Body Awareness and Control (Movement Patterns, Clapping, Body Directions, Finger Patterns), Visual-Perceptual-Motor (Copy Shapes, Visual Integration, Spatial Directions, Draw A Person), and Language (Serial Counting, Phrases, Sentences, Verbal Reasoning). Three additional subtests are ungrouped: General Information (for children 4-3 and under), Quantity Recognition, and Read Shapes.

For screening use, the authors advise that the test be administered either by a nonprofessional volunteer or a trained professional tester, "whichever is more economical." For nonprofessionals, they recommend a training program of several hours, followed by a "checkout" by an experienced examiner.

Several different versions of the PSS are provided. A short form, consisting of five selected subtests, is proposed for use as a "pre-screen" in the event that "there are large numbers of children entering school or few personnel to do the screening." Children scoring below the short form cutoff would then be given the remainder of the PSS. A non-language version consisting of five subtests that can be administered using pantomime in place of verbal instructions is proposed for children with a hearing or language problem, or "from another language background." Finally, a Spanish version of the PSS is available, and translations into various other languages (e.g., Chinese, Vietnamese, Italian, Portuguese, and Greek) are reported to be in progress. A group administration procedure is also described in detail, which the authors endorse as "a far better screening method overall." Groups of eight children at a time are screened by a team of four or five adults, with certain tasks assessed as part of a large group (e.g., gross motor activities are administered in a "Simon Says" format), and other tasks in small groups or individually. Since one hour is required to screen each group, there is no advantage in terms of time saved. The opportunity to observe children in both individual and group situations, and the collaboration by screening personnel are proposed to be the advantages of this procedure.

A parent measure to supplement the PSS, the Developmental Questionnaire, consists of three sections: Child behavior (28 items covering such activities as play, dressing oneself, listening to stories, and reactions to social situations), medical background, and developmental milestones. The authors propose that it be administered either as part of an interview at screening, or by mail.

Scores and Interpretation

Tables are provided by converting both PSS and Developmental Questionnaire raw scores into deciles (i.e., percentile ranges of 0–9, 10–19, etc.). A choice of norms is provided for children in the 4–4 to 5–9 age range: decile scores can either be computed for the screening population's "grade level" (using the 4–4 to 5–4 norms in the spring before kindergarten and the 4–9 to 5–9 norms in the fall), or by age ranges, broken down by four- and five-month intervals. The 2–6 to 4–3 form of the PSS is broken down into seven norm groups, most of which encompass a span of three months of age. Norm tables are also provided for computing various types of cluster scores from PSS results. The diagnostic information yielded by these scores is presumably not for screening use.

The authors recommend using as a screening cutoff point the bottom decile, or tenth percentile, based on the fact that this approximates national incidence figures for handicapping conditions. These guidelines are then qualified by two further considerations that may modify decision rules: (1) in order to identify less seriously handicapped children, a second and higher cutoff might be used as well, and (2) socioeconomic differences among communities introduce the need for alternative cutoff points. The authors propose that SES differences are best accounted for by setting local norms over a period of time, and guidelines for doing so are provided.

The most straightforward analysis of results would consist of a single decile score for the PSS and one for each of the three Developmental Questionnaire sections. The authors do not state how these four scores could be combined so as to arrive at a developmental screening decision. Since Developmental Questionnaire results are described as "useful in their own right . . . and as a comparison with the child test scores" (p. 91) and no other use is specified, one may conclude that screening decisions are primarily to be based on PSS scores.

Normative Sample

The normative group consists of 3000 children from inner city, city, suburban, and rural areas in the northeastern United States. Although the authors readily acknowledge the geographic limitations, the sample was weighted so as to approximate a nationally representative distribution by socioeconomic level at each grade and age level according to the following formula: 40 percent professional/managerial and white collar workers, 30 percent skilled and supervisory blue collar workers, and 30 percent semi-skilled, unskilled, and unemployed.

Research Data

Inter-rater and test-retest reliability were obtained with a sample of 20 children ages 3 through 5. Inter-rater reliability was investigated by having two trained examiners score PSS administrations simultaneously, one as examiner and one as observer. Four weeks later, children in the sample were retested by the same examiner as before to determine test-retest reliability. High inter-rater reliability and test-retest reliability correlations are reported, .94 and .99 respectively, for the PSS total score. These figures are well above minimum acceptable standards, but may be inflated due to the wide age range of children in the sample.

Studies conducted during the test development phase for purposes of subtest and item selection are cited as evidence of PSS validity. Also described in the manual is a study in which PSS results of entering kindergarten students were validated against ratings by kindergarten teachers two months later, however, the results as reported are uninterpretable because the predictive validity of the PSS cannot be disentangled from the effects of age and sex variables.

Two "longer-term" predictive validity studies are described, one in which prekindergarten PSS results are compared with teacher ratings of classroom skills at the end of kindergarten, and another in which prekindergarten PSS results are compared with reading series levels at the end of first grade. In both studies, children scoring in the bottom 40 percent were assigned to the at-risk group. For the kindergarten follow-up study, positive results are reported but insufficient data are provided to enable the reader to determine how many children with poor classroom skills were accurately identified by the PSS. The first grade follow-up study, however, is reported complete with a "hit rate" contingency table, which reveals interesting results. The criterion for classifying first graders as poor readers was apparently far too inclusive. While 32 of the 37 children who were classified at risk by the PSS were in the poor reader group in first grade, so were almost half of the not at risk group (14 of 32), despite the fact that the not at risk group was selected from children with PSS scores in the "upper 30–40 percent of the class."

Cost

The manual, which constitutes a complete administration kit for the PSS, is $15. The cost per child for a record form and Developmental Questionnaire, both of which are available in sets of 100, is approximately 30¢.

Critique

The Preschool Screening System embodies some of the most positive as well as some of the least desirable characteristics of screening procedures. On the positive side, the emphasis is not simply upon the test, but upon the overall screening process. The authors apply their considerable experience in the area of early identification and intervention in giving explicit guidance about program organization, training of personnel, interpretation of test results, providing feedback to parents, etc. Also to their credit, the PSS was developed through an extensive process of empirical research and pilot testing. Its content appears to be quite appropriate for preschool screening. One might expect the PSS screening instrument, when integrated into a well designed system, to accomplish the basic objectives of preschool screening.

The end result, however, is a system that is so elaborate and inclusive that the basic objectives of screening are obscured. First, the value of clear and straightforward screening guidelines is lost due to their seemingly random placement throughout the busy and disorganized manual. Much of the confusion arises from the insertion of the authors' follow-up assessment and early education curriculum materials in the middle of the manual. The follow-up model raises serious questions because it appears to advocate diagnostic use of screening results (PSS cluster scores together with classroom observations data are proposed for identifying remedial needs of children), in spite of the authors' emphatic warning, "never diagnose or determine a child's needs on the basis of a screening test." In a similar vein, the PSS is proposed to yield *screening data* in the hands of a paraprofessional, but *diagnostic information* when incorporated into the professional's battery. While it may be argued that guidelines for more sophisticated scoring and interpretation are provided, the validity data to justify this practice are lacking. Instead, the end result of introducing a plethora of scores for various types of interpretation, e.g., grade norms, age norms, cluster scores, age equivalents, etc., is detrimental to the basic objective of screening. Users are likely to become confused and to apply scores inappropriately.

Administration and scoring introduce some points of concern. The paucity of materials may be a problem in holding the attention and interest of the young child. The PSS manual and record forms nearly constitute the entire "test kit." The user supplies the few additional materials needed: pencil and paper and, for children below age 4-4, a small box, penny, and cube. Maintaining the child's attention towards the end of the test may be difficult, since none of the last six subtests involve manipulation of objects or motor responses. The placement of three gross motor subtests at the beginning of the test may also cause problems. Because many preschool children are reluctant to attempt gross motor tasks in a testing situation, this may have a negative effect upon rapport.

The use of nonprofessional examiners should be considered cautiously. Given the number of different subtests, and particularly the difficult-to-administer Body Awareness and Control subtests, it appears that nonprofessionals would require a more extensive training period than the authors suggest. The scoring criteria for many subtests are adequate, however some rely overly upon the examiner's subjective judgment. For example, on an item from the Visual Integration subtest in which the child must provide a verbal label for an abstract line drawing, the acceptable answers listed are: "Chair, upside-down 4, small h, milk in carton, or any reasonable response." Scoring samples are commendably provided for the Copy Shapes subtest, but there are too few samples for two items and none at all for the two easiest items.

These observations may seem inconsistent with the high inter-rater reliability figures reported, but caution is advised in interpreting the reliability study results. A serious limitation of the study is that only two examiners were involved. Furthermore, there is no indication of whether they were the authors, other professional examiners, teachers, or trained paraprofessionals. Study results obtained with two professionals who are highly familiar with the instrument cannot be expected to generalize to paraprofessionals who have been trained under typical conditions.

The Developmental Questionnaire places high demands upon both the parent and the examiner/scorer. A parent must be alert and more than minimally literate to accurately complete the instrument by mail given the reading level required and the alternation between multiple response, fill-in, checklist, and yes-no format items over the three sections. Scoring of the Developmental Questionnaire is complicated and time-consuming. Responses cannot be simply tallied; the scoring key in the manual must be consulted item-by-item to determine the number of points scored for each response that is checked. Most responses are scored as 0, 1, or 2 points (higher scores indicate problems or symptomatic behavior), but some receive scores of 3 and 4. In the absence of any interpretation guidelines, one wonders why the authors bothered to provide a scoring system for the Developmental Questionnaire.

Other shortcomings of the Preschool Screening System appear to result from an emphasis on practical considerations and clinical impressions over scientific rigor. For example, being faced with too many children or a shortage of screening personnel is not an acceptable rationale for using a prescreening approach with the Short Form, as the authors suggest. More to the point is the question of how well the Short

Form and total PSS scores correspond, a matter never addressed by the authors. The group administration approach with the PSS also lacks supportive evidence, and is inconsistent with standard practice. Finally, the rationale of setting a cutoff score at a level that matches the percentage of children in the target population disregards the realities of measurement error, i.e., that screening tests yield imperfect results and, therefore, a higher referral rate must be set (see Chapter 5).

Denver Developmental Screening Test

The Denver Developmental Screening Test (DDST) (Frankenburg & Dodds, 1967) was created to provide a brief developmental screening method to aid in the early detection of delayed or abnormal development in infants and children up to age 6. It was intended for use by physicians, nurses, and aides with no training in psychological testing. A Spanish language edition is available.

The DDST consists of 105 items that measure development in the first five years. Items are grouped into four areas: Gross Motor, Language, Fine Motor-Adaptive, and Personal-Social. The item content by areas and by age level may be appreciated by inspection of the DDST recording form (Fig. 4-3), and Table 4-7, which summarizes the number of items by area and by age level. While there are 75 items for measuring development from birth to age 2, for ages 2–5 there are only 30 items.

The test kit contains all materials, blocks, bell, ball, bottle, raisins, rattle, yarn, and pencil, required for screening. The test kit, a manual of instructions that includes technical data, recording forms, and a workbook for training examiners are all available separately.

Administration takes about 10–20 minutes and may be done by a trained paraprofessional. Following the standard administration procedure, only those items at or below a child's chronological age are administered. An abbreviated administration procedure takes only about half the time. While the DDST is primarily a test of the child, about half of the 105 items may be credited if the mother reports that she has observed the behavior required by the item.

Revisions and variations of the DDST have included (1) the revision of the original scoring system, (2) a brief parent report form, the Denver Prescreening Developmental Questionnaire (Frankenburg, van Doorninck, Liddell, & Dick, 1976), and recently, (3) a shortened method of administering the DDST using a revised format (Frankenburg, Fandal, Sciarillo, & Burgess, 1981).

Table 4-7
DDST Items By Area and Age Interval*

Age Interval	Gross Motor	Language	Fine Motor-Adaptive	Personal-Social	Total
Birth–1 year	16	8	15	12	51
1–2 years	6	5	7	6	24
2–3 years	3	3	3	2	11
3–4 years	4	3	1	3	11
4–5 years	2	2	4	0	8
Total	31	21	30	23	105

*Items located within age interval within which over 50 percent of children pass.

Scores and Interpretation

On the Denver recording form (Fig. 4-3), each item is represented by a bar that spans a certain age range. The left end of the bar is located at the age level by which 25 percent of children in the norm group pass the item; the right end of the bar is located at the age level by which 90 percent of children pass the item. For a given item, the interpretation of "delayed" development of that behavior is made when a child of a given age fails an item that 90 percent of children younger than the child pass. That is, the bar for the failed item lies entirely to the left of the vertical line indicating the child's age. Results are interpreted globally as "abnormal, questionable, normal, or untestable" according to guidelines based on the number of delays per area and delayed areas of development noted.

Normative Sample

The normative sample on which the 105 items were standardized consisted of 1036 Denver children between the ages of 2 weeks and 6.4 years. Of the total tested, 543 were male and 493 were female. All children with high risk of developmental abnormalities were excluded; that is, children born prematurely or via breech delivery or those with gross physical defects. Subjects were located through private pediatricians, well-baby clinics, schools, churches, and labor union auxiliaries. Although the location of the subjects necessarily involved unknown selection factors, the sample was evenly distributed throughout the city and reflected racial/ethnic and occupational group characteristics of the Denver population according to 1960 census data.

Research Data

An extensive reliability study by Frankenburg, Camp, Van Natta, and Demersseman (1971) provided data on tester-observer (i.e., inter-rater) agreement and test-retest reliability for children from 1.5–49

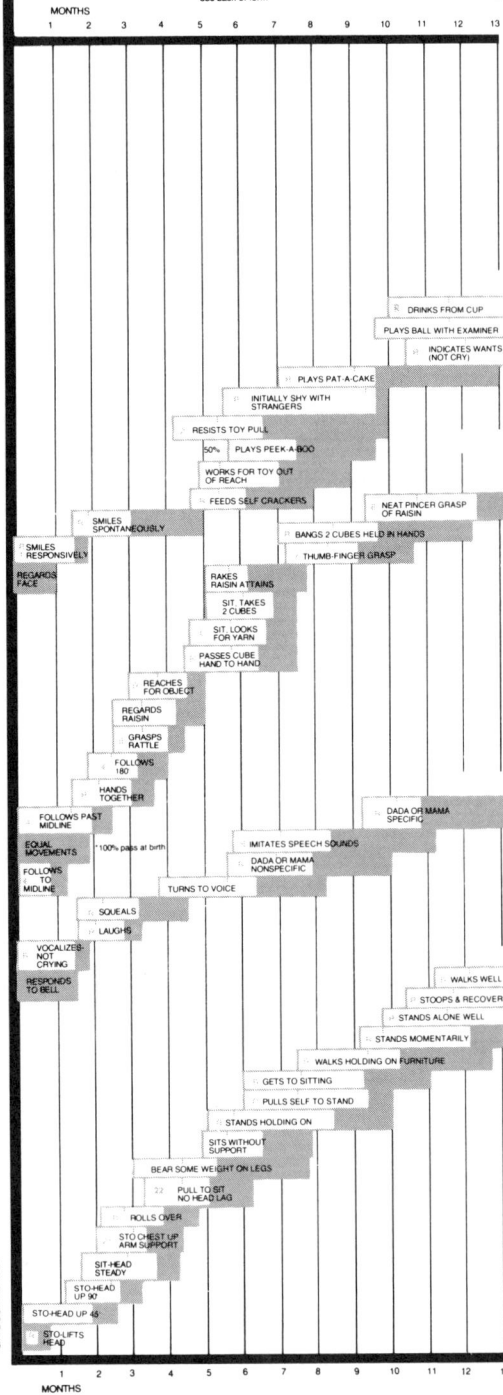

DENVER DEVELOPMENTAL SCREENING TEST
REVISED DDST-R

STO. = STOMACH
SIT. = SITTING

PERCENT OF CHILDREN PASSING

25 50 75 90

May pass by report →
Footnote no. →
see back of form

Test Item

Date:
Name:
Birthdate:
Hosp. No.:

© 1978 W.K. Frankenburg, M.D.

MONTHS
1 2 3 4 5 6 7 8 9 10 11 12 13

PERSONAL-SOCIAL

- DRINKS FROM CUP
- PLAYS BALL WITH EXAMINER
- INDICATES WANTS (NOT CRY)
- PLAYS PAT-A-CAKE
- INITIALLY SHY WITH STRANGERS
- RESISTS TOY PULL
- 50% PLAYS PEEK-A-BOO
- WORKS FOR TOY OUT OF REACH
- FEEDS SELF CRACKERS
- NEAT PINCER GRASP OF RAISIN
- SMILES SPONTANEOUSLY
- BANGS 2 CUBES HELD IN HANDS
- THUMB-FINGER GRASP
- SMILES RESPONSIVELY
- REGARDS FACE

FINE MOTOR-ADAPTIVE

- RAKES RAISIN ATTAINS
- SIT. TAKES 2 CUBES
- SIT. LOOKS FOR YARN
- PASSES CUBE HAND TO HAND
- REACHES FOR OBJECT
- REGARDS RAISIN
- GRASPS RATTLE
- FOLLOWS 180
- HANDS TOGETHER
- FOLLOWS PAST MIDLINE
- EQUAL MOVEMENTS   *100% pass at birth
- DADA OR MAMA SPECIFIC
- IMITATES SPEECH SOUNDS
- DADA OR MAMA NONSPECIFIC
- FOLLOWS TO MIDLINE
- TURNS TO VOICE

LANGUAGE

- SQUEALS
- LAUGHS
- VOCALIZES-NOT CRYING
- RESPONDS TO BELL
- WALKS WELL
- STOOPS & RECOVERS
- STANDS ALONE WELL
- STANDS MOMENTARILY
- WALKS HOLDING ON FURNITURE
- GETS TO SITTING
- PULLS SELF TO STAND
- STANDS HOLDING ON
- SITS WITHOUT SUPPORT
- BEAR SOME WEIGHT ON LEGS
- PULL TO SIT NO HEAD LAG
- ROLLS OVER

GROSS MOTOR

- STO. CHEST UP ARM SUPPORT
- SIT-HEAD STEADY
- STO-HEAD UP 90°
- STO-HEAD UP 45°
- STO-LIFTS HEAD

MONTHS
1 2 3 4 5 6 7 8 9 10 11 12 13

152

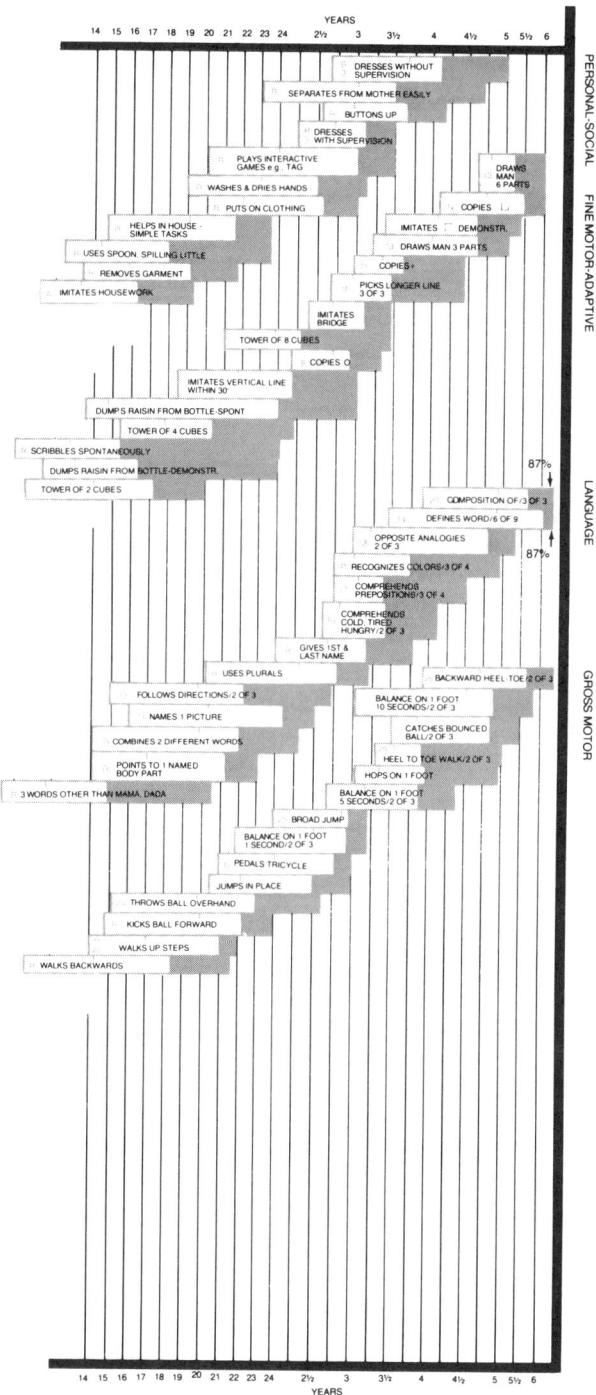

Fig. 4-3. Denver Developmental Screening Test revised scoring form. (Reprinted from Frankenberg, Fandal, Sciarillo, & Burgess, 1981. With permission.)

months of age. Tester-observer agreement was consistently high, with a mean of 96 percent agreement for administered items and only two items lower than 85 percent. Test-retest reliability (one-week interval) for 13 age groups ranged from .66–.93, with a median of .78. Only the oldest of these age groups included children over 3 years old, for which the reliability correlation was .86 (N = 17). High test-retest reliability for classificational scores was reported by Frankenburg, Goldstein, and Camp (1971), however, only a single score of abnormal was recorded in this sample of 186 children.

The DDST has been validated against various developmental and intelligence tests such as the Yale Developmental Schedules, the Bayley Scales, and the Stanford-Binet Intelligence Scale. This research has stressed classificational analysis of validity data; that is, the correspondence between abnormal vs. normal classifications generated by the screening test and by the criterion test.

A validity study (Frankenburg, Goldstein, & Camp, 1971) using the revised (and current) scoring system found a strong relationship between an abnormal DDST rating and intelligence in the mentally deficient range (i.e., Stanford-Binet or Bayley IQ less than 70). Table 4-8 presents the relationship between DDST classification and classification based on intelligence testing. The study sample included 246 infants and children to about age 6, of which 5 percent had an IQ less than 70. An "abnormal" DDST (8 percent of the sample) was associated with a 60 percent chance of obtaining an IQ less than 70, while "questionable" and "normal" DDST outcomes were associated with only a single instance of IQ less than 70. A questionable DDST (22 percent) was associated with only a 2 percent occurrence of IQ less than 70. Of 13 children with IQ's less than 70, 12 (92 percent) were identified by having an abnormal DDST rating. This analysis was not done by age, so that the discriminating power of the DDST for various age groups was not established.

Table 4-8

Relationship Between DDST Classification
and Classification Based on Intelligence Test Results

| DDST | Revised Bayley DQ or Stanford-Binet IQ | | | |
	Abnormal (below 70)	Borderline (70 to 79)	Normal (80 and above)	Total
Abnormal	12	2	6	20
Questionable	1	17	36	54
Normal	0	10	162	172
Total	13	29	204	246

(Data from Frankenburg, Goldstein, & Camp, 1971)

Table 4-9

Relationship Between DDST Outcome
and Reading Achievement in First Grade

DDST	Gates-MacGinitie Reading Tests			Total
	Below 25th percentile	25th to 75th percentile	Above 75th percentile	
At risk	26	18	11	55
Not at risk	64	154	78	296
Total	90	172	89	351

(Data from Lindquist, 1982)

Lindquist (1982) studied the relationship between DDST results obtained in the spring prior to kindergarten entry and reading achievement in first, second, and third grades as measured by the Gates-MacGinitie Reading Tests. While a significant correlation (.46) was obtained with reading achievement in first grade, the relationship was not strong enough to have practical significance for predicting academic problems. As shown in Table 4-9, 55 out of a total sample of 351 children (15 percent) were identified by the DDST as being at risk. Of these 55 children, 26 were found to be below the 25th percentile on reading achievement, while 29 scored in the average or above average range. Furthermore, 64 of the 90 children with reading scores below the 25th percentile were not identified as at risk by the DDST.

Cost

The DDST is relatively inexpensive. The cost of a complete set of DDST materials, including test kit, manual, and 100 scoring forms, is $27.50. The cost of additional scoring forms is less than 5¢ per child. Training films and videotapes are also available from the publisher.

Critique

The DDST appears to have achieved the purpose for which it was intended, namely, the early identification of children who are not developing normally. This goal has been achieved, first, by carrying out a conscientious program of instrument development and validation (research on the DDST is the most extensive in the field of developmental screening); second, by doing it in a way that is practical and acceptable to many pediatricians and other health professionals; and third, by creating training materials and programs for health care professionals. The DDST has also been widely used in early identification programs for special educational services under P.L. 94-142.

Research indicates that the DDST does a good job of identifying young children with IQs less than 70. However, for preschool screening of 3–5 year olds who may suffer lesser degrees of delayed development or more specific developmental disabilities (e.g., language disabilities), use of the DDST is open to question. Examination of DDST content in the 3–5 year age range reveals a rather limited sample of items relevant to school functioning. Consistent with this, the study by Lindquist (1982) shows limited validity of the DDST in predicting academic achievement in the primary grades.

It can be argued that predictions of early school performance from a prekindergarten DDST is an unfair test of the validity of the DDST. The DDST neither focuses on educational attainment nor on the prekindergarten age range. While the DDST has been used in preschool screening, it appears to be in the process of being displaced by instruments specifically designed for pre-academic screening of 3–5 year olds. The DDST appears to be most useful in identifying younger children who are relatively more delayed, and least useful with older children with lesser degrees of developmental lag.

Developmental Indicators for the Assessment of Learning

Developmental Indicators for the Assessment of Learning (DIAL) (Mardell & Goldenberg, 1975), a multidimensional screening instrument for children ages 2½–5½, has been widely adopted for use in screening programs throughout the country. The instrument grew out of the Learning Disabilities/Early Childhood Research Project funded by the State of Illinois. A survey of existing prekindergarten assessment measures undertaken as part of this project "confirmed the lack of a comprehensive screening device that would quickly but accurately assess all domains of learning for the young child" (Mardell & Goldenberg, 1975, p. 25). With this in mind, the authors constructed DIAL according to a theoretical framework encompassing six major components of functioning: language, conceptual, motor, social, affective, and sensory.

The first three components, language, conceptual, and motor, are directly assessed through a standardized screening test. To obtain social and affective information, examiners note behavioral observations in a checklist format. These observations serve as clinical aids, rather than as an integral part of the measure. Vision and hearing screening procedures are not actually part of the DIAL, but recommended accompaniments. Thus, while a broad ranging screening model is promoted by the authors, direct testing of language, conceptual, and motor functioning is the primary focus of the DIAL.

DIAL is divided into four areas, Gross Motor, Fine Motor, Concepts, and Communications, with seven subtests in each area. Most subtests consist of multiple items, so that the measure actually contains a total of over 150 items. Estimated administration time is 25–30 minutes. DIAL is specifically designed for use in a mass screening program. The DIAL manual specifies an overall procedure for administration as follows:

1. DIAL is administered by a team of five to eight persons. This includes a professional coordinator, four professional or paraprofessional "operators" (examiners), and, optionally, three volunteers as facilitators.
2. Each of the four areas constitutes a set of developmental tasks to be administered by an operator at a separate station. The order for proceeding through the four areas is interchangeable.
3. In addition to stations for the four areas, there is a registration area and play table for orientation purposes, a photo station where a Polaroid picture is taken, and a parent observation area.
4. The manual provides a detailed plan specifying how stations should be set up around a large open room, and how children are to rotate through the various stations.
5. After administering the subtest in an area, operators record scores and administration time, and indicate whether any of 12 numerically-coded symptomatic behaviors were observed.

Selection of subtests and items appears to be consistent with the stated objective of reflecting "school behaviors which could be expected from children in a regular classroom situation." Most of the subtest names, which are listed on the scoring form shown in Figure 4-4, are clearly descriptive of the task involved. Building involves constructing block towers to match models set up by the examiner; Sorting Blocks requires that the child classify blocks by color and arrange same-color sets of four into a square; Telling A Story has the child make up a story from stimulus pictures and is scored on the basis of sentence length and number of parts of speech used. Subtests that are less apparent from their names include Positioning (the child is instructed where to place a block relative to a box), Coping ("What do you do when you're sleepy . . . cold . . . ?"), and Remembering (sentence and digit repetition).

Following administration of a DIAL area, the examiner indicates whether any problematic behaviors from a list of 12 behavior descriptions were observed by circling the corresponding number on the scoring form. Examples from this list include:

DIAL™ SCORESHEET

yr. mo. day

Name _____   School _____   Date Today _____
Address _____   Child # _____   Birth Date _____
  Street   City   State   C.A. _____
Phone No. _____
  Mother   Father   Boy _____ Girl _____
Parents' Names
  1 2 3 4

Hearing + −
Vision + −

DECISION		
OK	REDIAL	FOLLOW-UP

GROSS MOTOR

	FUNCTIONAL LEVEL			
	Under 2½	2½–3½	3½–4½	4½ & Up
	SCALED SCORE			
	0	1	2	3
1. Throwing Right Left Both	0	1	2	3
2. Catching	0	1	2	3
3. Jumping	0	−	2	3
4. Hopping 1 2 3 4 5 R / 1 2 3 4 5 L	0	1-4	5-8	9-10
5. Skipping	0	1	2	3
6. Standing Still	0-9	10-19"	20-29	30
7. Balancing	0	1-2	3-4	5-6

TOTAL (Max = 21) _____
OBSERVATIONS 1 2 3 4 5 6 7 8 9 10 11 12
TIME _____ Min _____ Sec

Cut-off Points

Age (Yrs.-Mos.)	Boy	Girl
2-6 - 2-8	4	5
2-9 - 2-11	5	6
3-0 - 3-2	6	7

FINE MOTOR

	FUNCTIONAL LEVEL			
	Under 2½	2½–3½	3½–4½	4½ & Up
	SCALED SCORE			
	0	1	2	3
1. Matching	0	1-3	4-7	8-10
2. Building	0	1	2	3
3. Cutting Right Left	0	1	2	3
4. Copying Shapes	0	1-5	6-9	10-12
5. Copying Letters	0	1-5	6-9	10-12
6. Touching Fingers	0	1	2	3
7. Clapping Hands	0	1	2	3

TOTAL (Max = 21) _____
OBSERVATIONS 1 2 3 4 5 6 7 8 9 10 11 12
TIME _____ Min _____ Sec

Age (Yrs.-Mos.)	Boy	Girl
3-3 - 3-5	7	8
3-6 - 3-8	9	10
3-9 - 3-11	11	12

CONCEPTS

	FUNCTIONAL LEVEL			
	Under 2½	2½–3½	3½–4½	4½ & Up
	SCALED SCORE			
	0	1	2	3
1. Sorting Blocks	0	1-5	6-8	9-12
2. Naming Colors R Y B G O P	0	1-5	6-10	11-12
3. Counting 1 2 3 4 5 6 7 8	0	1-4	5-12	13
4. Positioning on under next back front	0	1-2	3-4	5
5. Following Directions	0	1	2	3
6. Identifying Concepts big/little, fast/slow, hot/cold, empty/full, day/night, more/less	0	1-5	6-11	12-14
7. Identifying Body Parts Mouth/Chin, Eye/Elbow, Nose/Shoulder, Ear/Ankle, Neck/Hip, Knee/Wrist	0	1-4	5-8	9-12

TOTAL (Max = 21) _____
OBSERVATIONS 1 2 3 4 5 6 7 8 9 10 11 12
TIME _____ Min _____ Sec

Age (Yrs.-Mos.)	Boy	Girl
4-0 - 4-2	12	13
4-3 - 4-5	13	14
4-6 - 4-8	14	15
4-9 - 4-11	15	16
5-0 - 5-2	16	17
5-3 - 5-5	17	18

COMMUNICATIONS

	FUNCTIONAL LEVEL			
	Under 2½	2½–3½	3½–4½	4½ & Up
	SCALED SCORE			
	0	1	2	3
1. Articulating bed, knife, match, pin; hammer, wagon, kuig, garage; fork, dog, jump, rat; tail, fish, dress, chair	0-16	17-21	22-26	27-32
2. Remembering [2] [5-3] [7-14] I am a big boy (girl) Grass is green in the summer Alligators always brush their teeth	0	1-3	4-5	6
3. Naming Nouns, Verbs dog/car/eating, fish/TV/swimming, horse/train/walking, bird/phone/flying, cat/sleeping, girl/washing	0-16	17-24	25-30	31-32
4. Coping hungry 0 1 2, sleepy 0 1 2*, cold 0 1 2*, toy 0 1 2	0-4	5-6	7-8	—
5. Naming Self, Age & Sex	0-1	2	3	4
6. Classifying Foods	0-1	1-3	4-5	6
7. Telling a Story noun pron. adj verb adv conj prep inter) Sentence Length	0-2	3-4	5-6	—

TOTAL (Max = 21) _____
OBSERVATIONS 1 2 3 4 5 6 7 8 9 10 11 12
TIME _____ Min _____ Sec

Age (Yrs.-Mos.)	Boy	Girl
5-6 - 5-8	18	19
5-9 - 5-11	19	20
6-0 - 6-2	20	21

Fig. 4-4. DIAL scoring form. (Reprinted by permission of Childcraft Education Corporation.)

(2) clumsy; child's movements are awkward and unsteady
(4) cries/whines
(8) hyperactivity: restless, fidgety, "antsy"

The DIAL kit, which is packaged in a large, round orange drum that doubles as a target for the Throwing subtest, contains a considerable amount of materials, including stand-up plastic dials for each of several subtests. The dials have stimulus items printed on a plastic disc that are rotated to appear through a window. Other materials, i.e., blocks, beanbags, scissors, and paper, also help to maintain the interest and attention of the young child. Administration instructions are printed on a separate laminated card for each area, in keeping with the team approach.

Scores and Interpretation

DIAL subtests may involve a single task (e.g., Skipping) or as many as 16 separate items (e.g., Articulating), but responses to each subtest translate into a scale score of 0–3. With each area containing 7 subtests, a child receives total scores for each area out of a possible 21 points. A cutoff score based upon the child's age and sex (lower cutoffs are set for boys) is then applied to each of the area totals. In this manner, a child's results are reduced to an outcome of either "OK" or "follow-up" for each area. For example, a boy of 4–1 might earn scale scores of 13, 14, 17, and 11 in the four areas. Given the cutoff score of 12 for his age, the boy scores "OK" in the first three areas and "follow-up" in the fourth. The pattern of results by area then determines the overall screening decision. Below cutoff performance in Communications or in all of the other three areas yields a screening decision of "follow-up." Therefore, in the example above, the child would be referred for further assessment. Below cutoff scores in two areas other than Communications yields an outcome of "re-DIAL," and the child is retested in those two areas. A passing score in the Communications areas and in two or three of the remaining areas gives a screening outcome of "OK", i.e., no follow-up required.

The stated goal of the DIAL is to discriminate between children whose development appears satisfactory and those whose development seems seriously "delayed." Delayed is "operationally defined as being in the lowest ten percent in performance on the item." Presumably, this means that cutoff points were set so as to identify the lowest 10 percent of the normative sample.

Normative Sample

The DIAL standardization sample was stratified so as to balance representation by sex, race, demographic setting, and socioeconomic status. This sample of Illinois children is comprehensively described, and item-by-item test construction data are presented for this group. Concern about representativeness may be raised given the proportion of black (30 percent) and low SES (65 percent) children included in the sample. It is, however, unclear whether norms are actually based on this sample. The manual reports that, since the standardization sample had a skewed age distribution, the norms were "reconstituted" in 1973 with a sample of 3100 children, 100 children at each month of age. This matter was clarified by the authors (Mardell-Czudnowski & Goldenberg, personal communication, 1983), who indicated that the original sample of 4356 children is the true normative group.

Research Data

Inter-rater reliability was computed by comparing examiners' scoring with the test authors' on videotaped administrations. The study involved 2 videotaped administrations in each of the 4 areas, and were scored by 16 examiners. Scoring agreement was always over 80 percent and usually over 90 percent for each videotaped administration, with lower reliability for the gross motor and fine motor areas.

The manual contains an allusion to test-retest reliability, but presents no data. The outcome of a one-year test-retest reliability study is summarized only as follows:

Half of these children [N = 520] were randomly selected from the upper 90 percent according to DIAL scores while half of these children were in the lower 10 percent. The two groups remained very distinct, indicating high test-retest reliability, even after a full year (Mardell & Goldenberg, 1975, p. 56).

The manual presents validity studies by the authors and by others. One concurrent validity study compared DIAL outcomes with an evaluation by an interdisciplinary diagnostic team. Although a figure of 85 percent agreement is cited, insufficient information is provided to determine false positive and false negative error rates. Results from two other concurrent validity studies are described as "most encouraging . . . although limited": reference is made to the DIAL Project final report, but no details are included in the manual other than the study locale.

Six pages of the manual are devoted to a correlational study by Sarff (1974) relating DIAL area scores and total scores to Peabody Picture Vocabulary Test (PPVT) scores, with a complete breakdown of correlations by sex, age, and DIAL classification. Correlations of overall DIAL score (i.e., sum of scaled scores) with PPVT mental age were .64, .63, and .37 for 5 year-olds, 4 year-olds, and 3 year-olds, respectively. No data based on classificational DIAL scores are supplied.

A predictive validity study (Hall et al., 1974) describes a two year follow-up of 249 kindergarten and first grade children using readiness or achievement test scores as criterion measures. Results are presented as multiple correlations between the four DIAL area scores and criterion measure subtest scores; however, this is of limited value (also incomprehensible, given the way results are abstracted from the original report). This use of multiple correlations is inappropriate because these research results are based on weighted DIAL area total scores, whereas DIAL decisions are not.

Additional research data from the literature is referenced in a later article by the primary author (Mardell-Czudnowski, 1980). A research report on a study of 71 preschool children by Matusiak (1976) favored the DIAL over the Cooperative Preschool Inventory and the Dallas Screening Test, but solely on the basis of correlational statistics, not screening decision accuracy. More recently, a comprehensive follow-up study (Lichtenstein, 1982) involving a battery of preschool screening measures administered to 428 preschool children revealed relatively high validity hit rates for the DIAL, but not as high as those obtained for a shorter instrument included in the screening battery.

Cost

Initial outlay for the DIAL kit is $140. In addition, a balance beam and Polaroid camera must be supplied by the user. The cost per child is relatively high if a Polaroid snapshot is taken of each child for use in the Naming Self, Age and Sex subtest; if this is dispensed with, the cost is approximately 15¢ per administration.

Critique

The DIAL has considerable potential as a screening instrument; its content appears well suited for preschool screening. Upon close inspection, however, concerns arise regarding both qualitative and psychometric characteristics.

The breakdown of DIAL subtests by area (Gross Motor, Fine Motor, Concepts, Communications) is not as "neat and clean" as the area divisions suggest. Two examples: (1) the Positioning and Following Directions subtests in the Concepts area have a substantial language component, and (2) some Communications subtests (e.g., Classifying Foods, Coping) depend heavily upon reasoning and conceptual knowledge. While rational consistency is claimed for the arrangement of DIAL subtests by area, no empirical support is provided (e.g., through factor analysis).

Administration and scoring may introduce complications. While the manual states that examiners might be either professionals or para-professionals, it does not indicate the extent and nature of training required. The amount of preparation required of paraprofessionals appears to be considerable. Gross Motor and certain Fine Motor sub-tests are particularly demanding, as the examiner must read instructions word-for-word, demonstrate tasks to be imitated, carefully observe responses, and apply scoring rules. Scoring criteria for most Concepts and Communications subtests are unambiguous and several subtests are accompanied by sample responses, but some Fine Motor and Gross Motor tasks require subjective judgments on the part of the examiner. It appears that paraprofessionals could learn to master administration and scoring in one day of intensive training, but only if they concentrate upon just one area, as directed.

With regard to the behavioral observations supplied by the examiner, the descriptions of problem behaviors are so general that much subjective judgment is involved and inter-rater reliability would expectedly be low. The manual provides neither guidelines nor research data indicating how to interpret these observations. Users should be extremely cautious about applying this information towards screening decisions.

The team administration format of the DIAL raises some interesting questions. Is time saved or lost by having children rotate to various testing stations? Are shy or distractible children likely to have difficulty adjusting to a series of different testing situations, resulting in a higher percentage of invalid administrations?

The DIAL manual does not use space to best advantage. Much technical information is included without a clear explanation of what it represents, or without sufficient detail. Administration instructions are condensed in a format that makes reading difficult for the examiner. On the positive side, recommendations for organizing a screening program that uses the DIAL are provided.

More research is needed on reliability and validity. Despite the amount of technical material presented in the manual, there is no solid evidence to indicate how consistently the DIAL classifies children, or how accurately it identifies children with learning or developmental difficulties. Research is also needed to test DIAL's structural elements, e.g., the use of separate sets of cutoff scores for males and females, and the arrangement of subtests by area. An element that raises particular questions about the measurement properties of the DIAL is the manner in which cutoff scores are applied to each area. It is possible that the same cutoff score will be optimal for each of the four areas at certain age levels. For this to be the case at every age level, and for these cutoff scores to systematically increase with each successive three-month age range, is in all probability for convenience and simplicity, rather than due to technical precision.

The DIAL's comprehensiveness appears to be both a strength and a drawback. Although extensive coverage of developmental functions is one of DIAL's strong points, the scope of information collected and the time required are more on the order of a diagnostic instrument than a screening test. And while the manual cautions against diagnostic interpretation, statements such as the following by the test's first author encourage this practice:

> Children's performances can be recorded, observed, and plotted as a functional profile. Even for children who are developing within the expected normative range, it is possible to plot the strengths and weaknesses for all the DIAL areas and to make suggestions to parents . . . (Mardell-Czudnowski, 1980, p. 43)

Hopefully, the revision of the DIAL (DIAL-R) that is planned for 1984 will address these concerns. Major changes include combination of the Gross Motor and Fine Motor areas, replacement of Illinois norms with national norms, and expansion of the age range to include ages 2 through 6.

Early Screening Inventory

The Early Screening Inventory (ESI) (Meisels & Wiske, 1983) is designed to identify children ages 4–6 who are at risk for experiencing school failure. First introduced as the Eliot-Pearson Screening Inventory (Meisels & Wiske, 1976), the ESI has been the subject of considerable pilot testing and research by the authors since 1975.

The authors describe the ESI as primarily a measure of developmental abilities rather than of readiness or achievement, and state that poor performance therefore suggests "a delay or disorder in the child's potential for acquiring knowledge" rather than a lack of current skill achievement. Developmental areas sampled include cognition, language, speech, perception, and gross and fine motor coordination. The authors also note that the ESI comprises only one part of a comprehensive screening battery, and should be accompanied by input from parents (a questionnaire is included in the manual), a medical examination, and hearing and vision screening.

Administration of the ESI usually requires 15–20 minutes. Some "formal background in early childhood behavior and development" is recommended for examiners, who might be "experienced teachers of young children, students of child development, school psychologists, occupational and physical therapists, nurses, or physicians." A videotape of an ESI administration plus other instructional material is available from the publisher.

ESI test items are arranged into three general sections: Visual-Motor/Adaptive, Language and Cognition, and Gross Motor and Body Awareness. Visual-Motor/Adaptive tasks include copying of forms, building blocks to match a model arranged by the examiner, and a Visual Sequential Memory subtest that bears some similarity to the card game "Concentration." Language and Cognition tasks involve counting blocks, describing common objects (for which responses are scored for giving the name, color, shape, and use), completing verbal analogies (e.g., "A horse is big; a mouse is———"), and repeating digits. The child's speech is also noted and subjectively described by the examiner. The Gross Motor and Body Awareness sections include four subtests: Balance, Imitate Movement (i.e., arm positions), Hop, and Skip.

A parent questionnaire, provided in an appendix to the manual, is mostly devoted to the child's medical history, current health, and developmental functioning. No information on scoring or interpretation of the parent questionnaire appears in the manual.

Scores and Interpretation

Most items are scored on a 0–1 or 0–1–2 scale. The Verbal Expression subtest is a notable exception. The child is shown toy models of four common objects and asked to tell about each in turn. For each object, up to 12 points are credited for describing the object by name, color, shape, and use. The point total on this subtest is then translated into a scale score from 0 to 3. The arrangement of the ESI by sections is disregarded in scoring; only a total ESI score is computed. Cutoff scores are provided for each six-month age range from 4–0 to 6–0, yielding one of three recommendations: "OK", "rescreen," or "refer." The "OK" category includes scores from one standard deviation below the mean (about 16th percentile) on up based on the normative sample scoring distribution. The "rescreen" category covers the range between one and two standard deviations below the mean, which corresponds to the range from approximately 2nd to 16th percentile. The authors recommend that children in this group be rescreened in eight to ten weeks. Children in the "refer" category are to be referred immediately for further assessment. The actual referral rates for the normative sample are not specified, although the proportion of four year olds and of five year olds passing each item is given. Users are advised by the authors to develop local cutoff points to insure that recommendations are appropriate for the particular community.

Normative Sample

The normative sample consists of 465 children from low to lower-middle SES urban families. The sample is described as primarily white, although no racial breakdown is given. The normative sample contains approximately 200 children in each of the two middle age ranges, 4–6 to 4–11 and 5–0 to 5–5, but only 50 children in the 4–0 to 4–5 range. The highest age range includes only a handful of children (although not specified, the number can be deduced to be 13), and cutoff scores for this group are extrapolated from the other age ranges.

Research Data

Inter-rater reliability was assessed by having an examiner and an observer simultaneously score ESI administrations with 18 children. Three examiners rotated between the tester and observer role for this study. A correlation of .91 between total scores is reported. A second study that involved 6 examiners and 57 four and five year old examinees assessed test-retest reliability over a one-week period. The correlation between ESI total score on the two occasions was .82. Neither study analyzed reliability data in terms of classificational outcomes.

Concurrent validity of the ESI was investigated using the McCarthy Scales of Children's Abilities (MSCA) (McCarthy, 1972) as a criterion measure. The ESI and MSCA were administered to a sample of 102 children that, by design, included a high proportion of at risk children. The correlation between the two measures was .73. Classificational outcomes on the MSCA were established by setting cutoffs on the General Cognitive Index (GCI) at one and at two standard deviations below the mean (standard scores of 68 and 84, respectively) to yield three categories that correspond to ESI classifications. As shown in Table 4-10, the ESI referred 17 of the 23 children with MSCA scores more than one standard deviation below the mean. In doing so, the ESI referred 8 children who were within normal range on the MSCA. Of the

Table 4-10

Classification Agreement Between ESI and
Intelligence Test Outcomes

ESI	McCarthy Scale of Children's Abilities			
	GCI < 68	GCI = 68-84	GCI > 84	Total
Refer	8	9	8	25
Rescreen	2	1	9	12
OK	0	3	62	65
Total	10	13	79	102

children classified "rescreen," 3 of 12 were in the MSCA at risk categories.

Two predictive validity studies are reported. The first compared ESI scores of 472 children screened at kindergarten entry with Metropolitan Readiness Test (MRT), Form II scores obtained late in the kindergarten year. Agreement between ESI and MRT outcomes was based on cutoffs at the 15th percentile for both tests. Of the 66 children scoring below the 15th percentile on the MRT, the ESI referred 22.

A long-term predictive validity study by Wiske, Meisels, and Tivnan (1982), reported in the ESI manual, followed a sample of 115 children who were screened near the time of kindergarten entry through fourth grade. Screening results were validated against three different criteria of school performance obtained at the end of each school year: report card grades, referral for special educational services, and grade promotion/retention. ESI scores were shown to significantly improve prediction of these performance measures when added to other screening information (i.e., vision, hearing, and medical screening, and parent reports of medical and developmental history). Hit rate analyses indicated that ESI screening results consistently referred the greater part of those children who were later classified as having problems. From kindergarten through third grade, for all criterion measures, the ESI identified in the range of 72–100 percent of problem category children. These results were obtained with a relatively high referral rate, from 29 percent to 47 percent, depending upon the sub-sample available for each criterion measure. Consequently, overreferrals (i.e., children referred by the ESI but performing satisfactorily on follow-up measures) were generally in the range of 20–30 percent of the sample.

Cost

The cost of the ESI test kit is $39.95. Additional copies of consumable materials (score sheet and parent questionnaire) cost approximately 70¢ per child.

Critique

The ESI bears many positive indications of being an instrument designed explicitly for screening. A commendable collection of age-appropriate, time-efficient items that are clearly relevant to school performance cover a broad range of developmental functions. ESI results are presented in the form of screening recommendations. The manual specifies the various elements of the overall screening process, and presents case studies to demonstrate how ESI results might be interpreted within the context of a complete array of screening information.

As advised in the manual, screening with the ESI should be limited to individuals with formal training in child development and/or experience with young children. Considerable familiarity with the administration and scoring instructions appears to be especially needed for certain subtests. For example, the child's responses on the Verbal Expression subtest must be immediately evaluated by the examiner to determine what follow-up questions to ask. Also, much expertise is required for the examiner to subjectively describe and evaluate the children's articulation and syntax, as instructed, following administration of this subtest. On several subtests, the child's performance on one item determines whether another item is to be administered. Thus, administration and scoring errors may be compounded.

Other subtests appear difficult to score reliably regardless of the examiner's training and expertise. Scoring instructions for the Skip subtest are simply: "*2 points* if child can do a two-footed skip . . . *1 point* for a one-footed skip . . . no points for a gallop.*" For the Imitate Movements subtest, the following scoring rules are applied after observing the child's imitation of nine arm positions modeled by the examiner:

Score *2 points* if child performs consistently with hesitant and/or corrected movements on *no more than* two positions. Score *1 point* if the child shows hesitation and/or correction on *more than* two positions or uncorrected movements on *no more than* two positions. Score *0 points* if child shows uncorrected movements on *more than* two positions.

Although it is possible, as reported by Meisels (personal communication, 1983), to train examiners to achieve high scoring reliability on these subtests, it is likely that interpretation of these scoring rules will vary from setting to setting.

One of the Block Building items requires the child to balance a block rotated 45°, edge downward, between two other blocks, a difficult if not impossible task when the table surface or blocks are slippery. The test user is advised to provide a sheet of manila drawing paper for a "standardized" surface and to lightly sand slippery block surfaces. A simpler solution would have been to discard the item as a matter of convenience.

Some anomalies appear in the psychometric data. Although the lowest age range for which ESI norms are provided is indicated as 4–0 to 4–5, the normative sample had a lower age limit of 4–2. Thus, cutoff points for children ages 4–0 and 4–1 may be too high. Establishing local norms for the 4–0 to 4–5 and 5–6 to 5–11 age groups is well advised anyway, given the insufficient numbers in the normative sample. A questionable "adjustment" was made in reporting the results of the concurrent validity study with the MSCA—results that are already quite respectable as is. In summarizing hit rates, the authors assume that those children classified as "rescreen" will all be correctly assigned to either the "OK" or the "refer" group, whichever matches the MSCA classification, upon rescreening. Using this logic, no screening errors can ensue for children assigned to the "rescreen" category. Finally, the reported inter-rater reliability figures are computed in a less than ideal manner. By using correlations between testers' and observers' scores to reflect scoring reliability, it is possible for raters to disagree on individual items but for these differences to cancel out when a total score is obtained.

While a commendable amount of research has been conducted on the ESI by its authors since its original publication in 1976, this has not led to the correction of certain shortcomings of the instrument. In particular, there is the need for greater simplicity in administration and scoring procedures. Still, the ESI has high potential for situations in which the screening population is well centered between the ages of 4–0 and 6–0 (typically the case for prekindergarten screening) and qualified examiners are available.

McCarthy Screening Test

Simply put, the McCarthy Screening Test (MST) (McCarthy, 1978) is one-third of the McCarthy Scales of Children's Abilities (MSCA) (McCarthy, 1972). The Psychological Corporation created a screening test out of the MSCA, one of the leading tests of general intelligence for children, by selecting a set of six subtests from the parent, or "donor," test and presenting them exactly as they appear in the MSCA. The MST was published in 1978, four years after MSCA author Dorothy McCarthy passed away. The Psychological Corporation resolved the matter of authorship with the title page credit, "Adapted from the McCarthy Scales of Children's Abilities by Dorothy McCarthy."

The MSCA subtests chosen for the McCarthy Screening Test are Right-Left Orientation, Verbal Memory, Draw-A-Design, Numerical Memory, Conceptual Grouping, and Leg Coordination. While the test is designed for children ages 4–6½, the Right-Left Coordination subtest is administered only to children ages 5 and up. Typical administration time is 20 minutes, although younger children may require more time and older children less.

As reported in the manual, the subtests were selected on the basis of content, level of difficulty, administration time, and ease of administration and scoring. Subtests were chosen so as to measure "a variety of abilities that are important in achieving success in school," and certain subtests, i.e., Right-Left Orientation, Draw-A-Design, Leg Coordination, are said to be "of a type that has proved particularly useful in identifying children with learning disabilities or perceptual difficulties" (p. 2). In terms of difficulty level, subtests are described as being appropriate for the 4–6½ age range, and also comparable in difficulty for white and nonwhite children and for males and females.

Because the subtests were selected for ease of administration and scoring, the author(s) of the manual state that teachers and paraprofessionals, as well as psychologists and other qualified professionals, may serve as examiners. Thorough instruction and supervised practice under professional guidance are advised for inexperienced examiners, although no specific recommendations for training procedures are provided. It is also recommended that qualified professionals assume sole responsibility for interpretation of MST results.

Materials required for the MST are relatively few, so that the entire test kit fits into a soft plastic portfolio. A cardboard picture of a boy is used in the Right-Left Orientation subtests for the child to point out left and right body parts—knee, elbow, foot, and shoulder. Draw-A-Design requires the copying of shapes, for which a consumable booklet is provided. Conceptual Grouping makes use of a set of 12 brightly-colored plastic blocks that the child sorts by size, color, shape, and, as items become more difficult, combinations of these variables (e.g., "find all the big yellow ones," "which one goes best with the ones on this card?").

Scores and Interpretation

After computing raw scores for each subtest, the examiner consults a table to determine whether any of the scores are below the 10th, 20th, or 30th percentile for the child's age (rounded to the nearest half-year). The user is given the option of setting cutoffs at any of these three percentile levels, and then of assigning the "at risk" classification on the basis of one, two, or three failed (i.e., below cutoff) subtests. Thus, the user may select from a total of nine alternative decision rules, noting this choice on the record form (see Fig. 4-5).

The MST manual makes reference to a validity study in which two particular decisions rules were used with positive results: two or more failures at the 30th percentile, and three failures at the 30th percentile, which yield standardization sample referral rates of 24 percent and 10 percent, respectively. These two options, however, are not explicitly recommended to the exclusion of others, and decision rules that produce referral rates between these two levels may be selected, e.g., two or more failures at 20th percentile corresponds to a 13 percent referral rate for the standardization sample.

McCARTHY SCREENING TEST

Record Form

NAME _____ AGE _____ SEX _____

HOME ADDRESS _____

NAMES OF PARENTS OR GUARDIAN _____

SCHOOL _____ GRADE _____

PLACE OF TESTING _____ TESTED BY _____

TEST SCORES		
Test	Score	Pass-Fail
1. Right-Left Orientation	_____	_____
2. Verbal Memory	_____	_____
3. Draw-A-Design	_____	_____
4. Numerical Memory	_____	_____
5. Conceptual Grouping	_____	_____
6. Leg Coordination	_____	_____

	Year	Month	Day
Date Tested	_____	_____	_____
Date of Birth	_____	_____	_____
Age	_____	_____	_____

CRITERIA

Percentile	Number of Tests Failed
_____ 10th	_____ 1 or more
_____ 20th	_____ 2 or more
_____ 30th	_____ 3 or more

CLASSIFICATION

_____ At Risk   _____ Not at Risk

Ⓤ THE PSYCHOLOGICAL CORPORATION
A Subsidiary of Harcourt Brace Jovanovich, Inc.

78-110AS

(25) 8-189102   (100) 8-189150

Fig. 4-5. McCarthy Screening Test record form. (Reprinted by permission of the Psychological Corporation.)

Normative Sample

MST norms are based on the subset of 516 children from the MSCA's national standardization sample, which was "stratified according to age, sex, color, geographic region, and father's occupation." The MSCA standardization sample excluded "institutionalized mental defectives, children with severe behavioral or emotional problems, those with known brain damage, and those with obvious physical defects," but "likely" included "children with serious but less obvious problems, such as a learning disability" (p. 23). Approximately 100 children were included at each half-year age range from 4–6½ (4, 4½, 5, . . .) with the exception of age 6, for which norms were interpolated. Actually, the age ranges are labeled by their *midpoints,* so that the age 5 range covers ages 4–9 to 5–3, and the overall normative sample for the MST includes ages 3–9 to 6–9.

Research Data

All research data presented in the MST manual are derived from studies with the MSCA, for which scores were recomputed to simulate MST results. Test-retest reliability over three to five weeks was obtained for 40 children ages 5–5½. Reliability correlation coefficients, reported for individual subtests only, ranged from .32 to .69, with a median of .57. The reliability of classificational scores for subtests (i.e., pass or fail) and for the overall MST (at risk or not at risk) is not presented.

The manual describes a validity study in which 46 "learning disabled" and 14 "emotionally disturbed/behaviorally disordered" children ages 3–11 to 6–8 were administered the McCarthy Scales. The only outcome reported is a comparison between the percentage of this identified group that was referred by the MST and by the MSCA. Using the decision rule of two or more MST subtests below the 30th percentile and a comparable rule for the MSCA, the MST referred 67 percent of this group compared to 88 percent identified by the MSCA.

A predictive validity study correlated scores on the MST and the Metropolitan Readiness Tests (MRT), Level II for 52 children who were administered the MST in the fall of the kindergarten year and the criterion measure in the spring. Correlations between MST subtests and the MRT Pre-Reading Skills Composite, which includes auditory, visual, and language skills, ranged from .10 for Leg Coordination to .54 for Numerical Memory, with a median of .35. Only correlational validity data for this study are presented, none of which are based upon overall MST results.

Cost

The initial cost for the complete MST test kit is $47.50. The cost of consumables is approximately 70¢ per child.

Critique

Not surprisingly, strengths of the MST reflect the quality of the MSCA, while its weaknesses derived from failure to differentiate it from the MSCA as an instrument specifically for preschool screening.

The MST manual is extremely well written and organized. Instructions to the examiner are very clear and readable. In the administration directions, instructions to be spoken verbatim by the examiner are highlighted in red. Scoring criteria are explicit for all subtests, and ample scoring samples accompany the Draw-A-Design subtest. Essential information is easily located in the manual. In addition to typical sections on test purpose and selection, statistical information, and general testing guidelines, the manual devotes a section to "determining the risk classification."

One of the MSCA's greatest strengths, its national stratified standardization sample, does not apparently work to the advantage of the MST when translated into decision rules. While providing the user an option of decision rules is well and good in principle, the relative merits of selecting, say, one failure at the 10th percentile as opposed to two failures at the 30th percentile (both of which yield estimated referral rates of 24 percent) are not described in any way. Furthermore, the user's choice is limited to the options presented, none of which have an expected referral rate between 13 percent and 24 percent, an interval in which referral rates are typically set. Given the nature of the MST scoring system, developing local norms is no easy matter. (See Chapter 5 for help in this matter.)

Leaving the content of MSCA subtests exactly as is raises some question. Since the MSCA is standardized for children ages 2½ through 8½, there is no apparent reason to have included the most difficult MSCA items in the MST, which is intended for screening out low-functioning children below age 6½.

Finally, the lack of psychometric data on the MST, as distinct from the MSCA, is a serious problem. The MST was apparently never administered as a set prior to publication. The collection of MST subtests may not yield the same results by itself as when embedded within the complete MSCA. It should also be noted that reliability data derived from MSCA studies would have been obtained using professionally trained examiners, and should not be regarded as applicable to paraprofessionals and teachers.

All in all, there is insufficient evidence to allay the suspicion that the MST, as a commercial spin-off of a well-known test, was not adequately developed in its own right.

Developmental Profile II

The Developmental Profile II (Alpern, Boll, & Shearer, 1980) was designed to provide a standardized multidimensional assessment of development. The age range of the DP II is birth through 9 years. The DP II measures the child's current development by means of a standardized interview with the parent or other caretaker (e.g., a teacher who knows the child well). The interview can also be combined with direct assessment of the child. The interviewer/assessor need not be trained in psychological testing. Originally designed as an assessment technique, which requires 20–40 minutes to administer, the DP II may also be utilized as a screening device.

Items measure development in five areas: Physical, Self-Help, Social, Academic and Communication. Each scale typically has three items at each developmental age level. The age levels are set in six-month intervals for the first four years and in one-year intervals thereafter. The sample items in Table 4-11 are from the 4 year level (Preschooler II, 43–54 months).

Scores and Interpretation

Age credits are assigned for the behaviors the child is reported to demonstrate in each area, and totaled to yield an age score for that area. Results for the five areas are represented on a developmental profile, which pictures the child's levels of functioning in the various areas. In this way, developmental strengths and weaknesses, and their variance from the child's chronological age are graphically depicted. In addition, an IQ equivalency score (IQE) may be computed using the ratio of the child's Academic scale age to the child's chronological age.

A microcomputer system is also available that scores the instrument and generates (1) an Adaptive Age Report (test results in each of the five areas, discrepancy analysis between developmental and chronological age, and a summary developmental average), (2) a Teacher's Report, which can be used to develop the child's individualized education program (IEP), and (3) a Parent Report, which includes a list of activities to practice at home.

Standardization

Standardization and research data derive from studies conducted with the original Developmental Profile (Alpern & Boll, 1972), which included more items and covered a wider age range than the DP II.

Table 4-11

Development Profile II Content at the Four Year Level

Physical Scale

- Does the child catch a ball (any size) thrown by an adult who is standing five feet away? The child must catch the ball 50% of the time.
- Can the child hop forward on one foot for a distance of at least ten feet without having to stop and start again?
- Does the child jump rope with one or both feet at least twice; or can the child jump over a number of things in its path without stopping? The "things" should be at least eight inches high.

Self-Help Scale

- Does the child dress completely except for shoelace tying and other difficult fastenings? The child must manage regular shirt or blouse buttons and zippers.
- Does the child put toys away neatly when asked to do so? (The child may often have to be asked more than once.)
- Can the child fix a bowl of dry cereal? This must include getting the bowl, cereal and milk and pouring both cereal and milk into the bowl.

Social Scale

- Does the child draw a person so that an adult could tell what was drawn? It need not be a whole person, but there should be a head and a body or a head and eyes, nose or mouth which any adult could recognize.
- Is the child allowed to play in her/his own neighborhood without being watched by an adult? This does not mean the child is allowed to cross the street alone.
- Does the child know and use (though not always) the terms "thank you," "please," and "you're welcome" at the right times?

Academic Scale

- When asked to draw a person or when drawing a picture of a person does the child draw a head that looks like a head and at least one other body part?
- Can the child tell a penny from a nickel and a dime by naming or pointing to the penny when it is named? The child need not know the value of the coins.
- Does the child draw or copy a square? The square must have right angle corners and the sides of the square should be of about equal size.

Communication Scale

- Has the child sung a song of at least 30 words? Many of the words can be repeated in the song, but the child must sing the song alone.
- Has the child been able to buy something in a store without help? The child must have let the salesperson know exactly what was wanted, paid for the item, and waited for change.
- Can the child tell people (by speaking or holding up fingers) how old she/he is now, how old she/he was last year, and how old she/he will be next year?

(From Alpern, Boll, & Shearer, 1980. With permission.)

Student interviewers were trained to interview parents (mothers) about the developmental competence of their normal children, with "normal" defined by parents' response to a physical and social history questionnaire. Item norms were based upon reports for 3008 children from birth to age 12–6, with both sexes equally represented. Reports were obtained from parents in Indiana and Washington. Racial and socioeconomic data for the parents, who were disproportionately located in urban areas, were described as consistent with the distribution of the entire U.S. population. Fourteen percent of the children in the sample were black. Items were assigned to the age interval during which 75 percent of the children achieved the behavior. A small number of items found to discriminate on the basis of sex, race, or socioeconomic level were deleted from the final profile.

Research Data

Two studies provide information about consistency in scoring and about consistency over time by a single respondent. First, of a group of 36 teachers who concurrently scored a demonstration of a Developmental Profile interview regarding a 4 year old, 30 were within one item of matching the model score and all except one were within two items of perfect agreement.

The second study involved two administrations of the Developmental Profile to 11 mothers by two different interviewers, with a two to three day interval between interviews. The average test-retest difference among all scales was only 1.7 items. In one-fifth of the cases, scores obtained by the two interviewers on different days were identical.

The validity of the Developmental Profile for measuring the current developmental status of children was assessed by determining the degree of correspondence between the caretaker's report of the child's behavior and a direct measure of the child's functioning. The first step was to derive a test from the interview. Each of the 318 items of the original standardization version was examined to determine if they could be administered to a child by direct testing. For example, such items as hopping, using a fork, copying a square, or repeating sentences could all be administered to children as test items. In contrast, there were items concerning whether the child could engage in cooperative play with a peer for a one-half hour period, take a bath acceptably, and ride a bicycle, none of which lent themselves to direct testing. Following preliminary selection of items and a pilot study of the test version, a manual of 197 items (62 percent of all items in the standardization version) was developed with standard instructions for individual direction administration. The study's procedure called for two investigators working simultaneously, one interviewing the mother while the second tested the child in a separate room. All subjects were administered all five scales.

The study sample consisted of 100 children: 55 males and 45 females, 88 whites and 12 blacks. The age range was from 3 months to 12 years, with a mean age of 6 years. There were from five to thirteen subjects at each year level. Although allowed for by plan, no subjects were eliminated from the study because children were judged to be too uncooperative or mothers' reporting was judged to be too unreliable.

For a total of 8709 observations (i.e., items on which there were both a mother's judgment and the child's performance score), there were 7351 agreements (i.e., items where the mother's report and the child's performance coincided), resulting in an overall agreement rate of 84 percent. Scale by scale analysis for the standardization version showed item validity to be essentially at the same high level for all of the five scales.

The relationship of the IQ equivalency score (IQE), which is based on the academic scale of the DP II, and intelligence (IQ) measured by testing with the Stanford-Binet, was determined for groups of retarded and normal children. For half of the normal group and 69 percent of the retarded group, IQE and IQ were within ten points of each other. The group of 16 normal preadolescents had a mean Stanford-Binet IQ of 119 and a mean DP II IQE of 108. The 54 retarded preadolescents had a mean Stanford-Binet IQ of 51, five points lower than their mean IQE. Note that for the retarded group, IQE tended to overestimate IQ; for the normal group, IQE tended to be lower than IQ.

Cost

The cost of the manual is $18.25, and the cost per child for the scoring and report form is approximately 30¢. With the interview format used, there is no savings in personnel costs compared to an individually administered test.

Critique

The DP II could be, and probably is, one of the more valuable tools for assessing the development of children and for involving parents in that assessment. At the same time, it should be used cautiously as a screening tool.

The reported validity data appear to support the value of the DP II as a method for assessing the adaptive competencies of children. However, the DP II has not been systematically utilized and validated as a developmental screening tool. Abbreviated formats for administering items immediately below the child's age level need to be studied systematically. For those parents who will have difficulty with paper and pencil information gathering methods and with those children for whom some problem is suspected, the DP II would appear to be a valuable tool in the early identification process. Although the DP II is presented as a general use assessment measure, it was constructed in a manner that is highly appropriate for a screening measure. Items were written to permit easy administration by nonprofessional examiners, a wide range of content was sampled, readability and clarity of items was emphasized, and items were placed at an age level where the majority of children respond correctly. One possible drawback to its use in screening is the requirement of 20–40 minutes of an interviewer's time for each administration.

With its revision in 1980, the DP II appears to have been structured to dovetail with the purposes of Public Law 94-142. The DP II is described as both an assessment level and screening level instrument; as a structured interview for obtaining information from the parent, or possibly the teacher; and as one basis for individual educational programming. At this point, these statements must be treated as claims by the authors rather than as established facts documented by extensive research. Its best established use is as a developmental assessment tool based on a structured interview with the parent or teacher.

The claim that this instrument is appropriate for children regardless of sex, race (i.e., black or white), or social class may be overstated. The authors have dealt with the complex issues of fairness by eliminating items so as to reduce differences between various groups on scale scores. While this limits the possibility of discriminatory use of DP II results, absence of bias cannot be assured without research demonstrating comparable validity across groups. Also, it is possible that the procedure of equalizing group means may have a negative impact on the instrument's overall validity. In view of the correlation of socioeconomic status with intelligence and school performance, it may be unwise to eliminate this source of variance. The authors show a sensitivity to this dilemma in describing how group differences were reduced, but not eliminated. However, the net effect of the procedures instituted cannot be determined from the data presented.

Examination of the item content of the Academic scale at the 4 year and 5 year levels reveals that four of these six items deal with drawing a person and copying designs. None of the items at these two age levels deal with pre-reading skills, e.g., knowledge of letters. This is a serious omission in an instrument proposed for preschool screening.

Guidelines for interpretation of DP II results and for referral are presented with the appropriate caution that these are "clinical guidelines." However, neither a working definition of a range of normal expectations nor data regarding norms for the standardization sample are provided. The tables of Referral Guidelines appear to add clarity, but the logic on which they are based is not made clear and the broad age ranges that are provided could lead to problems. For example, at the 5 year level, which includes children from ages 4–7 to 5–6, a 5½ year old would be classified as developing normally in the area of Communication even though the child was functioning at a 4 year level, which is over 30 percent below the child's age level. It appears, but is not explicitly stated, that the referral cutoffs are stricter for the Academic area, followed by Communication, then Physical, and finally Self-help and Social. The critical point here is that the subject of "the range of normal" is not adequately addressed, and that no data regarding this range are provided.

Several areas of investigation might be addressed in determining optimal application and interpretation of the instrument for preschool screening: (1) establishing cutoff scores and decision rules for integrating results on the five scales, (2) developing a shortened preschool level form with a lower ceiling, and (3) studying the possibility of administering part or all of the instrument in written form rather than by interview.

The logic and structure (format) of the DP II appear to be quite sound. The empirically-based instrument development process and early research with the Developmental Profile were extensive and thorough. The resulting content is well balanced, straightforward, and clearly presented. Its value as a screening tool, both in terms of time and cost, and also validity remain to be demonstrated.

Minneapolis Preschool Screening Instrument

Development of the Minneapolis Preschool Screening Instrument (MPSI) (Lichtenstein, 1980b) was undertaken by the Minneapolis Public Schools through Project Search, an early identification research project funded through a grant from the Bureau of Education for the Handicapped. The objective was to develop a screening instrument to select out preschool children with special educational needs as part of efforts to fulfill the mandate of Public Law 94-142.

The test construction strategy combined practical, theoretical, and empirical elements. Practical guidelines were that the measure should be (1) brief to administer—20 minutes at the most, (2) inexpensive—in terms of materials, consumables, and personnel requirements, and (3) simple—so that both professionals and nonprofessionals could master administration and scoring without undue difficulty. The four year old age group was determined to be the primary target population on the basis of two considerations: children had to be screened far enough in advance of school entry to permit preschool intervention to be provided, but not so early that school-related material would be premature and invalid.

Closely related to age range considerations is the matter of difficulty level. A screening test should be designed to make discriminations at the low end of the continuum, that is, to distinguish between children functioning far below age expectations and those functioning within normal expectations. This is accomplished by selecting items that the majority of children in the population will pass. Since the measure was intended for use with a narrow age range, it was possible to apply the guideline of selecting items that are relatively easy for the target population, i.e., items that would be passed by a high proportion of four year olds.

Another theoretical concern was whether items should be divided into separate scales (e.g., language, fine motor, gross motor), with each scale scored separately, or whether a single overall score should be used. Studies with young children (Kaufman, 1975; Meyers, Orpet, Attwell, & Dingman, 1962; Ramsey & Vane, 1970; Wallbrown, Blaha, & Wherry, 1973) indicate that mental ability factors most directly related to academic achievement, i.e, reasoning, language, memory, perceptual/performance, quantitative, are both intercorrelated and are independent to some degree. Therefore, the case could be made to use either multiple scales or a single unidimensional scale. Two considerations guided the decision to use a single overall scale: (1) longer scales have higher reliability, and (2) the information from multiple scales was being combined into a single overall screening decision (i.e., to refer or not to refer). To compute separate scale scores would be of value for diagnostic purposes, but not for screening.

An empirical approach predominated in content selection. An extensive review of the preschool assessment literature identified the types of subtests most highly related to successful school performance, a multidimensional array that included language, reasoning, memory, motoric, and perceptual processing tasks. Data from published research and from original research studies in local screening programs were then used to select and develop optimal items with regard to (1) reliability, (2) validity, (3) difficulty level, and (4) overall coverage of target content areas. An excess of items was compiled with the intention that only the "fittest" would survive the extensive pilot testing that followed. Input from a wide range of contributors (special education teachers, speech and language clinicians, psychologists, measurement experts, administrators, and screening examiners) was instrumental in evaluating and reusing MPSI items. Item analysis data from pilot testing also provided an empirical basis for weeding out relatively weak items.

The MPSI contains 50 dichotomously-scored items (pass=1, fail=0) distributed over 11 subtests: Building, Copying Shapes, Information, Matching, Sentence Completion, Hopping and Balancing,

NAME _____
last   first

ADDRESS _____

ID# _____   SEX: MALE   FEMALE

DATE _____ SCREENING
       year month day   LOCATION _____

BIRTH-
DATE _____ EXAMINER _____
       year month day

AGE _____
       year month day

PASS ☐
REFER ☐

	CUT-OFF SCORES	
AGE	PASSING SCORE	
3:7-3:10	25	
3:11-4:1	28	
4:2-4:4	30	
4:5-4:7	33	
4:8-4:10	35	
4:11-5:1	37	
5:2-5:4	38	

COMMENTS

BUILDING

1.___
2.___
3.___
4.___

COPYING SHAPES

5.___ ○
6.___ +
7.___ Ε

INFORMATION

8.___ What do you wear on your feet?
9.___ How many eyes do you have?
10.___ What animal barks?
11.___ What is a window made of?
12.___ Which is bigger, a dog or a mouse?
13.___ What do we do with our ears?

MATCHING

14.___ ○
15.___ ш
16.___ ___
17.___ <

SENTENCE COMPLETION

18.___ Brother is a boy, sister is a ———.
19.___ Planes go up, rain comes ———.
20.___ A block is square, a ball is ———.
21.___ Running is fast, walking is ———.
22.___ A bird flies, a fish ———.

HOPPING BALANCING

23.___ Hops 1 time — 1st foot
24.___ Hops 1 time — 2nd foot
25.___ Balance 5 sec. — 1st foot
26.___ Balance 5 sec. — 2nd foot

COLORS

27.___ Green
28.___ Orange
29.___ Black
30.___ Yellow
31.___ White

COUNTING

32.___ 2 Blocks
33.___ 4 Blocks
34.___ 3 Blocks
35.___ Counts to 3
36.___ Counts to 7

PREPOSITIONS

37.___ On
38.___ Inside
39.___ Under
40.___ Beside

BODY PARTS

41.___ Knee
42.___ Thumb
43.___ Chin
44.___ Elbow
45.___ Ankle

REPEATING SENTENCES

46.___ (The) girl is big.
47.___ Sit on the kitchen floor.
48.___ The dog won't come home.
49.___ They like to play in the rain.
50.___ The boy will eat a big breakfast.

___ **TOTAL SCORE**

SPEECH INTELLIGIBILITY

___ 4-Always understandable
___ 3-Most words understandable
___ 2-Some words understandable
___ 1-Few words understandable

MINNEAPOLIS PRESCHOOL
SCREENING INSTRUMENT

198   **Graphic Services** — Print Shop

Naming Colors, Counting, Prepositions, Identifying Body Parts, and Repeating Sentences (see Fig. 4-6). In addition, a speech intelligibility rating is assigned by the examiner. Administration time for the complete instrument is approximately 12–15 minutes.

The MPSI can be reliably administered by paraprofessionals who have completed a four-hour training session and a one-hour follow-up session. The MPSI manual includes detailed guidelines for training. This insures greater consistency in training, and also enables examiners to refer back to the training guidelines for review.

Administration of the MPSI begins with the Building and Copying Shapes subtests, which are valuable for the examiner in establishing rapport. These subtests involve fine motor activity with familiar materials rather than verbal responses, which helps the shy or inhibited child become more comfortable in the testing situation.

For the Copying Shapes subtest, the manual provides scoring sample of "just passing" and "just failing" responses in addition to the scoring criteria in order to insure scoring reliability. On verbal subtests, all acceptable responses are listed, and specific questions are provided for the examiner to follow up on certain insufficient, but not inaccurate, responses. For example, if a child holds up fingers to indicate how many eyes he or she has (item 9), the child is then asked, "How many is that?" Administration procedures are also specified for instances where the child may need further clarification of task demands. The first items in the Matching, Sentence Completion, Prepositions, and Identifying Body Parts subtests are followed by demonstrations if the child responds incorrectly.

Scores and Interpretation

After administering the last subtest, Repeating Sentences, the examiner rates the child on speech intelligibility on a scale of 1 ("few words understandable") to 4 ("always understandable"). The child's overall score on the 50 pass/fail items is then totaled and, referring to the cutoff score for the child's age, a screening result of "pass" or "refer" is recorded. More comprehensive assessment is recommended for those children classified as "refer". The cutoff points established for each of seven age ranges were set to refer approximately 15 percent of the children in the Minneapolis normative sample. The manual stresses, however, that each screening program should develop its own cutoff points based on local norms.

An optional feature that can significantly reduce administration time is the intermediate decision rule, which is implemented after item 20 is administered. Children with eight or fewer correct responses at this point are scored "refer" and children with 17 or more correct are scored "pass". For these children, the remainder of the MPSI is not administered. However, it is recommended that the Repeating Sentences subtest still be administered so that a speech sample is obtained for rating intelligibility.

Normative Sample

Normative data for the MPSI were collected on 1320 Minneapolis preschool children screened over two consecutive school years. The sample consisted of children ages 3–7 to 5–4 from a cross-section of socioeconomic levels from lower to upper-middle class. Approximate breakdown of the racial composition of this group was 86 percent white and 14 percent black and other minorities.

Research Data

The technical adequacy of the MPSI was evaluated through a number of research studies. Early research data on 728 preschool children ages 3–8 to 5–1 supported the idea of introducing an intermediate decision rule. Examiners had been asking when they should terminate an administration with a child who was performing very poorly (or not responding at all) and was certain to be referred. Several alternative decision points were tested by comparing the number of items answered correctly up to that point by children who had an eventual outcome of "refer" and those who had an eventual outcome of "pass". Following item 20 proved to be the best point for making an early decision to refer. The 73 children scoring eight or less at this point all had a final outcome of "refer". Applying this rule could have terminated the test at this point for nearly half the referred children in this sample. Coincidentally, this same intermediate decision point was the most efficient point at which to make an early decision of "pass". All children with scores of 17 or more after item 20 had an outcome of "pass" after the complete MPSI administration. Following this rule, an early decision could have been made for over two-thirds of the children in this sample with an eventual score of "pass".

Reliability of the MPSI was investigated through a combined test-retest/inter-rater reliability study that involved 61 children in 8 Minneapolis-St. Paul preschool centers. For this study, paraprofessional examiners were trained according to the guidelines provided in the manual. The MPSI was administered twice one week apart to 51 children in the sample by different examiners. Test-retest reliability was .92 for this group. Reliability figures remained above .90 when computed separately for younger children (ages 3–8 to 4–4) and for older children (4–5 to 5–1). The pass/refer screening outcome was identical on both occasions for all 51 children.

Inter-rater reliability figures were obtained by having an examiner and an observer independently score a child's responses during a live administration. This was done during test administrations of 45 children in the sample. Reliability was computed as the percentage of examiner-observer pairs who agreed on the scoring of an item. Agreement on individual items ranged from 84 percent to 100 percent. Only two items had less than 90 percent agreement, while over half the items had 100 percent agreement. Summing over the items within subtests, inter-rater agreement on subtests ranged from 91 percent (Hopping and Balancing) to 100 percent (Prepositions). Over the entire set of MPSI items, scoring agreement averaged 97 percent.

Four separate concurrent validity studies showed moderate to high correlations between the MPSI and various assessment measures. One of these studies also provided results in terms of classificational outcome rather than correlations. In a sample of 48 at risk preschool children, all 11 children with Stanford-Binet IQ scores in the borderline range and below (i.e., under 80) were classified as "refer" by the MPSI.

The most important component of the research program was a large-scale predictive validity study (Lichtenstein, 1982) involving follow-up of preschool screening program results. A battery of screening procedures, which included the MPSI, DIAL (Mardell & Goldenberg, 1975), a brief test of speech articulation, and a short developmental inventory completed by parents, was administered to children screened by the Minneapolis Public Schools. The study sample consisted of 428 children ages 4–1 to 5–4 who were screened during the school year prior to kindergarten, and rated on a follow-up questionnaire by teachers during the spring of their kindergarten year. Since preschool screening took place throughout the school year, the prediction interval from screening to follow-up ranged from 1 to 1½ years. Return rate for the follow-up questionnaire was over 97 percent.

Although the purpose of the MPSI is to refer children who are in need of special education services, placement in special education programs proved to be an unacceptable criterion measure to validate screening decisions. The decision to place children in special education programs at kindergarten level was frequently determined by their initial placement as preschoolers, which was in turn dependent upon referral from screening. Therefore, the screening measure and criterion measure were not independent. Also, many kindergarten techers were hesitant to refer underachieving kindergarten students for special education services because of their reservations about premature classification, or because individualized educational services could be provided through the regular classroom. As a result, teacher judgment

PRESCHOOL SCREENING FOLLOW-UP QUESTIONNAIRE

Child's Name _____ _____ TR _____
            (Last)   (First)

Birthdate _____ _____ _____ Sex _____ (male = 1, female = 2)
       (Month) (Day) (Year)

Rater's Name and Position _____ School _____

A. Please rate the child's peformance on a scale of 1 to 4 for each of the areas described. The chart below explains each of the four ratings and shows the approximate percentages of kindergarten children that would be expected to fall into each category. Note that a child is most likely to receive a rating of 3.

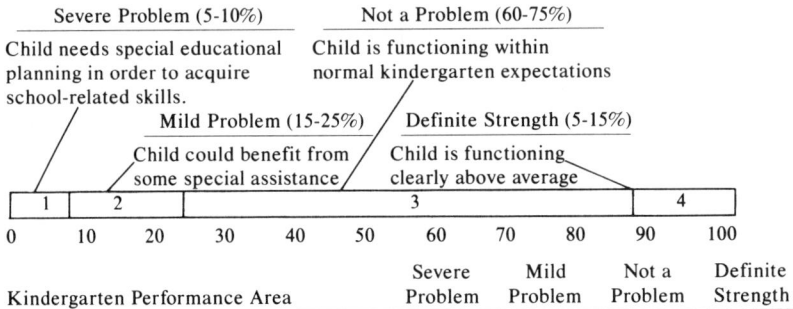

Kindergarten Performance Area	Severe Problem	Mild Problem	Not a Problem	Definite Strength
Learning Habits (Paying attention, following directions)	1	2	3	4
Reading Readiness (Visual and auditory discrimination, letter knowledge)	1	2	3	4
Speech (Articulation, voice quality)	1	2	3	4
Gross Motor (Walking, running, hopping, balancing)	1	2	3	4
Social-Emotional Development (Relationships with children and adults, frustration tolerance, emotional stability)	1	2	3	4
Pre-Academic Skills (Comprehension, memory, learning skills, concept knowledge, reasoning)	1	2	3	4
Language Development (Understanding language, vocabulary expressing ideas)	1	2	3	4
Fine Motor/Perceptual Motor (Copying, cutting, drawing, pasting)	1	2	3	4
Expected Readiness for First Grade (Based on current school performance)	1	2	3	4

Fig. 4-7. Follow-up questionnaire for predictive validity study. (Reprinted from Lichtenstein, 1980a.)

rather than current educational program status was used as a criterion measure of children's needs for special educational services.

The follow-up questionnaire developed specifically for this study, shown in Figure 4-7, defined rating categories in terms of special needs. Also, since teachers may differ in their judgments of what constitutes a "mild" or "severe" problem, normative guidelines were provided as to the approximate percentage of children that should be assigned to each category. Ratings of kindergarten performance were obtained for nine areas: learning habits, reading readiness, speech, gross motor, social-emotional development, pre-academic skills, language development, fine motor/perceptual motor, and expected readiness for first grade.

Ratings were averaged over the nine categories to classify children into three criterion groups: 29 children with an average rating of under 2.0 were classified as having "moderate to severe problems," 36 children with ratings from 2.0 to 2.5 were classified "mild problems," and 363 children with average ratings over 2.5 were assigned to the "no problems" group.

Comparisons between the MPSI and DIAL were of particular interest because the DIAL was the most widely used screening instrument in Minnesota at the time. Two alterations of standard DIAL procedures were used because of screening program constraints. First, the entire DIAL was administered by the same examiner. Second, children receiving a score of "re-DIAL" were not readministered the areas in which they scored below the cutoff, but were simply referred for further assessment. In reporting study results, these children are grouped with those scored as "refer".

The MPSI had higher predictive validity rates than the DIAL, as shown in Table 4-12. The MPSI correctly referred 25 of the 29 children (86 percent) with moderate to severe problems, and 41 of the 65 children (63 percent) in the two problem categories combined. The DIAL correctly referred 21 of the 29 children (72 percent) with moderate to severe problems, and 35 of the 65 children (54 percent) in the two problem categories combined. In terms of over-referrals, the MPSI referred 25 children in the no problem group, compared to 24 over-referrals for the DIAL. Overall teacher ratings correlated .74 with MPSI total score, and .69 with total DIAL scaled score.

The Metropolitan Readiness Test (Hildreth, Griffiths, & McGauvran, 1964), administered to 296 children in the sample at the beginning of first grade, provided a second criterion measure. Two different criterion groups were established by setting cutoffs at 1 standard deviation and at 1½ standard deviations below the mean according to national norms. The MPSI identified 11 of the 13 children in the sample who scored in the extreme low group on the Metropolitan

Table 4-12

Classificational Agreement Between MPSI and DIAL Outcome
and Teacher Ratings

	Overall Teacher Rating			
DIAL Outcome	Moderate to severe problems	Mild problem	No problem	Total
Refer	20	10	17	47
Re-DIAL	1	4	7	12
OK	8	22	339	369
Total	29	36	363	428
	Overall Teacher Rating			
MPSI Outcome	Moderate to severe problems	Mild problem	No problem	Total
Refer	25	16	25	66
Pass	4	20	338	362
Total	29	36	363	428

Readiness Test, and 25 of the 42 children who scored more than one standard deviation below the mean. By comparison, the DIAL identified 8 of the 13 children in the extreme low group, and 21 of the 42 children scoring more than one standard deviation below the mean. Correlations with Metropolitan Readiness Test total score were .70 for the MPSI and .61 for the DIAL.

Other findings from this study were of interest. First, the speech intelligibility ratings assigned by examiners had greater validity than a brief (eight item) speech articulation subtest in identifying those children with speech problems in kindergarten. Analysis of the validity data suggested that the speech intelligibility ratings might best be used as a "pre-screening" measure, with children receiving ratings of 1 through 3 referred for further screening. Following this rule, 24 percent of the study sample would have been screened further for speech.

Another aspect of this validity study involved analyses to determine whether MPSI screening decisions were biased with respect to SES or sex differences. The MPSI referred low SES children at a higher rate than high SES children, and referred males at a higher rate than females. However, these referral rate differences were consistent with group differences in special needs as indicated by criterion measures. Comparable predictive validity rates were obtained for different SES subgroups and for males and females, suggesting that the MPSI is free from SES and sex bias.

Cost

Cost of the complete MPSI kit is $35. Additional scoring forms are available in sets of 30 at a cost of approximately 12¢ per child.

Summary

As indicated by research, the MPSI is a promising instrument for educationally-oriented preschool screening. It is brief and economical to administer, and appears to be highly reliable and valid for a screening test. However, this must be qualified by the fact that MPSI norms and research findings have been limited to a particular geographic area. At a minimum, other screening programs using the MPSI should devise local norms that correspond to the needs of the specific screening situation. Optimally, validity data from other settings will contribute to a broader understanding of the applicability and usefulness of the MPSI.

Minnesota Preschool Inventory

The Minnesota Preschool Inventory (MPI) (Ireton & Thwing, 1979) was designed for preschool screening and to measure kindergarten readiness. The MPI is a standardized parent report inventory for obtaining mothers' observations about their preschool children's current development and readiness skills, adjustment, and symptoms. MPI norms and validity data were derived from mothers' reports obtained in the spring prior to kindergarten entry, for a sample of 360 4½–5½ year old children. There is also a 135-item version of the MPI for 3–4 year olds that is in the process of being validated.

The Minnesota Preschool Inventory consists of a manual, booklet, answer sheet, scoring templates, and a profile form for recording results. The first part of the booklet contains 87 statements that describe developmental behaviors of children from 2 to 6 years of age. The second part contains 63 statements that describe adjustment problems and symptoms. In the instructions, the mother is asked, first, to report any handicaps or special problems of her child, and, second, to indicate those statements in the booklet that describe her child's behavior by marking "yes" or "no" on the answer sheet. The MPI typically requires 15 minutes for the parent to complete.

The developmental items of the MPI were taken directly from the Minnesota Child Development Inventory (Ireton & Thwing, 1974). The adjustment items were selected from a survey of the literature, particularly from the work of Herbert Quay (1972). The adjustment items are included to assess psychological problems believed to be threatening to school performance. The symptom items are included to provide additional clues for detecting developmental, psychological, physical, or sensory problems. Certain symptom items describe the negative side of development, other items deal with physical or psychosomatic symptoms, and others reflect sensory deficits.

Scores and Interpretation

The items are grouped to form seven developmental scales, four adjustment scales, and four symptom clusters. The developmental scales include Self-Help (21 items), Fine Motor (17), Expressive Language (18), Comprehension (34), Memory (15), Letter Recognition (7), and Number Comprehension (9). Memory, Letter Recognition, and Number Comprehension are subscales of the Comprehension Scale. The Adjustment scales include Immaturity (18 items), Hyperactivity (8), Behavior Problems (20), and Emotional Problems (11). The symptom clusters are Motor (4 items), Language (5), Somatic (4), and Sensory (2) symptoms.

The results are summarized on the Minnesota Preschool Inventory Profile. The Profile organizes the data into four areas: (1) mother's description of the child's handicaps or problems, (2) the developmental scales, (3) the adjustment scales, and (4) the symptom groups. It pictures the child's development and adjustment in comparison to children of his or her age in terms of percentile norms. The extreme 5 percent and 10 percent (i.e., relative to the normative sample) are indicated to reflect significant degrees of developmental delay or maladjustment. A sample child study is presented in Figure 4-8.

The accuracy of MPI interpretation depends on the interpreter's knowledge and familiarity with the descriptive and statistical data reported in the manual. There is no simple formula that indicates the appropriateness of interpretations and decisions made on the basis of MPI results. Ideally local norms should be established in order to compare the child to his or her peer group. MPI results are only one source of information about the child that, ideally, will be used in concert with direct observations of the child and other screening and evaluative procedures.

Normative Sample

The normative sample was 360 white children from Bloomington, Minnesota who participated, with their mothers, in the schools' spring kindergarten roundup program. The children ranged in age from 4–8 through 5–7, with both sexes equally represented. Bloomington is a suburb of Minneapolis. Parents' socioeconomic status indicates that they are relatively well educated and occupationally successful in comparison to national norms. Elementary school officials report that the average IQ score of students in the district is approximately 110.

MINNESOTA PRESCHOOL INVENTORY PROFILE

Harold R. Ireton and Edward J. Thwing

Name _____ Date Completed _____ Age **5-2**

_____ Birthdate _____ Sex **M**

Mother's Education **HIGH SCHOOL** Mother's Occupation **Housewife**

Child's Problems or Handicaps **Very active**

DEVELOPMENT   ADJUSTMENT

MPI
(Spring – prior to kindergarten entry)

Problems: "Very active"
Developmental Scales in bottom five percent
Adjustment Scales in bottom five percent
Symptoms: Motor, Language, Somatic

PSYCHOLOGICAL EVALUATION
(Fall – in kindergarten)

Borderline ability, I.Q. of 79

TEACHER RATING
(end of kindergarten)

Bottom five percent
of students

Scale columns: SH FM EL Co Me LR NC Im Hy BP EP

SYMPTOMS

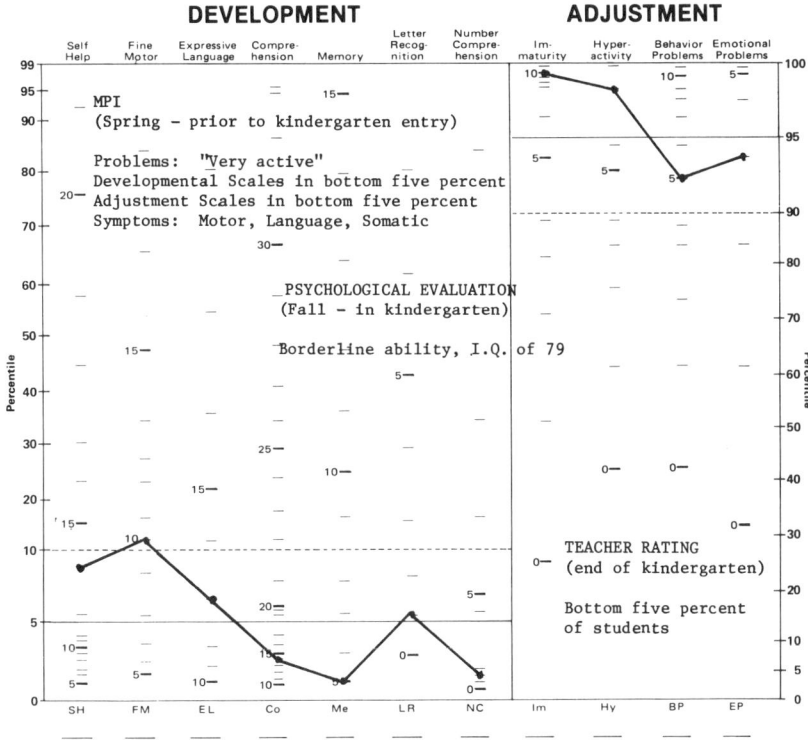

Motor	Language	Somatic	Sensory
136 Clumsy, awkward	140 Talks only in short phrases	145 Tired, sluggish, low energy	149 Vision?
137 Avoids physical games	141 Stutters, stammers		
138 Clumsy with hands			
	142 Trouble expressing ideas		150 Hearing?
	143 Speech difficult to understand		
	144 "Baby Talk"		
139 Draws, colors poorly		147 Eating problems	
		148 Aches and pains	

Fig. 4-8. Sample MPI Profile.

189

Research Data

The validity study (Ireton, Lun, & Kampen, 1981) included 287 of the 360 children in the normative sample. Seventy-three children were lost to follow-up for a variety of reasons, including family moves, school transfers, and age-eligible children who did not enter kindergarten. Validity was measured in terms of the relationship between Minnesota Preschool Inventory results obtained in the spring prior to kindergarten entry with kindergarten teachers' ratings obtained at the end of the school year. The relationship between MPI results and teachers' ratings of kindergarten performance was analyzed both in terms of correlations and classificational outcomes.

The results of the correlational analysis, showing the relationship between MPI scales and teachers' ratings of kindergarten performance, are presented in Table 4-13. The developmental scales, except for Self-Help, correlated with teachers' ratings to a statistically significant degree. The adjustment scales did not, with the exception of a significant but low correlation for the Hyperactivity scale.

For the classificational analysis, each child's MPI results were classified, first, as *delayed* or *within age range* on each of the developmental scales. The scores on each of the developmental scales were classified as delayed if they fell within the bottom 5 percent of the norm group. For the adjustment scales, scores were classified as either *maladjusted* (if above the 95th percentile) or *within normal limits.* For the criterion measure, teachers were first instructed to rate each child's overall performance according to a five-point scale: (1) poor performance, (2) below average performance, (3) average performance, (4) above average performance, and (5) superior performance.

Teacher's ratings of overall kindergarten performance on a five-point scale yielded a distribution of ratings skewed toward the high end of the scale, with 12 percent rated as superior and only 4 percent or 11 students, rated as poor. In anticipation of this reluctance of teachers to rate children's performance as poor, teachers were asked to make a second judgment in which they were to identify their poorest students, that is, the bottom 5 percent of the class group. In this manner 16 students were identified. By combining the results of the first and second ratings, 20 children were identified as doing poorly on the basis of one or both ratings. These 20 children (7 percent of the sample) became the *target group* for the purpose of identifying children who are at risk for poor kindergarten performance. Perfect identification would be to classify these 20 children as potentially poor performers on the basis of prekindergarten Inventory results while labeling no children as poor performers who subsequently perform adequately.

Of 19 children with delays only on the Self-Help, Fine Motor, or Expressive Language scales, none were among the target group of

Table 4-13

Correlations Between Developmental and Adjustment Scales
and Teacher Ratings of Kindergarten Performance

MPI Scale	Correlation
Developmental	
Self-Help	.07
Fine Motor	.41
Expressive Language	.20
Comprehension	.44
Memory	.51
Letter Recognition	.56
Number Comprehension	.24
Adjustment	
Immaturity	.07
Hyperactivity	.12
Behavior Problems	.04
Emotional Problems	.04

Table 4-14

Classificational Agreement Between Status on the Comprehension Scales and
Kindergarten Performance

Comprehension Scales	Kindergarten Performance		Total
	Poor	Adequate	
Delayed*	12	9	21
Adequate	8	258	266
Total	20	267	287

* Delayed on one or more of the following scales: Comprehension, Memory, Letter Recognition, Number Comprehension.

children performing poorly in kindergarten. These scales by themselves were clearly not predictive of poor kindergarten performance. A very different result is obtained by referring those children with delays on one or more of the Comprehension subscales or on the overall Comprehension scale. Table 4-14 shows the classificational agreement between Comprehension scale status and kindergarten performance. Of 21 children with delays on the Comprehension, Memory, Letter Recognition, or Number Comprehension scales, a total of 12 (57 percent) were rated as poor performers in kindergarten (significantly higher than the base rate of 7 percent). These scales were successful in identifying 12 of the 20 students who were rated as poor performers in kindergarten. Using these scales alone, only nine children out of 287 (3 percent of the sample) were mislabeled as potentially poor performers.

Data for the adjustment scales indicate that 27 of 28 children who scored in the extreme 5 percent on one or more of these scales, but who scored within age range on the developmental scales, performed adequately in kindergarten. In other words, extreme scores on the adjustment scales by themselves were not predictive of poor kindergarten performance.

It might be argued that the validity of the MPI is carried solely by the Comprehension scale; after all, the Memory, Letter Recognition, and Number Comprehension scales are simply subscales of the Comprehension scale. However, the information provided by the subscales is not redundant. Further analysis shows that the three subscales identify five children who would have been missed by the Comprehension scale.

The eight poor students who were not identified by the developmental scales of the Inventory are of particular concern. Five of these children had MPI results showing no indication of handicaps, problems, or parental concerns, with development and adjustment scale scores within normal limits, and with no symptoms reported. Three of these children had symptom items reported for them: two with both motor and language symptoms, and the third with the uncommon symptom of chronic fatigue. While individual symptom items are not indicative of poor school performance and, if regarded as such, could lead to serious errors in mislabeling and over-identification of children, their cautious use as a basis for further inquiry could increase the accuracy of identification of children with significant problems that may affect school performance.

Cost

The cost of the complete set of MPI materials is $49, which includes the manual ($10), plastic scoring templates ($12), reusable MPI booklets ($15, package of 25), and answer sheets and profile forms (6 dollars each for packages of 25). Cost of consumable materials per child is approximately 50 cents. The MPI is machine scorable.

Summary

From a research point of view, it could be concluded that much information provided by the MPI—reports of children's handicaps and problems; the Self-Help, Fine Motor, and Expressive Language scales; all four adjustment scales; and the symptom items—is not sufficiently predictive and, therefore, should be deleted. From a broader screening perspective, it is all relevant in that it systematically provides an array of potentially valuable screening information. For example, 10 percent of Bloomington parents expressed concerns about their children in response to the question regarding "handicaps or problems." Reported handicaps, problems, and concerns range from "muscular dystrophy" to "left-handed." All require inquiry, if not follow-up.

At a descriptive level, the Inventory provides a picture of the child's current development, adjustment, and symptoms. At a predictive level, low scores on certain developmental scales raise serious questions about the child's ability to meet kindergarten expectations. At an identification level, the developmental scales, adjustment scales, and symptom items all may point to a need for further assessment.

SUMMARY

A methodical approach to selecting screening instruments begins by framing the task appropriately. First, the screener must consider what options are most promising given situational factors such as program objectives, resources, and the nature of the community. The screener then considers specific options with regard to both the situational "fit" and the overall value of the instrument or procedure.

The overall value of a screening procedure may be judged on the basis of (1) psychometric characteristics, i.e., validity, reliability, and standardization, (2) qualitative characteristics such as administration and scoring procedures, manual and materials, interpretation, cultural fairness, and acceptability to participants, and (3) costs related to use of the particular procedure, including both materials and personnel. Procedures designed explicitly for screening are brief and economical, and easy to administer, score, and interpret. However, cost-effectiveness and convenience mean little if the procedure fails to meet the basic requirements of providing reliable and valid information. While the prospective user must take various factors into account, particular attention must be paid to validity and cost.

Various reference sources that provide data on specific screening instruments may aid the prospective user in the process of instrument selection. Although there are many screening instruments to choose from, the options are substantially reduced once measures that are inappropriate for the situation and those that are lacking in terms of essential characteristics are eliminated.

5

Making and Evaluating Screening Decisions

The basic task involved in preschool screening is to make the decision whether or not to refer each child for further assessment. Discussion to this point has focused on gathering screening information relevant to this task. Adequate information does not, however, insure accurate decision-making. Contrary to what may be implied by federal and state mandates, how-to guides, and screening program flow charts, accurate screening decisions do not magically evolve as a consequence of having the right kind of information on hand.

There is no single "correct way" of interpreting screening results to arrive at screening decisions. Screening decisions may depend entirely upon scores from standardized measures, or scores may be considered in the context of other information available about the child. Decisions may be based upon professional judgment or upon an empirically derived formula. Information may be interpreted by a single professional or by a team of individuals from various disciplines.

To select among alternative approaches, it is first necessary to be clear about the issues that are involved, about the logic of decision-making in screening, and about alternative strategies. This is a complex subject of which, at a minimum, the general structure must be well understood. Preschool screening attempts to identify that small percentage of the population that is at risk for developing school problems by means of relatively brief, cost-effective procedures. There are inherent limitations and hazards in this situation. In particular, screening errors are an inevitable consequence. Two possible erroneous decisions may be made at screening. First, we may fail to identify children with problems who need help, and leave them to struggle without assistance. Second, we may misidentify or mislabel adequately functioning children as high risk on the basis of screening results. In this case, parents and child are caused needless anxiety and expensive evaluations are unnecessarily performed. Given these hazards, let us consider how decision-making may be approached.

PIECES OF THE PUZZLE: PROBLEM BASE RATE, REFERRAL RATE, AND HIT RATE

Since preschool screening is intended to lead to the identification of those children who will experience problems in the early grades of school, it is advisable to begin by determining the frequency of such problems.The prevalence of the problem to be identified is referred to as the *base rate*. The percentage of children in kindergarten or first grade receiving special education services would provide one estimate, although probably a low one, of the problem base rate. A better estimate might be obtained by adding the percentage of children who are doing poorly in school and apparently need additional services to the percentage already receiving services. Once we have some notion of the extent of the problem, we are in a good position to determine what percentage of the screening population we may wish to refer.*

To better understand how referral rates and base rates are related and how this relationship affects screening decisions, we must take a closer look at the hit rate model introduced in Chapter 4.

The Hit Rate Model

In making screening decisions, the objective is to maximize the correspondence between the group of children that is referred and the group of children who have special problems. This relationship is best conceptualized using the classificational, or hit rate, model introduced in the previous chapter. Those who have written about evaluating the effectiveness of screening procedures (Barnes, 1982; Buck & Gart, 1966; Cochrane & Holland, 1971; Frankenburg, 1974; Gallagher &

---

*To avoid distortions when using the estimated base rate to determine a target referral rate, children who did not, or would likely not, participate in screening (e.g., severely handicapped children who were already identified) should not be included in deriving the base rate.

| | | "Actual" Status | |
		Child needs special services	Child does not need special services
Screening Outcome	Refer; High risk (+)	A accurate referral; valid positive	C over-referral; false positive
	Do not refer; Low risk (−)	B under-referral; false negative	D accurate non-referral; valid negative

Problem base rate: $\dfrac{A + B}{A + B + C + D}$

Referral rate: $\dfrac{A + C}{A + B + C + D}$

Sensitivity: $\dfrac{A}{A + B}$

Specificity: $\dfrac{D}{C + D}$

Efficiency of screening outcome "refer": $\dfrac{A}{A + C}$

Efficiency of screening outcome "do not refer": $\dfrac{D}{B + D}$

Fig. 5-1.   The hit rate model for evaluating screening decisions.

Bradley, 1972; Harber, 1981; Lichtenstein, 1979; Meisels, 1978; Wilson & Jungner, 1968) have all advocated the hit rate model for analyzing outcomes.

The hit rate model summarizes the relationship between outcomes of a screening procedure and "actual" status of individuals in a given population. For evaluation purposes, actual status is represented by a classificational outcome on a criterion measure such as a comprehensive psychoeducational evaluational or a classroom performance rating scale. As illustrated in Figure 5-1, possible outcomes of screening are that a child is either categorized as a screening *positive,* meaning the child is regarded as high risk and will be referred for further assessment; or as a screening negative, meaning that the child is low risk and not referred. (This paradoxical convention of calling an outcome "positive" when it suggests a problem or the need for treatment has its origins in medical terminology.) Performance on the criterion measure similarly divides the screening population into two categories—children needing special services, and those not needing services.

With children in the screening population falling into one of two screening outcomes and into one of two actual status categories, there are four possible results for each child. A child may be referred by the screening procedure and be found in need of special services; thus, an accurate screening decision. The other type of accurate screening decision is the case where a child is not referred, and the child does not require special services. Then, there are two possible outcomes that constitute screening errors. A child may be referred by the screening procedure, but not need special services, which is a *false positive,* or *over-referral,* error. The opposite case, where a child is not referred but should have been due to some problem, is a *false negative,* or *under-referral,* error. (The terms over-referral and under-referral will be used so as to avoid the mental contortions required to keep false positives and false negatives straight.) When, for a given screening population, frequencies for each of the four cells in the hit rate table are filled in, we can extract essential summary data about the screening situation, including (1) the proportion of children in the criterion measure problem group, i.e., the base rate, (2) the proportion of children referred for further assessment, i.e., the referral rate, (3) the proportion of children accurately classified by the screening measure, and (4) the over-referral and under-referral rates. (See Fig. 5-1.)

It would also be helpful to compute a single index or ratio that summarizes the level of screening accuracy represented by the overall table. However, this proves to be problematic. Several different methods for expressed decision making accuracy have been used. The most common approach is simply to report the overall hit rate, i.e., the proportion of accurate screening decisions out of the total number of screening decisions. In Figure 5-1, this is the ratio

$$\frac{A + D}{A + B + C + D}$$

Note that the actual number, or frequency, of accurate screening decisions is meaningless. The frequency is translated into a proportion by calculating the ratio of accurate decisions to the number of cases being considered. This proportion may be translated into a percentage by multiplying by 100.

The problem with this index of screening accuracy is that the overall hit rate for a screening procedure is highly dependent upon the criterion measure base rate (Meehl & Rosen, 1955). Generally, the "problem group," i.e., children needing special services, (the terms "problem group" and "normal group" being used, with apologies, for convenience) constitute only a small proportion of the total population. The smaller the base rate, the more likely that a referral screening outcome will be incorrect and a non-referral outcome will be correct. As a result, the screening procedure that makes the fewest referrals typically yields the highest overall hit rate. Consider an extreme example: if only 5 percent of the children in a population have special needs while a screening procedure refers no children at all, this screening procedure will have a 95 percent overall hit rate. (Not bad for a worthless device!)

A screening procedure, in order to be valid, must meet two basic objectives: (1) to refer those children in the problem group, i.e., to minimize under-referrals, and (2) to not refer children who are in the normal group, i.e., to minimize over-referrals. Both of these critical aspects must be reflected in summarizing hit rate efficiency. The overall hit rate method proves to be unsatisfactory because a screening procedure can fail completely on the first objective, yet have an impressive overall hit rate.

A straightforward means of accounting for both of the above objectives is to use an interrelated pair of validity figures. Commonly used statistics of this type are *sensitivity* and *specificity*.* Sensitivity represents a screening measure's capacity for identifying those children with special problems. Referring to Figure 5-1, sensitivity is computed as the proportion of children needing special services who are accurately classified as high risk by the screening procedure, that is, the ratio $A/(A + B)$. Specificity represents a screening procedure's accuracy in selecting out those children who do not have special needs. In Figure 5-1, it is the proportion of children in the "does not need special services" group who were not referred by the screening procedure, that is, $D/(C + D)$.

Computation of these hit rates is illustrated with the screening data shown in Figure 5-2. The sensitivity rate for the Minneapolis Preschool

---

*The terms *co-positivity* and *co-negativity* from Buck and Gart (1966) are sometimes used for technical reasons in place of sensitivity and specificity, respectively.

Metropolitan Readiness Test (first grade)

		Poor performance (below 10th percentile)	Satisfactory performance	
MPSI	Refer	17	27	44
(preschool)	Pass	5	247	252
		22	274	296

$$\text{Problem base rate} = \frac{22}{296} = .07$$

$$\text{Referral rate} = \frac{44}{296} = .15$$

$$\text{Sensitivity} = \frac{17}{22} = .77$$

$$\text{Specificity} = \frac{247}{274} = .90$$

$$\text{Efficiency of screening outcome "refer"} = \frac{17}{44} = .39$$

$$\text{Efficiency of screening outcome "pass"} = \frac{247}{252} = .98$$

Fig. 5-2. Illustration of screening hit rates.

Screening Instrument (MPSI) in this screening situation is .77, meaning 77 percent of the children scoring below 10th percentile on the Metropolitan Readiness Test (MRT) were accurately predicted by MPSI referrals. The specificity rate is .90; accurate screening predictions were made for 90 percent of the children with satisfactory MRT scores.

Another way to compute hit rates is to determine the likelihood that each type of screening outcome, pass and refer, will be accurate. This is accomplished by expressing the rates of accurate screening results (cells A and D in Figure 5-1) as a function of screening outcomes. The ratio A/ (A + C) indicates the probability that a screening decision of "refer" will be accurate in selecting out a problem group child. In Figure 5-2, this probability is .39, indicating a 39 percent chance that a preschool child referred by the MPSI will perform poorly on the Metropolitan Readiness Test in first grade. (In comparison to this hit rate, the base rate for poor MRT performance in the population is 7 percent.) The second hit rate in this pair is the proportion of screening outcomes of pass that prove accurate, which in Figure 5-1 is the ratio, $D/(B + D)$. In the example presented in Figure 5-2, there is a 98 percent chance that a preschool child with a screening outcome of "pass" will perform satisfactorily on the MRT in first grade.

An essential point to keep in mind when computing hit rates is that the figures obtained are situation-specific. They reflect the results obtained with a screening procedure when using a *given decision rule* (e.g., cutoff point), to predict a *given criterion measure* in a *given situation*. Different results are obtained if the decision rule is changed so as to refer more children or less children; different results are obtained if some other criterion measure is used; and the hit rate pattern will vary with the population screened.

Establishing a Referral Rate

The hit rate model helps us conceptualize the nature of the task of setting screening referral rates. We begin with the understanding that there is some percentage of the screening population that fits the description of the problem or conditions (e.g., educational handicaps) to be identified. Given this estimate, the referral rate should be some figure greater than this. After all, since screening is the first stage of a sequential assessment process, more children must be referred from screening than are eventually identified. Because a certain proportion of referrals will prove to be in error, this allows for the possibility that all target group children may still be picked up through screening. This could not occur if the screening rate were set equal to or less than the base rate, since each over-referral would then leave one less slot for a target group child, and cause an opposite type error in turn. To have even a statistical chance of identifying all problem group children, the referral rate must be at least equal to the base rate plus the screening over-referral rate. Of course, all of this can only be guessed at when establishing screening decision rules. The base rate is only an estimate at best, and the over-referral rate cannot be foreseen.

There is no standard formula to determine what is a safe margin between the base rate and referral rate—nor can there be. The options involve a difficult decision, one might say a predicament, as to the type of "costs" that must be paid. The referral rate can be set far above the base rate to insure that most children with problems will be identified. In doing so, however, a large number of children will be unnecessarily referred, at great expense. Setting the screening rate closer to the base rate reduces over-referral errors, but at a cost of failing to identify some children who need help (i.e., under-referral errors). This is the basic dilemma of the "prediction predicament." It is possible to set referral rates to minimize under-referral errors or to minimize over-referral errors, but not both at once. A reduction in one type of error results in an increase in the other. The following example should clarify the nature of this predicament.

The Cityburg School District uses a particular screening procedure to screen for preschool children who may need special educational services. This procedure might be a single instrument or a combination of measures. Regardless, let us assume that the procedure yields a score from 1 to 100. A cutoff score is to be selected such that all children with scores below the cutoff will be referred for further assessment. Ideally, the set of children scoring below the cutoff score will include all children in the screening population with special educational needs and few, if any, children who do not have special needs.

Let us assume that, one year after screening, all children in this sample (now in kindergarten) are evaluated to determine who actually needs special services according to the school district's special education guidelines. The result is that ten children are identified who should have been referred by the screening instrument. Let us further suppose that the screening program used a cutoff score of 65, with the result that the screening procedure referred 16 children. A hit rate analysis reveals that, of the ten kindergarten children who needed special services, seven were referred by the screening instrument and three were not. As shown by the first hit rate table in Figure 5-3, the screening procedure unnecessarily referred nine children (these being over-referral errors) and missed three target group children (under-referral errors). With seven of the ten target group children referred, sensitivity is 7/10 or .70. A screening outcome of pass for 81 of the 90 normal group children produces a specificity rate of 81/90, or .90.

Suppose now that the "powers that be" are alarmed that three children were missed using this decision rule (let's call it Cutoff A). The proposal is made to raise the cutoff score to 70 (Cutoff B) and refer more children in the future, thereby reducing the under-referral rate. The results that would have been obtained using the more inclusive Cutoff B are then analyzed. As shown in Figure 5-3, it is discovered that Cutoff B would have resulted in only a single under-referral error. Of course, there is a price to pay: this decision rule would have referred 32 children for further assessment, 23 of whom proved to be children not needing special services (but some of whom might be identified and served all the same). While the sensitivity rate is then .90, specificity drops to .74—one out of every four "normal" children is referred. The cost of comprehensive assessments for 32 children makes this intended course of action open to question.

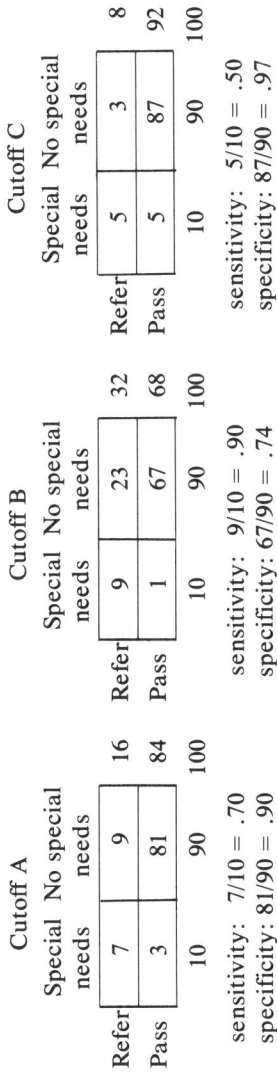

Cutoff A

	Special needs	No special needs	
Refer	7	9	16
Pass	3	81	84
	10	90	100

sensitivity: 7/10 = .70
specificity: 81/90 = .90

Cutoff B

	Special needs	No special needs	
Refer	9	23	32
Pass	1	67	68
	10	90	100

sensitivity: 9/10 = .90
specificity: 67/90 = .74

Cutoff C

	Special needs	No special needs	
Refer	5	3	8
Pass	5	87	92
	10	90	100

sensitivity: 5/10 = .50
specificity: 87/90 = .97

Fig. 5-3. Hit rates for a screening measure using three different cutoff points.

As administrators deliberate over this proposed change, Election Day arrives. A statewide tax-cutting proposal triumphs, while the City-burg school levy is voted down. In light of the radically changed budgetary situation, the "powers that be" review the consequences of even maintaining Cutoff A. They conclude that there are insufficient funds for comprehensive assessment of 16 children the following year (as per Cutoff A) and, furthermore, that special education services for as many as ten preschool children will be difficult to provide. A new proposal is then made to refer fewer children by lowering the cutoff score to 60, and to provide special services for fewer children, only those with relatively severe problems, in the future. Results that would be obtained using this alternative, Cutoff C, are calculated. In referring eight children, Cutoff C would have identified only five of the ten problem group children (a sensitivity rate of .50), but would have reduced over-referrals to three (specificity of .97). The Cityburg School District decides to resolve the dilemma by implementing Cutoff C next year. Under these circumstances, the price paid is the loss of early intervention services for those preschool children whose special education needs are not discovered until after school entry.

"Must this be such a no-win situation?" you may ask. In the case of the Cityburg School District, for example, might not better results be obtained with some other screening procedure? After all, studies commonly show that even brief instruments yield substantially higher scores for normal children than for target group children. But even strong group trends have marked limitations for making classification decisions about individuals. Figure 5-4 illustrates this phenomenon, using the Cityburg School District example. The large bell-shaped curve on the right represents the distribution of screening measure scores obtained by normal children (i.e., children who, according to follow-up evaluation results, do not need special services). The smaller curve to the left represents the scoring distribution for target group children. True the two distributions are dramatically different. How-ever, they overlap in that critical range at the low end of the distribution where cutoff scores are set, as is invariably the case. A decision rule such as Cutoff A, which divides the two distributions fairly well, still leaves some target group children above the cutoff point (area y in Figure 5-4) and some normal group children below the cutoff (area x). The alternative of setting a cutoff point as high as 70 (Cutoff B) so as to refer most of the target group would result in a substantial portion of the normal group being referred. Similarly, any cutoff point in the range of 55–70 would result in a trade-off between under-referral and over-referral errors.

The solution is simple, you may say. Devise a screening procedure that works even better, so that the scoring distributions for the two

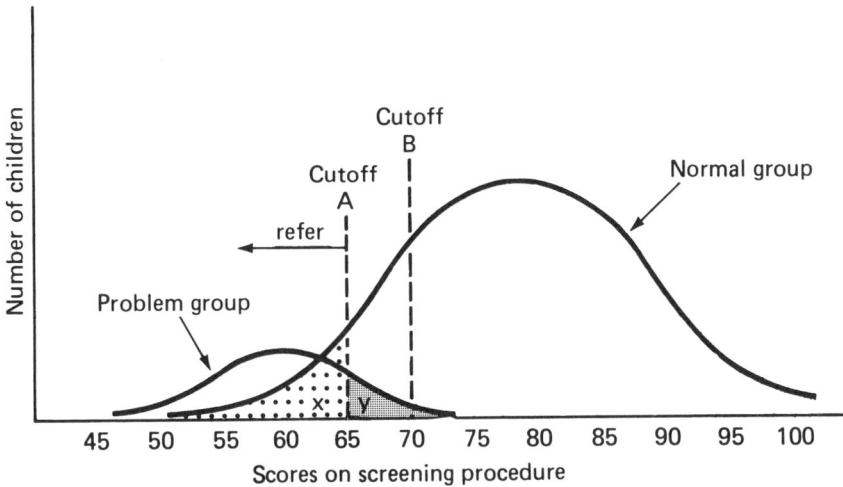

Fig. 5-4. Cutoff point selection and criterion group membership.

groups do not overlap as much. Find out what characteristics or test items identify those target group children who were missed, and add these indicators or items to the screening battery. This, in fact, describes the strategy that instrument developers typically follow to produce group distinctions as great as those shown in Figure 5-4. The Cityburg School District example cannot be dismissed as merely a mediocre screening effort. The hit rates presented in this example were purposely set at levels comparable to the highest rates reported in the screening literature, as will be documented in a later section of this chapter (The Limits of Prediction).

This example illustrates that there is no "correct" referral rate associated with a screening procedure, but that each alternative decision rule will yield a different hit rate pattern with distinct implications. None of the alternatives produce "ideal" results; the optimal referral rate is the one that yields the "most acceptable" (i.e., least troublesome) outcome for the given situation. It is a matter of local priorities and policies to weigh the relative disadvantages of over-referral and under-referral errors and to set a target referral rate accordingly.

A common guideline for setting screening referral rates is to regard under-referral as the more serious error, since over-referral can be corrected at the stage of further assessment while under-referral can not. However, this guideline has its limitations. A great number of over-referral errors may be necessary in order to identify a major part of the target group, especially with a screening procedure of limited validity (imagine the two curves in Figure 5-4 overlapping to a greater degree). This may overburden the follow-up assessment component of an early identification program, and may have the net effect of diverting critical resources away from direct service. Furthermore, there is no assurance that children who are erroneously referred will be weeded out during further assessment. Referring a child from screening may create a "self-fulfilling prophecy" that biases later evaluation. That is; a referral may create the expectation that some problem requiring special services should be found. A case in point is provided by a study by Algozzine and Ysseldyke (1981). Various raters, including regular and special education teachers, administrators, and school psychologists, were asked to make placement recommendations for hypothetical cases. Each case contained a referral statement stressing the need for the child to be evaluated, but test results were reported to fall "within normal limits." Still, the raters recommended special education placement in 57 percent of the cases reviewed.

Given all these qualifications and considerations about establishing a referral rate, the practitioner may feel more in need of guidance than ever. And so, we will offer some general rules of thumb based upon population prevalence figures and personal experience with screening. Typically, base rates for developmental and educational problems at the preschool and primary levels fall in the range of 5–10 percent of the population. This will be higher for a high risk sample, or if relatively mild problems are to be identified. Referral rates might reasonably be set at a value of 1⅓–2½ times the estimated base rate. The lower the base rate, the higher this ratio will need to be. For base rates as low as 1–3 percent, perhaps three times the base rate will need to be referred.

The discussion to this point has followed from the assumption that it is meaningful to establish referral rates on a statistical basis so as to refer some target percentage of the population. This approach corresponds to what is known as *norm-referenced measurement*. An alternative approach is to assume that some particular level of functioning, or degree of disability, that signals that a child needs special services can be identified. The decision process is then linked, not to arbitrary cutoff points or percentages, but to this criterion that directly reflects problematic functioning. Children who fail to meet this standard, by definition, constitute a high risk group. This approach is know as *criterion-referenced measurement,* since the child is assessed relative to criterion performance, rather than norm-based percentages. An example of criterion-referenced measurement is in screening for visual acuity. Irrespective of the total numbers that may be found within a given population, all children with eyesight worse than a certain level, that is, a level suggesting the need for corrected vision, are referred for an eye examination.

The essence of criterion-referenced measurement is to interpret screening information in terms of the child's functioning and future educational prospects. This is very similar to the process that should occur at the stage of further assessment, where the objective is to determine whether or not each individual child fits the criteria that the program is using to define a problem or a handicapping condition. But in actual practice, it is highly difficult to apply absolute standards to identification of developmental problems. One reason for this is the lack of clear standards or definitions for establishing when a child has a "problem," or is "disabled." A child's status may vary as a function of environmental circumstances. Characteristics of the educational setting, the teacher, and the peer group, in addition to characteristics of the child, will determine whether or not the child's developmental status is a problem in school. Also, criteria for determining whether or not a child qualifies for special services may differ as a function of population characteristics, assessment procedures, and policies of the particular school district or agency. As a result, it is difficult to apply criterion-referenced standards other than on a situation-by-situation basis.

Criterion-referenced measurement is also difficult to implement in actual practice because of the measurement problems involved in reliably determining what a preschool child can and cannot do with regard to all relevant developmental functions (after all, the objective of criterion-referenced measurement is to assess actual functioning, rather than to estimate an individual's relative standing from a sample of relevant behaviors). Prospects of this are particularly prohibitive in screening, where less extensive and less valid data are obtained. To apply the criterion-referenced model to screening would require that the criterion level be regarded as an estimate at best, and be set safely high so as to refer the majority of children who would be identified at the further assessment stage. The end result is not appreciably different than with norm-referenced measurement; in either case, the screening process is designed to refer children at a rate that is higher than the problem base rate indicated by follow-up evaluation or some other criterion measure of "actual" status.

FROM SCREENING DATA TO SCREENING DECISIONS

Referral rates, base rates, and hit rates provide a framework for understanding the mechanics involved in transforming screening data to screening decisions. Interpretation of screening data in various forms will be considered, beginning with the simplest case and progressing to more complicated types of screening data.

Interpreting Results of Individual Screening Procedures

Let us first consider the case where screening decisions are primarily, or exclusively, based upon results of a single screening procedure, most likely a multidimensional screening test. This was the nature of the screening process in the Cityburg School District example in the previous section. In such a situation, the screening process is essentially a matter of translating the results of this one procedure into a screening recommendation.

One way of making screening decisions, which sidesteps the complications associated with establishing referral rates, is to simply rely upon the decision rule (e.g., cutoff score) that is supplied with a published screening instrument. The user makes no decisions regarding an appropriate referral rate, but simply accepts what the instrument offers. In computer talk, this is called a *default* option, a procedure that applies when no alternative instructions are specified.

The obvious drawback to the default approach is that a given decision rule cannot be optimal for all situations and settings, and the user may or may not find the results acceptable. This drawback is frequently disregarded; that is, until the early identification program is burdened by an excessive number of referrals, or when children who should have been identified are missed. The disgruntled user may be inclined to blame the screening instrument, but perhaps the fault lies mainly with the decision rule used. No instrument user should institute a default decision rule without first finding out (1) the percentage of the normative sample referred by the decision rule, and (2) the composition of the screening instrument's normative sample. This information should always be supplied with a screening instrument. By considering these two factors, the user can make a rough guess as to the numbers that will be referred by the screening instrument in the local setting.

Still, the user may institute the default decision rule and find the results unsatisfactory. The user has two choices at this point: (1) to try again with a different screening instrument and a different "default option" decision rule, or (2) to continue using the screening instrument, but devise decision rules that work better in the local setting. Let us take up this second strategy, devising local decision rules; a strategy that the screener might have used initially as well.

Presumably, the screener has some notion in advance as to what constitutes a reasonable referral rate in the particular situation. Standardized screening instrument's typically provide normative data indicating what percentage of the instruments normative sample is referred by recommended decision rules or cutoff scores. The user might use this information to estimate what percentage of the local screening population will be referred by the recommended rule. (This figure is already known to the user who has first tried the instrument with the default decision rule.) However, normative data are of limited value to the user if the normative sample and the local population differ appreciably. For this reason (among others), it is preferable to select a measure developed with a sample similar to the local population.

Some instruments provide data indicating the percentage of the normative sample that would be referred by each of a variety of different cutoff scores or decision rules. From this, the user may be able to adjust for differences between the two samples. For example, the user might initially guess that a cutoff score at the 12th percentile for the normative sample will refer 15 percent of the lower-functioning local population. Suppose, however, that the actual result is an 18 percent referral rate. The user might then switch to a cutoff point at the norm group's 10th percentile in an effort to obtain a local referral rate closer to 15 percent.

With continued use of a screening measure, local norms that indicate the percentage of the local population referred by alternative cutoff scores can be established. Local norms are constructed by compiling the distribution of scores obtained by the local population on a given screening measure. In addition to scores, information that should be recorded for each child includes age of the child (to the nearest month), the child's sex, and relevant demographic data. After results are compiled for a large number of children, a summary table is constructed from which cutoff points can be established.

Table 5-1 shows percentile norms that have been compiled for a hypothetical instrument (the Acme Screening Test) that yields a single overall score. These norms are only for children in the local school district's screening population who were 4–4½ years old at the time of screening. The frequency column in Table 5-1 shows the number of children scoring at the corresponding raw score; the cumulative frequency column indicates the number scoring at or below the raw score. The far right column indicates the percentage of children scoring at or below the corresponding raw score; for example, 5 percent of the sample received a score of 28 or below. Alternative cutoff points could be selected as desired. The bottom 10 percent of this group would be referred by setting the cutoff point between the scores of 35 and 36. If the decision were made to set the referral rate at 15 percent, the cutoff point would be between 38 and 39. (Note that, in this example, percentiles are not given for raw scores of 50 and above; there is no reason for a screening test to make distinctions between children with high scores on the measure.)

Table 5-1.

Metroville School District Norms for the Acme Screening Test, 4½ to 5 Year Old Age Range ($N = 212$)

Raw score	Frequency	Cumulative frequency	Percentile
50–60	75	212	65–100
49	6	137	64
48	10	131	61
47	9	121	57
46	12	112	53
45	11	100	47
44	11	89	42
43	13	78	37
42	8	65	31
41	11	57	27
40	7	46	22
39	7	39	18
38	4	32	15
37	4	28	13
36	3	24	11
35	2	21	10
34	3	19	9
33	1	16	8
32	1	15	7
31	2	14	
30	1	12	6
29	1	11	
28	2	10	5
27	1	8	4
26	1	7	
25	1	6	3
24	1	5	
22	1	4	2
19	1	3	
18	1	2	1
15	1	1	

Certain factors must be considered to insure that local norms are adequate. The first consideration is the size of the normative sample. Normative groups of less than 100 children yield fairly unstable norms; that is, the percentile figure associated with a given cutoff might be in error by a matter of several percentage points. In the example above, the screening population was large enough to enable norms to be devised for each half-year age range. However, while it would be desirable to devise norm groups for three-month age ranges, further subdividing a sample of this size would be of questionable value. In the other direction, the age range for a norm group cannot be adjusted indefinitely to fit the sample size. If the local sample size required that the norm group span an age range of a full year, it would perhaps be best to collect more data before using local norms.

Selection factors also affect the adequacy of local norms. If a screening program serves a nonrepresentative sample of the local population (e.g., if children whose parents suspect that they have developmental problems are disproportionately represented), norms based on this screening sample would be meaningless to apply to the local population in general. Or, the demographic characteristics of a local sample may change over time, in which case norms compiled in previous years may be no longer appropriate. Continuous collection of screening data for the local population enables norms to be kept current. Guidelines for updating local norms are provided in an article by Elliott and Bretzing (1980).

The process gets more involved as other dimensions of screening data, e.g., demographic factors, are taken into account. Alternative cutoff scores may be devised for children in different SES or cultural/racial groups. In order to do so, a separate table is compiled for each distinct group. Of course, each group must include a sufficient number of children in order to yield useful norms.

Establishing local decision rules becomes more involved when the results of a multidimensional screening instrument are broken down into separate scores by area. In general, there are two alternative strategies for interpreting multidimensional assessment data. These two strategies follow from two competing approaches to assessment, which Keogh (1971) describes as the compensatory model and the deficit model. A brief discussion of these models should help to clarify the logic behind different types of decision rules.

The *compensatory model* is based on the assumption that a child's functioning in different developmental areas is interrelated. As strengths in some areas offset weaknesses in other areas, the child's overall functional capacity is assumed to average out to some in-between level. Thus, a child with delayed language development would be considered less at risk for experiencing school problems if the child also demonstrated strengths in abstract reasoning and memory. In applying the compensatory model to interpretation of a multidimensional screening instrument, a child's overall functioning would be reflected by combining different scales or subtest scores into a total composite score. In this way, strengths and weaknesses across areas balance out. This combining strategy may be referred to as an *additive* approach.

(A technical caution regarding additive scores: given that raw scores on different scales may be highly discrepant in size and range, scores that are added together may need to be weighted so that the variance—not total score possible, but variance—of each scale is approximately equal, or else proportional to the importance associated with the scale.)

The *deficit model* treats developmental areas independently. The assumption is that a certain minimum level of competency in each area is necessary to insure adequate educational progress. Like the weak link in a chain, an area of deficient performance signals a limitation that may be cause to regard a child as being at risk. With this model, it is the pattern of developmental functioning rather than the overall level that is most relevant. Since each scale is regarded as potentially significant for decision-making purposes, a combining procedure that preserves these distinctions is needed. The corresponding strategy is the *multiple cutoffs* approach, whereby a child is referred if he or she scores below the cutoff point on any scale, or on some particular set of scales.

The suitability of one approach versus the other depends upon several factors. First is the extent to which the areas assessed are interrelated. The additive approach is best suited to scales that are related, particularly when strengths in one area may be used to compensate for weaknesses in another area. How closely related must scales be so that they may be meaningfully added? This is a matter on which opinions vary. Consider, for example, a screening instrument that contains sections on language development and on concepts (e.g., size, shape, and number). Professor A might argue that adding these scores together is like adding apples and oranges, and it therefore should not be done. Professor B might respond that the two are indeed different, but sufficiently correlated that a "total fruit" composite score would be meaningful for screening purposes. On the other hand, both professors would likely agree that measures of social-emotional development and of academic readiness are as different as apples and asparagus, and should be interpreted separately using the multiple cutoffs approach.

A second factor is the degree of importance assigned to each respective area assessed. A given area may be regarded as so critical to educational functioning that a deficit in that area alone justifies a screening referral, thereby calling for a multiple cutoff scoring system. The DIAL screening test applies the deficit model in this manner. The Communications area is the only one of the four DIAL areas in which scoring below the cutoff score automatically results in a screening outcome of "refer." Presumably, any area so critical as to constitute a certain referral would be emphasized in the intervention services provided. For example, significant delays in motor development alone would warrant a referral if the identification/intervention program placed such great importance upon this area as to provide perceptual-motor training or occupational therapy services.

A third factor that may be of concern is the measurement error associated with scales of different length. As a general rule, longer scales are more reliable. If a scale is so brief that its reliability is suspect, it is inappropriate for that scale to determine a screening decision by itself, as may result with the multiple cutoffs approach. The additive approach enables a composite scale of satisfactory reliability to be constructed from several scales with low reliability.

Given this introduction to the additive and multiple cutoffs approaches, let us consider how screening information is combined by multidimensional instruments, and how alternative strategies may be used to adapt an instrument's decision rules for local use. The simplest case is the multiple scale instrument that provides a total score to which cutoff points are applied in making screening decisions. The screening test from the Preschool Screening System (PSS) is of this type. Scores and percentile norms are derived for each of three scales, but only the total score is used to generate screening recommendations. Local norms could be devised for this total score, just as illustrated earlier in the case of the Acme Screening Test that yielded only a single score. Another option would be to establish local norms for one or more individual scales, presuming that the scales were of particular relevance to the given screening program. Of course, the user needs to be concerned about the reliability of any scale to which a separate cutoff is applied. Reliability data for the PSS indicate that the Language scale would clearly be adequate for this purpose.

The more complex case of an instrument that employs a multiple cutoffs scoring system can best be illustrated by example. With the Minneapolis Preschool Inventory (MPI), a child is classified as "delayed" if a score below the 5th percentile is obtained on any of the seven developmental scales (see MPI profile, Figure 4-8). Using this scoring system, 14 percent of the normative sample was classified as "delay." (Note that the referral rate is higher than 5 percent because different sets of children constitute the bottom 5 percent for each of the seven scales; but the referral rate is lower than 35 percent because there is overlap among the lowest 5 percent on the various scales.)

The user might first consider using the scoring system provided. If the local population is similar to the MPI normative sample and the 14 percent referral rate is acceptable, this would be an attractive choice. If the local population is dissimilar to the normative sample but a referral rate near 14 percent is desired, the user could apply the original scoring system with local norms, that is, establish new cutoff points at the 5th percentile on each scale using local norms. An alternative means of modifying the decision rule would be to use the percentiles provided by the MPI profile, but to select a cutoff point higher or lower than the 5 percent figure to bring the referral rate closer to the target level. Trial-and-error experimentation with MPI data collected on the local screening population may be the best way to arrive at a new cutoff level that produces the target referral rate.

The user might also consider using the multiple cutoffs approach with a subset of the developmental scales in light of the nature of the screening decisions to be made. As demonstrated by Ireton, Lun, & Kampen (1981), the validity of the MPI for the purpose of identifying early school problems may be optimized by applying the multiple cutoffs scoring system to four particular scales: Comprehension, Memory, Letter Recognition, and Memory.

Referral rates for some instruments are difficult to adapt because they use idiosyncratic decisions rules—usually, some modification of the multiple cutoffs approach. The DIAL is one such example. A cutoff score is applied to each of the four areas, but there is a direct correspondence between a below-cutoff score and a screening result of "refer" only for the Communications area. Outcomes on the other three areas are considered interdependently to reach a screening decision (i.e., two delayed areas are scored "rescreen," three delayed areas are scored "refer"). One way in which DIAL decision rules may be adapted is to raise or lower the cutoff score (the same cutoff score applies to all four areas), but still use the recommended scoring system to arrive at screening decisions. Another option is to convert to an additive approach by adding the scale scores for the four areas together and devising local norms for this total score. In one Minnesota school district where this procedure was used, validity of the revised scoring system proved to be greater than for the original scoring system (Lichtenstein, 1978).

The Denver Developmental Screening Test (DDST) also uses a modified multiple cutoffs scoring system, but is more difficult to adapt because it does not provide normative data for a total score or for individual scales. The DDST scoring system is based upon the number of items within the child's age range that are passed and failed in each area. Establishing local norms in the same manner as the original scoring system is clearly impractical, as it would involve renorming all 105 items. However, several strategies could be used to modify decision rules while retaining the same general scoring system. First, the DDST yields an intermediate screening outcome of "questionable." Children in this category may be grouped together with results of "abnormal" to yield a higher referral rate, or with results of "normal" to yield a lower referral rate. Second, adjustments can be made in the direction of increasing referral rates by computing item delays based on the 75 percent pass level or 50 percent pass level indicated on the scoring form (shown in Fig. 4-3), instead of the 90 percent level.* While this method permits a consistent adjustment of cutoff levels across all items, there is less flexibility to adjust referral rates to a particular target level. A third possibility is to adjust the vertical line indicating the child's age from which item delays are determined, adding months to each child's age to raise referral rates, or subtracting months to lower referral rates. Through trial-and-error, cutoffs could be adjusted to any target referral rate.

A fourth option is to dispense with the scoring system provided and establish local norms for an overall score that consists of the total number of items passed. In addition to simplicity and flexibility, this strategy has the advantage of making each scale's contribution roughly proportional to the number of items in each scale, which Table 4-7 shows to be rather uneven at the 4 and 5 year levels.

Next, let us consider a category of screening procedures for which it may appear impossible to apply systematic decision rules, let alone local norms: observational data interpreted via professional judgment. Judgmental ratings are not standarized, since every rater operates from a personal set of guidelines. Yet, a professional's judgment can be expressed quantitatively, and a set of "personal norms" can be compiled for each rater. Subjective judgments can be translated into numerical form, just as you might ask someone to make a judgment "on a scale of 1 to 10." Instead of using word descriptors like "low risk," "high risk," or "extremely high risk," a professional might judge that the likelihood of school success is an 8, a 3, or a 1. The meanings of different ratings can be made more consistent across raters if numerical scores are "anchored" by descriptors (e.g., 3 = "high risk", 5 = "borderline").

Quantifying and compiling screening results enables each rater to establish personal norms, which are useful for estimating referral rates and reviewing decisions rules as well as for determining the consis-

---

*The percentages of each item, which are coded on the scoring form, represent the age at which that percentage of the standardization sample pass the item. These alternative scoring levels are described in the DDST validity study by Frankenburg, Camp, and Van Natta (1971).

tency of judgments across raters. Consider, for example, the following set of rating categories assigned by speech and language clinicians after evaluating a child's speech in a brief interview:

1- Definitely in need of remediation
2- Slightly delayed; refer for further assessment
3- Within/above age expectations

Reviewing the ratings assigned in the course of screening, a speech and language clinician may discover that he or she is rating only 2 percent of the screening population as "definitely in need of remediation" and 6 percent as "slightly delayed", which, given local prevalence rates for language problems, suggests that children in both of these categories should be referred. A second speech and language clinician might be assigning 9 percent of children to category 1, which would appear to be equivalent to a rating of 1 or 2 by the first rater, and 12 percent to category 2.

Understanding the various ways in which decision rules may be established for individual screening procedures is of primary importance when one procedure largely determines the screening outcome. It is often the case, however, that screening data from several sources contribute to an overall screening decision. In such instances, it is not the decision rule for each screening procedure that is of importance, but rather the method of integrating the results of these various procedures to arrive at an overall screening decision.

Interpreting Results for the Overall Screening Process

There are two general ways in which screening information from several sources may be resolved into a single screening decision. One approach is to establish regular rules, perhaps even a quantitative formula, for generating a screening decision from relevant information. Screening information of all types can be entered into a systematized decision process of some kind. This systematizing of all decision-making variables may be referred to as the *statistical* method.

The other major approach is to rely upon human judgment to integrate multiple screening variables. A professional or team of professionals might review the relevant information and reach a screening decision based on a combination of factors, e.g., experience, technical knowledge, and perhaps intuition. This approach to making decisions, known as the *clinical* method, is commonly used by institutions and agencies that provide educational and psychological services.

The relative merit of these two approaches has been a long-standing point of debate. Meehl's (1954) classic work, *Clinical versus statisti-*

cal prediction, approaches the subject in a manner that is highly relevant to decision-making in screening. Although Meehl acknowledges that the clinician (psychologist, in this case) has the range of experience and integrating skills to synthesize complex data, he raises the question of how the overall value of the clinical approach compares with alternative approaches. After all, given the cost of a professional's time and the relative value of the various services they might provide, there is little justification for having the professional concentrate upon assessment and decision-making if a paraprofessional using "cookbook" interpretation of standardized tests can do as well. To investigate this matter, Meehl (1954) reviewed outcome studies in diverse areas of psychology, and concluded that the validity of the statistical method was consistently superior to the clinical method. However, further study on this question (Holt, 1970; Sawyer, 1966) has suggested that the case is not yet closed.

In the area of screening and early identification, research comparing the clinical and statistical methods is insufficient to show a clear trend. Perhaps this is just as well, since there is little reason to regard this as a simple either-or choice. The differences between the two approaches become less distinct when considering that a statistical decision-making process may incorporate professional judgment and other qualitative data, and conversely, a clinical decision-making process typically includes statistically-interpreted scores among other input. The basis for the statistical-clinical distinction is the nature of the final stage of the process at which the decision or prediction is made.

Statistical method

The statistical method in particular requires further elaboration. The name itself is a bit misleading in that its defining characteristic is not the use of formulas or quantitative data, but the systematic, rule-bound nature of the process. Rules can be devised to take all kinds of information into account, not just scores from standardized measures, but also professional judgment, behavioral observations, demographic variables, and results of prior evaluations. Thus, for example, if there is reason to interpret screening test results differently depending upon a child's SES, this adjustment might be systematized by using different cutoff scores for each SES group. Variations in the screening process itself can also be systematized. For example, observation of certain child behaviors might, according to plan, automatically warrant administration of an additional social-emotional adjustment measure. The critical element of the statistical method is that information is interpreted using predetermined, mechanical decision rules, rather than subjective judgment that may vary with the decision maker.

The same general approaches that were introduced as options for interpreting multidimensional scales, the additive approach and the multiple cutoffs approach, may be applied in combining the results of several different screening procedures. Of the two, the multiple cutoffs approach, in its basic form, is the easier to implement. Data from multiple procedures is combined by treating the outcome of each screening procedure independently. In the simplest case, a child who is referred by any of the procedures in the screening process receives a final screening decision of "refer."

The situation is complicated by the fact that the overall referral rate for a screening process increases with the inclusion of each additional procedure. As an example, it may appear that using three screening procedures, each of which refers 15 percent of the screening sample, represents an improvement over using just one of the three procedures because more children with special needs are identified. Although an increase in sensitivity will indeed result, the cumulative effect of using multiple procedures is a higher overall referral rate— say, 25 percent in this case—and an accompanying increase in over-referral errors. Ignoring this trade-off creates the erroneous impression that a decision-making process automatically improves with the incorporation of additional data.

The importance of this point may be appreciated by considering the situation in practical, rather than statistical, terms. The usual rationale for introducing additional screening procedures is to remedy perceived deficiencies of the screening process, i.e., the user is concerned because "some children with problems are being missed." A likely scenario is where one of more specific-area screening measures are proposed as supplements to a multidimensional instrument. There may be reason to suspect that many of those "missed" children would have been picked up by some screening procedure (e.g., a test of language development) or indicator (e.g., early hearing problems) that is not currently a determinant of the screening outcome. However, while obtaining this additional information seems like a logical course of action, to systematically incorporate it into a statistical decision-making process may or may not bring about gains in screening accuracy. As each new procedure picks up previously missed children, it also refers some "normal group" children who would not otherwise be referred, so that under-referral errors are reduced at the expense of increasing over-referral errors (a familiar predicament). Are the extra "hits" worth the extra "misses"? This is similar to the choices presented by changing the referral rate for an individual screening procedure, which may offer no clearly preferable alternative.

To determine whether the addition of supplementary screening procedures actually results in improved screening accuracy (i.e., through a criterion-related validity study) requires that the screening referral rate be maintained at a fairly constant level, presumably in the vicinity of a target referral rate established in the manner discussed earlier. Regulating referral rates with the multiple cutoffs approach might be accomplished in either of two ways. First, referral rates for each individual procedure can be adjusted downward. In the example of the three screening procedures, each with a 15 percent referral rate, the cutoff points for each instrument would need to be revised probably to below the 10th percentile to yield an overall referral rate near 15 percent.* A second strategy is to establish a decision rule such that a certain number of "high risk" or below-cutoff outcomes on individual procedures results in a final screening decision to refer. For example, the decision rule might be that a child scoring in the bottom 10 percent on two of the three screening measures would be referred. This is quite similar to the scoring system for the McCarthy Screening Test, which allows the user several options of this nature. A decision-making procedure of this type was also used in the well-known study on early identification of reading problems by de Hirsch, Jansky, and Langford (1966), in which children with below-passing scores on seven of ten tests were classified as high risk for reading failure. With these referral rate adjustments, however, there is no systematic way to predict how manipulation of decision rules will affect the referral rate for the overall screening process. Trial and error appears to be the best method for achieving a desired referral rate.

Upon establishing decision rules that yield referral rates in the desired range, follow-up data can be effectively used to compare various options. Hit rate patterns can be analyzed to gauge the value of adding each successive procedure or variable to a multiple cutoffs screening process, or to compare alternative decision rules or sets of screening procedures. Again, as with adjusting referral rates, trial-and-error appears to be the most workable method for arriving at optimal decision rules when using the multiple cutoffs approach (Wiggins, 1973).

A variation of the multiple cutoffs approach, which Meehl and Rosen (1955) call the "successive hurdles" approach, involves administering multiple screening procedures in sequence, as needed. The most economical (and, presumably, least valid) procedures would be administered first, and on the basis of these results, children whose functioning is clearly satisfactory would be ruled out from further

---

*As an alternative, in the case where one procedure (e.g., a multidimensional instrument) is to be given greater weight, cutoffs might be set at, perhaps, the 10th percentile for the primary measure and the 5th percentile for each supplementary procedure.

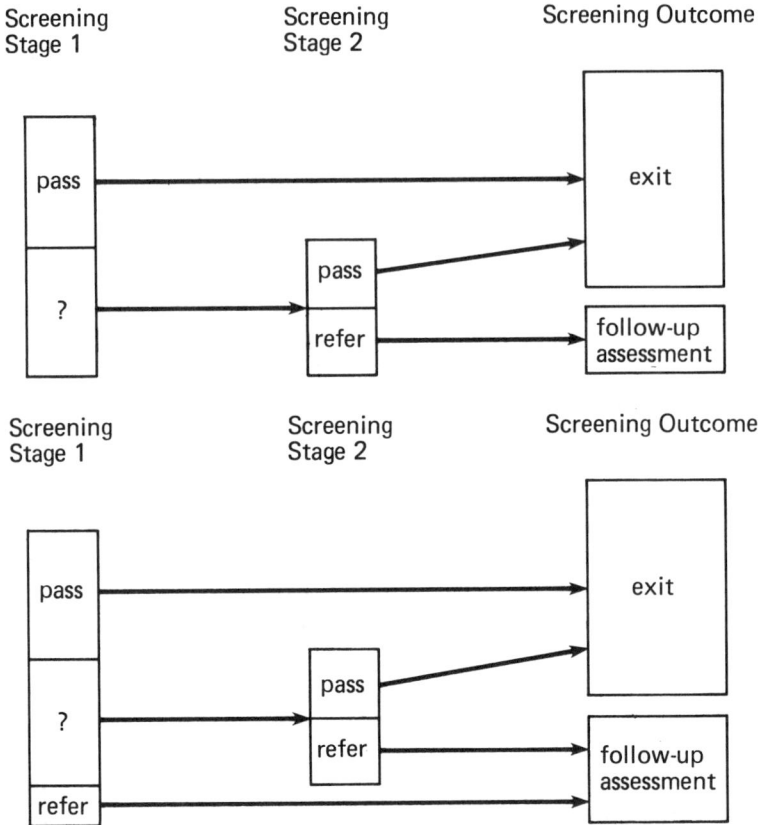

Fig. 5-5. Alternative strategies using the successive hurdles approach.

screening. All children for whom some question still remains would continue on to the next "hurdle" of more costly and valid screening procedures. This strategy parallels the successive decision-making process of "screening followed by further assessment," except that the several stages are all part of the screening process.

Figure 5-5 illustrates two different ways in which the successive hurdles approach might operate. In the first case (top diagram), children who are functioning adequately and assigned an outcome of "pass" are ruled out at each successive level, leaving only "higher risk" children to be screened further. The Denver Prescreening Developmental Questionnaire (PDQ) is designed to be used in this way together with the Denver Developmental Screening Test (DDST). The recommended procedure is that only those children scoring below a certain cutoff on the PDQ are then screened with the DDST.

A second variation on this approach (Fig. 5-5, bottom) is to allow a screening decision of either pass or refer to be made at each stage for children with sufficiently high or low scores, leaving only those children in the indeterminate range to continue on in the screening process. This strategy corresponds to the "intermediate decision rule" devised for the MPSI, whereby children with especially low or high scores at a point midway through the test are assigned a screening outcome and the test administration is discontinued. This midway point thus becomes the first screening stage, and the end of the MPSI the second screening stage. To carry out this strategy through an additional stage, children who are administered the entire MPSI could be assigned a third outcome besides pass and refer, a borderline category indicating that the child should be administered additional screening procedures or, possibly, be rescreened at a later date. These and other decision strategies are discussed at length by Cronbach and Gleser (1965), who assign them impressive names such as "pre-reject double-stage strategy" (referred to here as "top diagram").

The additive approach is the second general strategy for combining data from multiple screening procedures. This approach involves computing a composite total score from results on different measures, and then setting cutoff points to generate referral decisions from this score. (Again, the need to weight scores so as to equalize or prioritize the contribution of each procedure must be kept in mind.) As noted earlier, it is presumed that the procedures to be added together have aspects in common that justify their being combined additively; for example, all might tap developmental functions that directly bear upon academic functioning. A ground rule is that, if procedures are to be combined additively, the end result should be an overall process that has greater utility than any of the individual procedures used singly. As an example, let us consider a screening battery that consists of a multidimensional screening test (Procedure A), a parent inventory (Procedure B), and a screening test of language development (Procedure C). Each measure is transformed into a scale score that ranges from 0 to 25 and has a similar distribution. Cutoff points are then devised for each procedure and for each combination of procedures, so that 15 percent of the screening sample is referred in each case. A follow-up study is then conducted from which hit rates can be computed and the sensitivity of each alternative screening process can be compared. (Since referral rates are held constant, the procedure with higher sensitivity will also have higher specificity, and therefore specificity is disregarded in this example.) As shown in Table 5-2, the highest sensitivity rate for an individual procedure is the .66 figure for Procedure A. Thus, in order for a screening process composed of two or three procedures to warrant consideration (assuming similar costs and acceptability for each procedure), the .66 figure must be exceeded. Furthermore, the margin of improvement with the addition of each

Table 5-2
Comparison of Sensitivity Rates for Additive Combinations
of Screening Procedures (Referral Rates Held Constant)

Predictor	Sensitivity
Procedure A	.66
Procedure B	.52
Procedure C	.56
A + B	.72
A + C	.59
B + C	.64
A + B + C	.73

procedure should justify the cost of including it in the process. The sensitivity figures in Table 5-2 show that Procedure A and Procedure B together produce a sizable increase in validity over Procedure B alone, and this is the best rate obtained by any pair of procedures. Although the highest sensitivity rate is obtained by combining all three procedures, the slight increase that results from including Procedure C as well does not justify its use. Therefore, the most likely choice is a screening process that consists of Procedures A and B.

A more sophisticated method of combining the results from different screening measures involves the use of *multiple regression,** a statistical procedure for establishing ideal weights to be assigned to each predictor. A multiple regression analysis can be conducted when two types of data are available for a good-sized sample: (1) screening data, i.e., screening measure results plus any other predictors of interest (age, demographic factors, etc.), and (2) follow-up data, i.e., criterion measure results that distinguish between target group and normal group children. These data should be obtained from a sample that is representative of the intended screening population. The equation that is produced indicates how screening measures should be weighted so as to best predict the given criterion measure. The equation can also indicate how variables such as age, sex, or SES should be taken into account when these have a consistent effect upon validity. A competent statistician, with the help of sophisticated computer software, can readily conduct this type of analysis. The resulting regression equation might appear to be rather unwieldly, as an example:

$$(\text{Procedure A} \times .24) + (\text{Procedure B} \times .67)$$
$$+ (\text{Procedure C} \times .88) + (\text{months of age} \times -.15) = Y$$

---

*Technically, when predicting group classifications, a statistical procedure closely related to multiple regression called *discriminant analysis* is the procedure of choice.

where Y is the total score to which cutoff scores are applied. On-site computation can, however, be easily done with the aid of a programmable hand calculator.

The multiple regression version of the additive approach may seem ideal. An optimal combining procedure can be precisely defined, and variables that contribute little to decision-making can be identified and discarded. The catch is that the "optimal equation" is specific to the sample and criterion measure with which it was devised. The statistical decision rule that results from this process is not a true prediction of an unknown outcome, but a custom-tailored fitting of the decision rule to the data already in hand. This optimal decision rule may not be nearly as effective when applied to another screening situation, or even in subsequent use under highly similar circumstances. The same phenomenon occurs when a "best cutoff point" is identified for a single screening procedure on a trial-and-error basis so as to maximize hit rates in predicting known criterion measure results. To determine how well the decision rule really works, it is necessary to try it out in a second validity study with some other sample. This verification procedure is known as *cross-validation*.

The reduction in validity rates that occurs when a sample-specific (i.e., custom-fit) decision rule is cross-validated is referred to as *shrinkage*. The greater the number of variables in the prediction equation and the fewer subjects in the study sample, the more shrinkage can be expected. The need to cross-validate also applies when a multiple cutoffs decision rule is worked out to maximize hit rates with a known criterion rather than to match a target referral rate. Wiggins (1973) warns that a sample-specific multiple cutoffs decision rule is unlikely to generalize to other samples if it includes more than two or three predictors. The need to cross-validate sample-specific decision rules is important to consider when evaluating research study results. It is common for highly favorable validity data to be reported without including a caution that shrinkage may be expected upon cross-validation.

A difficulty with the additive approach is that information of a qualitative nature cannot readily be added to quantitative scores. How, for example, might screening test results be combined with the information that a parent is "highly concerned" about the child's development, or that a professional has observed "strong indications of emotional problems"? To fully apply the additive approach, a system for quantifying each variable is needed. Thus, rating scales (e.g., from 1 to 10) might be devised for assessing the level of parent concerns or severity of emotional problems.

It is possible to use the additive and multiple cutoffs approaches together at different levels of the data interpretation process, such as in situations where it is inappropriate to add all screening inputs together but still desirable to combine certain screening results additively. For example, both direct testing and parent reports might provide data regarding a child's language development. If each is a valid source of information, these could be added together to yield a more reliable measure of language functioning. This composite score might be one of several composite scores covering different areas, each of which is then interpreted separately using multiple cutoffs. In this manner, features of both statistical approaches could be combined.

Clinical Method

The most troublesome limitation of the statistical method is that information can be incorporated into the screening process only if there is advance planning to systematically collect this information. When professional (i.e., clinical) judgment is the basis for arriving at a screening decision, there is no limit to what information can be taken into account. An unusual incident reported by a screening examiner, an atypical physical or sensory problem, reports of dramatic changes in behavior, or a written summary of a recent psychological evaluation—all of which would be passed over by a mechanical decision rule—could be considered by the decision-making professional or team. The clinical strategy also allows for greater flexibility. A missing piece of information may render the statistical decision rule useless, whereas a professional can simply make a mental adjustment or, perhaps, draw upon other information that can serve as a substitute.

Despite all of these apparent advantages of clinical decision-making, the results may or may not be more valid than the statistical approach. As Meehl (1954) argued, consistent interpretation of valid standardized instruments may be more predictive than the flexible and all-encompassing judgment of the professional. Each professional or team of professionals will integrate screening data differently, and while some may be able to "beat" the statistical decision rule, many will do no better or worse.

A systematic decision rule can and should improve over time. The cutoff points and combining procedures of a statistical decision process can be evaluated against outcomes, and the results used to determine what works best. While overall hit rates for a clinical decision process can also be computed, it is difficult to determine how the process can be adjusted so as to improve screening accuracy in the future. This would require that decision-making professionals make their reasoning process explicit by identifying and quantifying the variables that contribute to their decisions, which, in effect, would make the clinical process considerably more statistical.

It should be apparent to the reader that the interpretation of the overall screening process is unlikely to be purely statistical or clinical in nature. In fact, Sawyer (1966), in reviewing the "clinical vs. statistical" controversy, maintains that the best strategy is to base decisions upon statistical interpretation of both clinical and statistical data. There are various ways in which both strategies can be integrated into an overall screening process. The following illustration of a hypothetical screening process should further clarify how various approaches to making screening decisions may be applied.

Illustration of a Screening Decision Process

A suburban school district has planned a comprehensive early identification program that involves mass screening in the spring for children who will enter kindergarten in the fall. The screening program consists of four components: medical, vision, hearing, and developmental. Each of these components is independent; if a referral is made for just one part, further evaluation focuses only on that component. For this illustration, only the developmental component is discussed.

Three distinct areas are assessed as part of developmental screening: educational (i.e., school readiness), speech articulation, and social-emotional adjustment. Screening procedures have been selected so that there is more than one source of screening information for each of the three developmental areas.

Screening Procedures

A developmental screening test, the Minneapolis Preschool Screening Instrument (MPSI), is individually administered to each child by paid paraprofessional examiners. The MPSI yields a total score and screening outcome for educationally-related areas of development. In addition, a speech intelligibility rating is assigned by the examiner. While the child is being screened, the parent completes the Minnesota Preschool Inventory (MPI), which provides information regarding the child's development, school readiness and social-emotional adjustment, and also assesses parent concerns. Behavioral observations by the screening examiner, recorded on a checklist such as the one shown in Table 2-2, provide a second source of information regarding adjustment. Finally, a screening examiner administers a screening test of speech intelligibility, the Denver Articulation Screening Exam (DASE), as needed.

Given the relative homogeneity of the screening population, no demographic differences are taken into account in interpreting screening data. Screening results for males and females are interpreted alike,

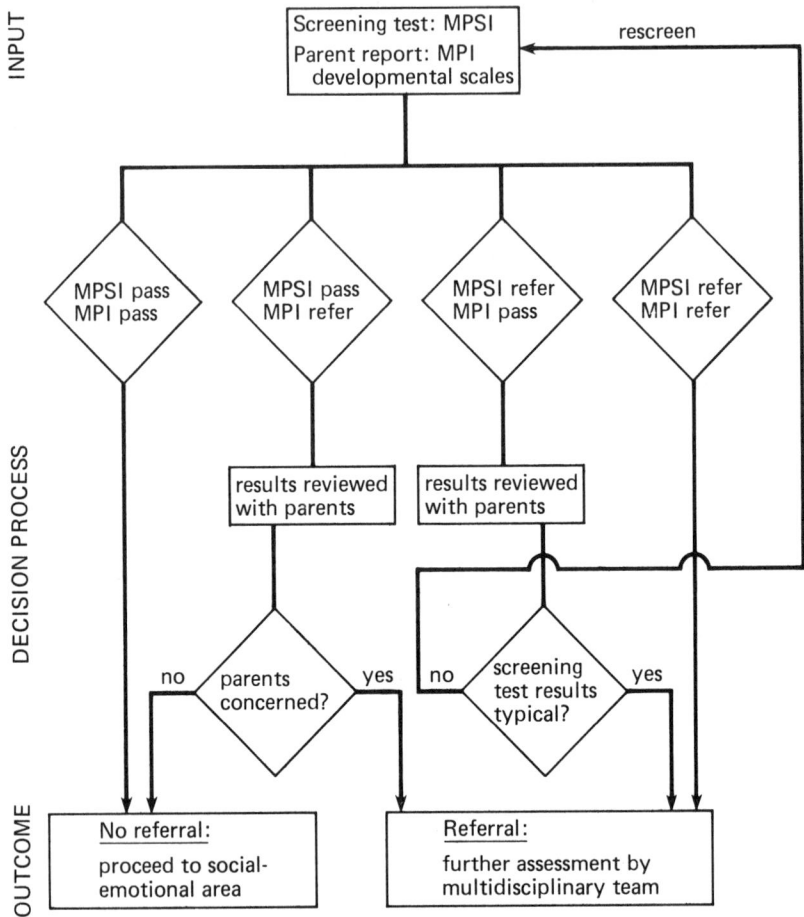

Fig. 5-6. Educational area decision process

although this policy is subject to review on the basis of follow-up evaluation. Children's age differences are accounted for by the age-based norms of the MPSI and MPI.

The decision processes established for the educational, speech, and social-emotional areas are diagrammed in "flow chart" fashion in Figures 5-6, 5-7, and 5-8. The three areas can be considered independently, with one exception: the educational and social-emotional areas are interrelated in that a screening decision for social-emotional adjustment is unnecessary for a child who has been referred in the educational areas, and thus will be assessed further by a psychologist regardless.

Educational

A referral in the educational area is jointly determined by results on the screening test (i.e., the MPSI) and the parent report (i.e., MPI) as shown in Figure 5-6. MPSI results are interpreted using local norms, with cutoff scores set so as to refer 15 percent of the screening population. Interpretation of the MPI developmental scale profile focuses upon four scales, Comprehension, Memory, Letter Recognition, and Number Comprehension, as suggested by Ireton, Lun, and Kampen (1981). A child scoring below the 5th percentile on any of these four scales receives an MPI outcome of "refer."

MPSI and MPI results are interpreted using a successive hurdles type strategy, with inconsistencies between screening test and parent report data being resolved through a follow-up procedure involving professional judgment. Four possible combinations may result from a child receiving pass or refer outcomes on each of the two instruments: (1) the MPSI and MPI both yield an outcome of pass, i.e., no referral recommended, (2) the MPSI result is pass while the MPI result is refer, (3) the MPSI result is refer while the MPI result is pass, and (4) the MPSI and MPI both indicate referral. Naturally, a child receiving a matching screening outcome on the two instruments will be referred or not referred accordingly. In the event of disagreement, the following decision rules are to be followed:

- A child may receive an MPSI outcome of pass and an MPI outcome of refer, indicating that the parent's impression of the child's development is below age norms, even though the child performed adequately in the testing situation. If a brief parent interview indicates that there is a high degree of concern on the part of the parent, the child is referred for further assessment. Otherwise, the parent is advised of the child's performance on the screening test and no referral is made.

- If the MPSI yields an outcome of refer while the MPI outcome is pass, the possibility must be considered that the child's response to the testing situation was atypical and invalid. The screening coordinator notes any remarks or observations recorded by the screening examiner, and then reviews the discrepancy between the two outcomes in a brief, on-the-spot interview with the parent(s) to determine whether the child's performance on this occasion was atypical due to shyness, fearfulness, fatigue, etc. If the MPSI administration is judged to have been invalid, rescreening at a later time is arranged. But if the child's performance was apparently representative, the child is referred for further assessment.

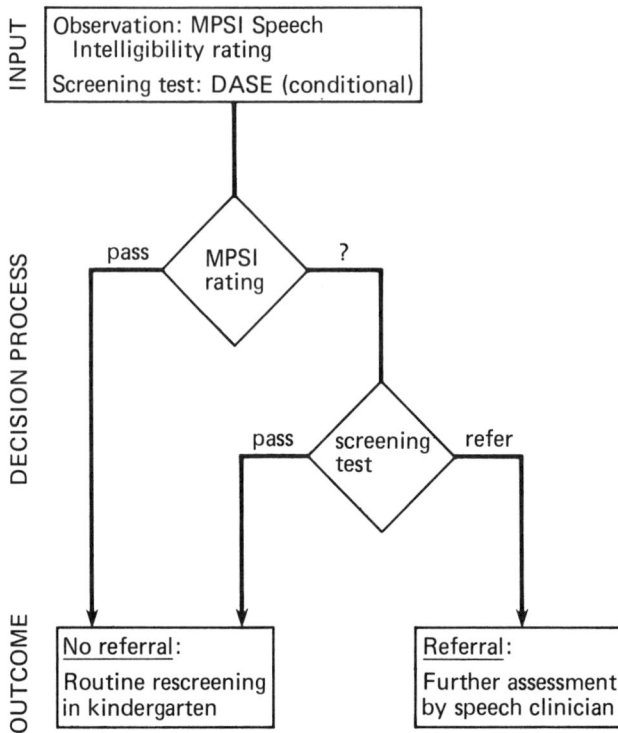

Fig. 5-7. Speech articulation area decision process

Note that while the decision process is highly systematized, professional judgment plays an important part. The successive hurdles approach is applied in such a way that the first hurdle involves a statistical decision rule, and the next hurdle, if required, involves clinical decision-making.

Speech

A two-stage process is involved in screening for speech articulation, as Figure 5-7 illustrates. An initial screen is provided by the Speech Intelligibility rating assigned by the examiner following administration of the MPSI. Based on recommendations in the MPSI manual, only children with a rating of 4 ("always understandable") are excluded from further speech screening. Children with ratings of 1, 2, or 3 are administered the Denver Articulation Screening Exam by the screening coordinator. Children scoring below the cutoff point on this instrument are referred for a comprehensive speech evaluation by a speech and language clinician.

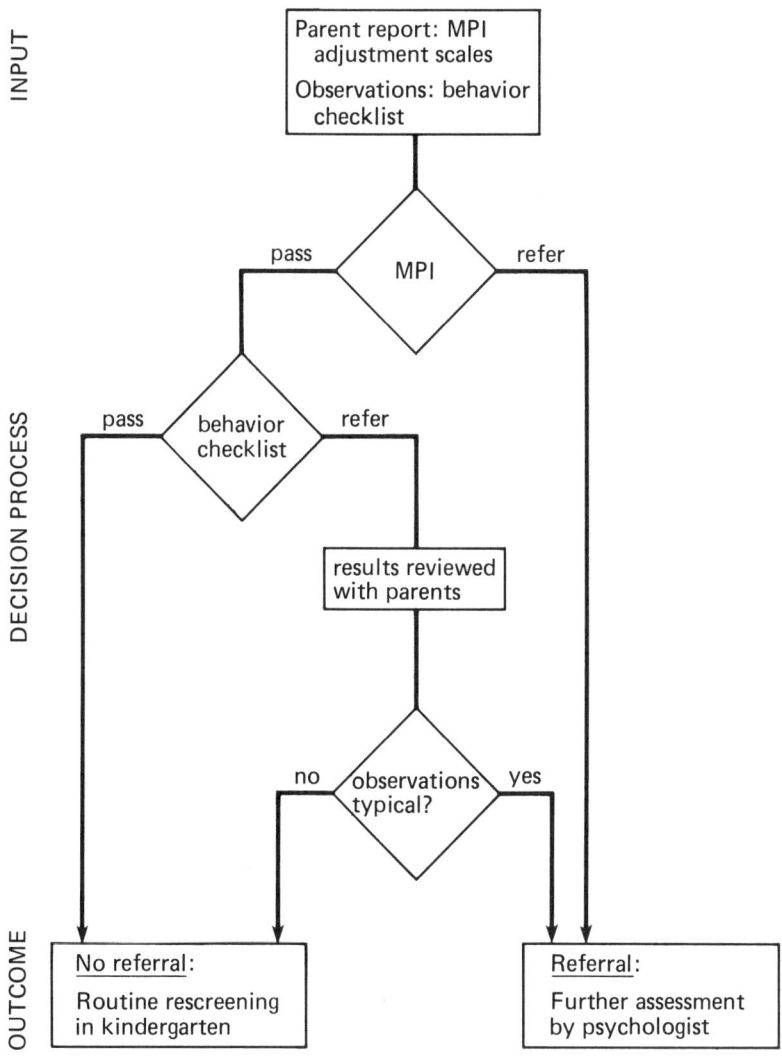

Fig. 5-8.   Social-emotional area decision process.

Social-Emotional Adjustment

Children not referred for educational concerns are screened for social-emotional adjustment. This decision process is outlined in Figure 5-8. Screening data for this area include the MPI adjustment scales and the behavior checklist completed by the examiner. Children scoring in the bottom 5 percent on one or more of the MPI adjustment scales are referred for further assessment of social-emotional development by a school psychologist. A child not referred by the MPI might nevertheless be considered for referral if observations during testing reveal atypical behavior, as defined by three or more ratings in the maladaptive range (e.g., the far right column in Table 2-2). In this event, the screening program coordinator briefly interviews the parent(s) to determine whether the behavior observed was a representative sample of the child's behavior. If so, the child is referred for further assessment in the social-emotional area.

As indicated in the flow charts (Fig. 5-6—5-8), a distinct type of follow-up assessment is provided for children referred in each area. Those children not referred are routinely screened the following year in kindergarten.

The particular decision process illustrated here offers several advantages. It makes full use of standardized screening instruments for which validity has been demonstrated in similar situations. The statistical aspects of this decision-making process introduce economic and administrative advantages by eliminating the need for extensive case by case review (e.g., by a multidisciplinary team) at the screening level. Yet, flexibility is programmed into the decision process in order to account for various contingencies. For example, parents are asked to review results when their observations are inconsistent with the child's performance or behavior in the testing situation. Thus, an invalid test administration, if identified as such, is not used inappropriately in making a screening decision.

Of course, the advantages of this approach are of significance only if the resulting decisions are at an acceptable level of accuracy. As with many questions regarding alternative procedures, this matter can best be resolved through empirical evaluation of screening decisions to determine what works best.

EVALUATION OF SCREENING DECISIONS

The basic concepts involved in evaluating screening decisions have already been introduced. This section is intended to expand upon some key points, to address special issues, and to collect some loose ends.

The central point to reemphasize is that the hit rate model provides the basic methodological tool for determining the validity of a screening process or for comparing one prospective screening process with another. The model is deceptively simple in certain respects. Conducting a criterion-related validity study is complicated by such considerations as selection of criterion measures, confounding effects of early intervention, and group differences in validity rates.

Before addressing these matters, which may have the effect of discouraging the research-shy practitioner, a caveat is in order. Evaluation is not an expendable extra or a superfluous academic exercise, but an essential component in providing high-quality professional services to children and their families. It is highly unrealistic to expect a screening process as initially implemented to function at full potential. Aspects in need of review or revision can invariably be identified if the effort is made. A corollary to this caveat is that some evaluation is always better than none. Without implementing a large-scale research effort, certain basic evaluation procedures can yield a substantial payoff.

The most basic and necessary evaluation procedure is to maintain systematic records of screening outcomes from which referral rates can be determined. Data should be compiled so that referral rates can be computed for each area in which screening decisions are made (see sample data card, Figure 5-9, that doubles as an organizing system for screening cases). In addition to variables such as age, sex, and demographic characteristics, which may be used in categorizing referral trends, screening data recorded for each child might include scores on specific measures, and other variables that contribute to the decisions process or might be considered in the future.

Further evaluation data that can be obtained without introducing special research procedures concern a child's progress and placement within the school system. Records of which children are referred for further assessment, which are recommended for special services, and which actually receive special services should be kept. Table 5-3 provides an example of how early identification program outcomes might be summarized. Data might also be compiled for all children in the screening population on subsequent eligibility for and receipt of special services, grade retention, etc. for the purpose of estimating problem base rates and comparing them to referral rates.

Keeping good records need be no more complicated than maintaining a basic index card filing system. (To facilitate data analysis, machine scorable forms might be used.) Investigating key questions about the screening process is infinitely easier when the questions are posed in advance, and the necessary information is collected on an ongoing basis.

Another valuable source of evaluation data is feedback from participants in screening (i.e., parents, children, and screening personnel).

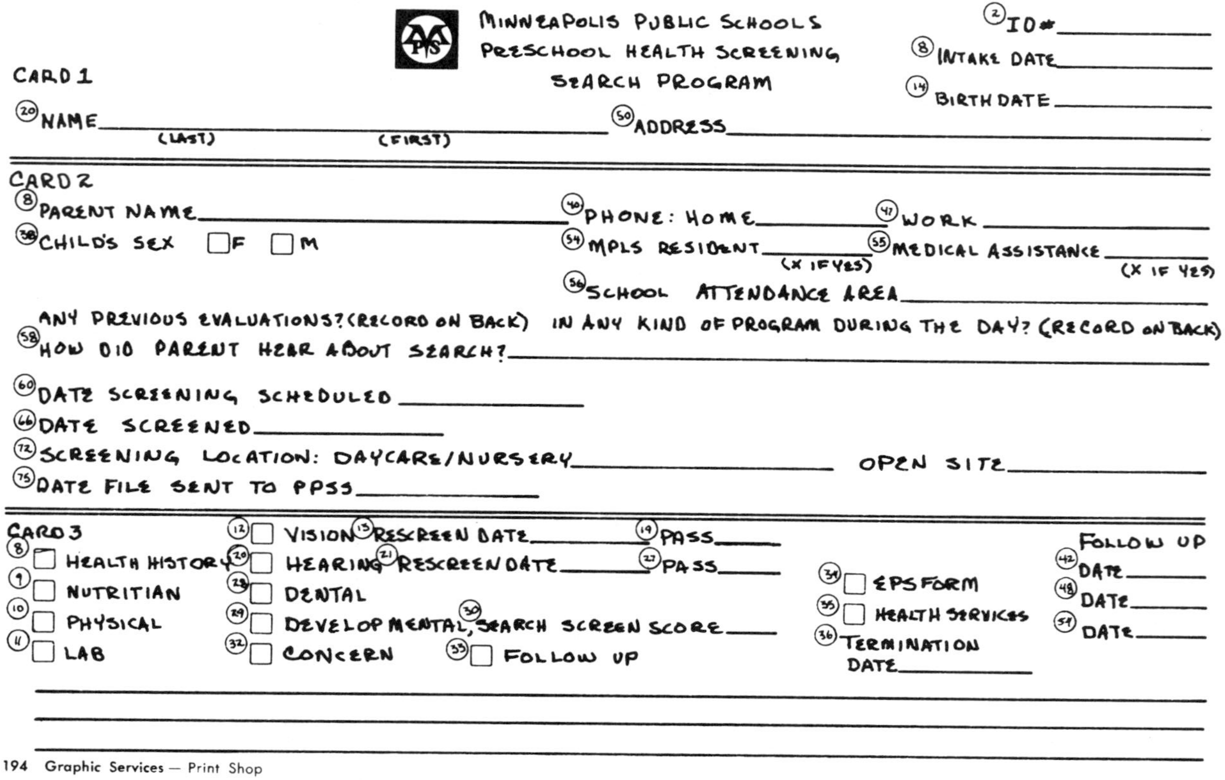

CARD 1

🏫 MINNEAPOLIS PUBLIC SCHOOLS
PRESCHOOL HEALTH SCREENING
SEARCH PROGRAM

② ID #

⑳ NAME _____ _____
      (LAST)   (FIRST)

⑧ INTAKE DATE _____
⑭ BIRTH DATE _____

CARD 2
⑧ PARENT NAME _____
㉚ CHILD'S SEX ☐ F ☐ M

㊿ ADDRESS _____

㊴ PHONE: HOME _____ ㊼ WORK _____
㊶ MPLS RESIDENT _____ (X IF YES) ㊿ MEDICAL ASSISTANCE _____ (X IF YES)

㊾ SCHOOL ATTENDANCE AREA _____

㊾ ANY PREVIOUS EVALUATIONS? (RECORD ON BACK) IN ANY KIND OF PROGRAM DURING THE DAY? (RECORD ON BACK)
㊿ HOW DID PARENT HEAR ABOUT SEARCH?

⑥ DATE SCREENING SCHEDULED _____
㊽ DATE SCREENED _____
㊼ SCREENING LOCATION: DAYCARE/NURSERY _____ OPEN SITE _____
㊀ DATE FILE SENT TO PPSS _____

CARD 3
⑧   ⑫ VISION ⑮ RESCREEN DATE _____ ⑲ PASS ☐
① HEALTH HISTORY ☐   ⑲ HEARING ⑳ RESCREEN DATE _____ ㉒ PASS ☐
① NUTRITION ☐   ㉕ DENTAL _____
⑩ PHYSICAL ☐   ㉚ DEVELOPMENTAL, SEARCH SCREEN SCORE _____
④ LAB ☐   ㉝ CONCERN ㉟ ☐ FOLLOW UP

㉞ ☐ EPS FORM
㉟ ☐ HEALTH SERVICES
㊱ ☐ TERMINATION DATE _____

FOLLOW UP
㊷ DATE _____
㊸ DATE _____
㊹ DATE _____

Fig. 5-9. Sample data collection card for preschool screening program.

Table 5-3
Early Identification Program Annual Summary (Developmental Area)

	0–3 yrs.	3–5 yrs.	Total
Inquiries/requests received*	113	403	516
Children screened	88	306	394
Referred to multidisciplinary team	45	127	172
Placed in early intervention program	18	33	51
Referred to community agency	11	21	33
Referred to school program	3	76	79
Information provided	11	60	71
Consultation provided	20	70	90
Scheduled for future screening	21	62	83
Referral Sources			
Parents	52	163	215
Agencies	32	124	156
Preschool programs	8	81	89
Physicians/professionals in private practice	19	28	47
Other	2	7	9

*Program uses an outreach/referral system, rather than mass screening. (Adapted from reporting form used by Madison Metropolitan School District. With permission)

Spontaneous comments may signal various concerns: parents may regard a questionnaire as irrelevant or unnecessarily intrusive; screening examiners may find it difficult or too time-consuming to administer a given procedure; on-site coordinators may find themselves unable to ask the parents key questions or to provide screening results at the proper time; children may be bored or scared or puzzled by the screening situation. Such input goes beyond the matter of how well the screening process is working (as is indicated by psychometric evaluation data) to reveal what is occurring and why, and what might be done differently. Some of the problems that are pinpointed may affect the acceptability or efficiency of the screening process, and thus bear directly upon its utility.

A limitation of spontaneous feedback is that it is provided by a self-selected reporting group, and therefore cannot be assumed to be representative of the views of all screening participants. Feedback can be more systematically elicited through an evaluation questionnaire or, as may be more appropriate for reviewing the process with screening personnel, through informal discussion.

Addressing, more narrowly, the matter of evaluating the accuracy of screening procedures, we return once again to the hit rate model.

While screening measures have been discussed at length, attention is now devoted to issues concerning criterion measures.

Selecting Criterion Measures

A criterion measure should be a meaningful indicator of what the screening process is intended to measure, i.e., whether or not a child is in need of special services. Criterion measures provide the yardstick with which accurate screening decisions are distinguished from screening errors. But the use of criterion measures to determine which were the "right" children to have been referred should be accompanied by a caution: identification of educational or developmental problems is not precise or infallible. The criterion measure addresses the same challenge, and limitations, as the screening measure in trying to assign children to discrete categories. As a result, validity studies provide an estimate at best of screening accuracy, an estimate that is dependent upon the validity and appropriateness of the criterion measure. In order to evaluate screening procedures fairly, highly adequate criterion measures must be selected.

Thorndike and Hagen (1969) propose four qualities that are desired in a criterion measure: relevance, freedom from bias, reliability, and availability. *Relevance* in validating preschool screening procedures pertains to how well the criterion measure reflects the presence of, or possibility of, educational problems. (This is essentially the same thing as validity.) For screening procedures that address specific content areas, the criterion should provide a good match with that content area. *Freedom from bias* concerns the need for each child to have the same opportunity to perform well on the criterion measure. This may relate to standardization of criterion measure, to the appropriateness of its content for all children in the population, or to the objectivity of a third-person rater. *Reliability,* as introduced earlier, is the degree to which a measure is reproducible and stable. *Availability* refers to practical considerations such as cost and acceptability that determine whether the criterion measure is feasible to administer in a given situation. These points should sound familiar; basically, the same general factors that characterize good screening procedures apply to criterion measures as well.

Criterion measures may be classified into two categories depending upon the nature of the validity study. Criterion measures for a concurrent validity study, obtained at or around the time of screening, determine how well screening procedures identify children's current problems. For a predictive validity study, criterion measures are obtained later in time (i.e., after the screening population has entered school) and determine how well screening procedures predict subsequent problems. Let us first consider criterion measures for concurrent validity.

Criterion Measures for Concurrent Validity

A natural choice for validating screening decisions is the outcome (i.e., whether or not the child needs special intervention) of the further assessment process to which children are referred from screening. After all, screening is intended to be a first-stage approximation of this more elaborate and costly identification process. Typically, further assessment involves collection of personal history and family data, testing, and observation by professionals who have special expertise in assessment. An elaborate and "ecologically-valid" assessment process might also incorporate observational data from a trial classroom placement such as described in Chapter 2.

The drawback to using the further assessment process as a criterion measure is cost; it is generally provided only for that small subset of children referred from screening. Criterion data are needed for both referred and non-referred children. Further assessment of non-referred children would require special arrangements at a considerable cost. While it may be economically and practically unfeasible for non-referred children to be assessed strictly for purposes of evaluation, this could be done for a randomly selected sample of non-referred children. The number of non-referred children recommended for special services would provide an estimate of the under-referral rate.* In conducting a study of this type, it is best to include as many non-referred children as resources will allow. Therefore, this could be done only on an occasional basis, and should be reserved for a point in time when the screening process is sufficiently established to merit rigorous evaluation. Of course, this type of evaluation study requires that parents be informed and permission be obtained for further assessment of non-referred children.

An alternative to conducting a comprehensive assessment for all validity study children is to adminster one of the general cognitive measures (a.k.a. IQ tests) that are usually central to a psychoeducational evaluation, e.g., the Stanford-Binet Intelligence Scale, the Mc-

---

*Under-referral errors could alternatively be interpreted as illustrating *self-fulfilling prophecy* bias in the assessment process; that is, the tendency to look for, and therefore to find, problems when a child is referred. Assuming, however, that the assessing professional or team is aware of the study design (i.e., that some children have been referred at random), this phenomenon would be far less likely to operate and the validity of the criterion measure should be greater as a result.

Carthy Scales of Children's Abilities, or the Wechsler Preschool and Primary Scale of Intelligence. To identify a criterion "problem group" from the IQ scores yielded by these measures, the cutoff is typically set in the range from 68 (2nd percentile) to 80 (10th percentile). Figure 4-10 provides an example in which the Early Screening Inventory is validated against the McCarthy Scales of Children's Abilities.

Criterion Measures for Predictive Validity

Concurrent validity measures provide a more definitive "second-opinion" regarding a child's apparent needs at the time of screening. A predictive validity study goes beyond this to consider the actual condition that the screening process is intended to predict, i.e., whether or not a child performs satisfactorily in the school setting. Predictive validity criterion measures tend to focus on actual achievement, on situationally-relevant behaviors, and on skills (e.g., reading, following directions) that require integration of various developmental functions. Primary options for obtaining follow-up data on school functioning include standardized tests, teaching ratings, diagnostic evaluations, and "administrative indicators" of a child's educational status.

Well-constructed *standardized tests* of readiness or achievement tend to be highly useful as measures of criterion performance. The obvious advantages of standardized tests are careful standardization and technical adequacy, which insure objective and consistent comparisons between children. Also, test content typically consists of a comprehensive sample of skills and abilities in the areas measured. The Metropolitan Readiness Tests (Nurss & McGauvran, 1976) is the most commonly used group achievement test in the early grades. For kindergarten children, however, an individually-administered test is often preferable given the young child's limited capacity for concentration and for independent work, and sometimes necessary, such as when verbal or motoric responses are required. The Woodcock-Johnson Psycho-educational Battery (Woodcock & Johnson, 1977), given its scope, technical properties, and standardization range, is well-suited for this purpose.

Teacher ratings are useful for assessing areas that are less conducive to measurement by standardized testing. A teacher who has observed a child over a period of time may be expected to provide more valid data on a child's social-emotional adjustment, maturity, or adaptive behavior than standardized psychological tests. The difficulty is to insure that ratings across different classrooms provided by different teachers are comparable. In order to summarize teachers' observations in a valid and standardized manner, a rating scale might break an area down into well-defined components or behaviors, thereby increasing consistency among raters. For example, rather than asking about emotional stability in general, a measure might be composed of items regarding mood shifts, frustration tolerance, aggressive behaviors, etc.

Teacher ratings may also be used to rate academic areas, which is of particular use when children are too young for group achievement tests. Teacher ratings have been shown to be valid measures of school performance at the kindergarten level (Feshbach, Adelman, & Fuller, 1977; Keogh & Smith, 1970; Novack, Bonaventura, & Merenda, 1973; Tobeissen, Duckworth, & Conrad, 1971). The degree of standardization among teachers depends upon the uniformity of performance demands across classrooms and upon the specific rating measure used. To insure adequate consistency across raters, a rating measure must clearly define the behaviors or dimensions to be rated and provide objective standards upon which to base judgments. While many rating scales are too vague, others address the need for objectivity by asking highly specific questions (e.g., "Can the child work independently on an assignment for at least 10 minutes?") or by requiring raters to select among response options that involve precise estimates of frequency (e.g., the behavior is observed "more than half, but less than 90 percent of the time"). The goal of objectivity is lost if a teacher does not have such specific knowledge about the child, or is unable to make such precise judgments. Or, it is possible that a rating scale containing many specific items is highly valid, but too lengthy to elicit the cooperation of teachers who may be requested to complete a large number of them. If questions arise regarding the utility of rating measures, a sample of teachers should be asked to review the measure.

A rating measure format that is specifically geared to validation of preschool screening measures has teachers rate children's functioning in terms of their apparent needs for special educational services. An example of this is provided by the questionnaire in Figure 4-7. In addition to defining response categories using descriptions of a child's level of needs, this questionnaire provides normative guidelines to insure greater consistency in rating standards. For example, the "severe problem" category is defined as "child needs special educational planning in order to acquire school related skills," and is proposed to include the bottom 5–10 percent of the population.

The most thorough type of criterion measure is a *diagnostic evaluation,* which is typically initiated only when substantial concerns are raised about a school-age child. This is analogous to the further assessment process that follows screening. A diagnostic evaluation may involve standardized tests, clinical observation, information provided by teachers and parents, and other data assembled by a psychologist or educational specialist. Due to the cost involved, the number of diagnostic evaluations that may be conducted expressly for a predictive validity study would likely be limited. As in the case of preschool level assessments, an individually-administered general cognitive measure could serve as a more cost-effective substitute for a complete evaluation.

Another possible criterion measure is the child's *educational status* as defined by administrative decisions such as grade promotion and placement in special education programs. This may at first appear to be an ideal criterion measure. First, decisions about a child's educational status incorporate information from all other types of follow-up data, i.e., achievement tests, teacher judgment, and diagnostic evaluation. Second, the child's status constitutes the school system's operational definition of whether or not the child is having special problems. But anyone familiar with the nature of referral, placement, and retention decisions in schools will recognize that consistency is a major drawback to using administratively-defined status as a criterion measure. For example, some kindergarten teachers are hesitant to refer children who are having difficulty for special education services because of their reservations about premature classification. Or, special services may perhaps not be pursued because individualized instruction can best be provided for a child in the regular classroom. Also, placement decisions may be based upon situation-specific factors such as characteristics of the specific regular vs. special settings considered, or upon the availability of an open slot in a special program. An additional concern is that a child's special placement may have initially originated with the screening/early identification process; therefore, it may be impossible to determine whether a screening referral is the direct cause of the criterion measure status or whether the child would have been identified as needing special services regardless. Use of administratively-determined criterion measures is most appropriate in a school system where standards for special educational placement and grade retention are clearly established and uniformly applied. As a rule, however, standardized tests and teacher ratings provide criterion data of greater validity.

Throughout this section on criterion measures, it has been assumed that follow-up data will classify children into groups, as required for hit rate analysis. Criterion measures such as assessment process decisions and educational status are already in classificational form, and naturally sort children into categories that correspond to problem base rates. Continuously-scored measures such as standardized test scores can be dichotomized by setting cutoff scores at levels corresponding to problem base rates (i.e., in the general vicinity of the 5th to 10th percentile, or some other level established by the local programs).

Special Issues in Validating Screening Procedures

Evaluation of screening procedures introduces some complex and troublesome issues. The first two issues to be taken up, involving the screening/follow-up time interval and the effect of interventions upon a validity study, pertain specifically to the case of predictive validity.

Time Interval Between Screening and Follow-up

How far into the future should early identification decisions predict? One position is that there is no real need for preschool screening to predict far into school years, since information obtained after the child is in school will be far more useful than preschool screening results for predicting school performance in later grades. Thus, the practical importance of preschool screening is to identify children with special needs through that point in time when cost-effective measures such as group achievement tests and teacher ratings attain high validity. Research suggests that this point is reached by the end of kindergarten or beginning of first grade (Eaves, Kendall, & Crichton, 1974; Lichtenstein, 1980a; Novack, Bonaventura, & Merenda, 1973). Following this logic, follow-up evaluation should extend no further than first grade at the latest.

Another line of reasoning, however, is to argue that long-term prevention is the ultimate objective of an early identification program; that is, children are identified and served at a young age because they are at risk for developing substantial problems in future years. Therefore, long-term follow-up studies are needed to determine which children are truly in need of early intervention, and how accurately they can be identified. *The Children of Kauai* (Werner, Bierman, & French, 1971) is a classic example of a study investigating these questions. Perhaps this issue can be resolved by regarding long-term longitudinal studies as the domain of academic research, while either concurrent validity or predictive validity through the kindergarten or first grade level is sufficient for "in-house" evaluation of preschool screening procedures.

A Methodological Confound Due To Intervention

A matter that seriously complicates evaluation of screening procedures concerns the effect that early intervention may have upon a child's status by the time follow-up measures are obtained. The purpose of early identification is to identify those children who are likely to experience school problems and to intervene so as to prevent such an occurrence. To the extent that this is successful, predictive validity study results are distorted. Consider the case of a child who is referred from screening and receives special services, but when follow-up evaluation takes place the child is classified as not having special educational needs. It cannot be determined whether the child was incorrectly identified, or whether the child improved markedly due to the success of the intervention. Hence, the problem is that the ultimate objective of preschool screening, providing early intervention for children who are predicted to fail in school, is to confound this prediction.

How can it be determined whether the prediction would have been right? The ideal procedure in terms of research design would be to provide intervention for no children at all, and thereby determine just how accurate these early predictions of school problems prove to be. This, of course, is unacceptable given ethical and legal obligations to provide special services when there is an apparent need. Given these constraints, a predictive validity study must be implemented with a less-than-ideal design.

One such design is to use different criterion measures for children who receive special services and for those who do not. For children receiving services, the criterion measure might be derived from evaluation of the child's functioning early on in the intervention program, that is, some time after the child has had a chance to adjust and there has been sufficient opportunity to observe his or her performance, but before significant gains could be attributed to the intervention (perhaps six to eight weeks into the program). Those children not receiving intervention services would be evaluated using other follow-up measures following school entry such as described earlier.

Another approach, which might be considered in situations where only children with moderate to severe handicapping conditions are identified, is to reason that a child with substantial problems would still be distinguishable as a problem group child in the early years of school even with the benefit of an effective intervention program. If this is the case, the confound due to early intervention might simply be ignored. Follow-up data, although subject to some distortion, would still suffice for comparing the accuracy of one screening procedure or process versus another. As for estimating base rates that would be obtained in the absence of intervention programs, the possibility that certain children are classified upon follow-up as not having special needs due to intervention-induced gains might be investigated on a case by case basis.

The complications of a predictive validity study may outweigh its potential value. The simplest solution of all is to confine evaluation of screening procedures to concurrent validity. To the extent that the predictive validity of concurrent criterion measures is known, this may be used to estimate the predictive validity of screening procedures in turn. The drawback to this, however, is the failure to address the critical question of whether early identification procedures, and screening procedures in particular, are able to predict a child's future status.

Comparing Alternative Screening Procedures

Validating screening results against a common criterion measure provides a basis for comparing individual screening procedures or alternative sets of screening procedures. Examples of such comparisons have already been presented where referral rates are fairly well matched, which greatly simplifies matters. If two procedures have similar sensitivity rates, then the one with higher specificity may be regarded as having greater validity (assuming that the comparison is based on the same population). Similarly, if specificity rates match, the procedure with higher sensitivity has greater validity.

What of the situation where one procedure has a higher sensitivity rate while the other has the higher specificity rate, which is quite likely when referral rates differ considerably. Or suppose the screener wishes to compare the accuracy of two screening processes for various purposes, each involving different referral rates. As noted earlier in this chapter, overall hit rate (i.e., proportion of accurate screening decisions) is not an effective means of summarizing hit rate table results. Comparison of overall hit rates tends to favor the procedure with the lower referral rate.

One solution to this dilemma involves representing the sensitivity and specificity rates associated with hit rate tables as points on a two-dimensional graph (Harber, 1981; Lichtenstein, 1980a). Figure 5-10 shows how graph points for various hit rate patterns, each derived from a separate cutoff point or decision rule for the given screening procedure, describe a curve that characterizes the procedure's validity. Screening procedures A and B, which could just as well be alternative screening processes, are validated against the same criterion measure. The two can be compared on specificity for a given level of sensitivity, and vice versa. In the example, Procedure A has higher sensitivity than Procedure B when cutoff scores are set to achieve low or moderate levels of specificity. But at a specificity level of .95, Procedure B has higher sensitivity. Validity data presented in this manner is extremely valuable to other potential users. Unfortunately, validity studies reported in the literature rarely provide sufficient data from which to generate a validity curve.

Some screening procedures cannot be manipulated so as to match referral rates across alternatives. Comparing them is like trying to compare Procedures A and B in Figure 5-10 given one point towards the upper-left for Procedure A and one point toward the lower-right for

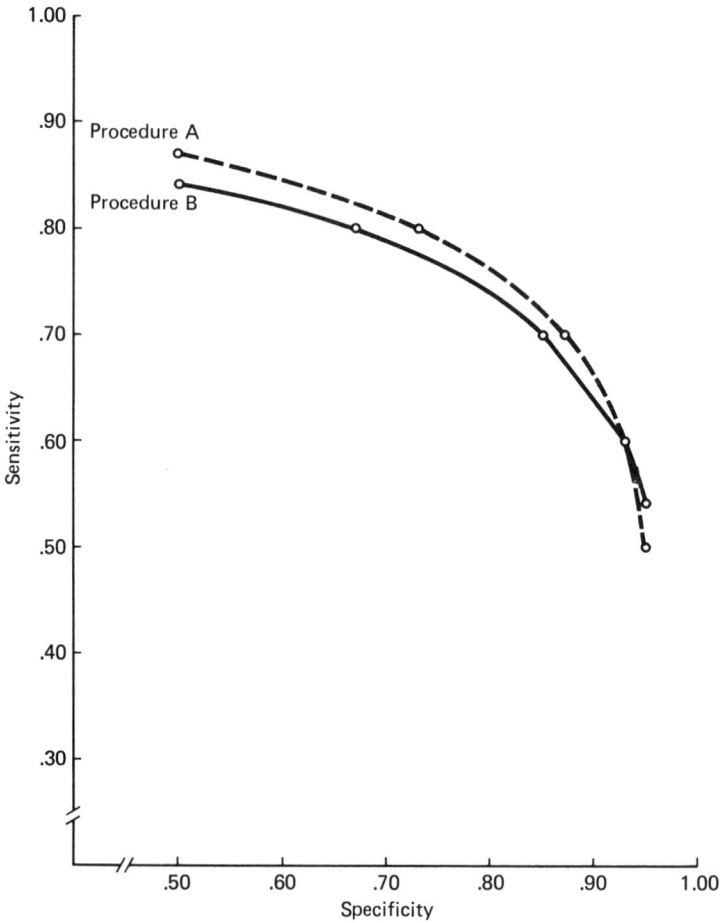

Fig. 5-10. Graphic representation of sensitivity and specificity.

Procedure B—not the entire curves. A comparison of this sort presents the same predicament as choosing between two different cutoff points for the same procedure, as illustrated by the Figure 5-3 example early in this chapter. Unless one procedure has higher sensitivity *and* specificity, or unless there is a striking disparity in the trade-off between under-referral and over-referral errors for the two, it is a matter of preference as to which hit rate pattern is more desirable.

As a reminder, validity data comparing alternative screening procedures provide the user with valuable information, but this should not serve as the sole criterion for selecting measures. One cannot designate one option as more favorable than another without also taking other factors into account, including the utility of the overall sequential decision-making process of which the procedure is a part. Harber (1981) makes this point in an excellent scholarly article on utility of decision-making in special education:

> . . . a test that requires little time investment in terms of administration and interpretation, is inexpensive, can be administered by relatively untrained personnel, and/or is suitable for group administration, may yield a greater proportion of incorrect decisions than does a test that requires great time investment, trained personnel, expensive equipment, and individual administration; and yet the former test may be found to have greater utility than the latter. (p. 423)

That is, the briefer and less valid test, used in combination with other measures, enables the overall process to have greater value.

IDENTIFYING BIAS IN SCREENING

Over the past 20 years, policies concerning the assessment and educational placement of children have come under attack for being unfair to certain groups—particularly minorities. Standardized tests have been a primary target of this controversy. Mercer (1973) heightened awareness of this issue with documentation that minority groups are over-represented in restrictive special classes, and that inappropriate and persistent labels may result from poor performance on standardized intelligence tests. The 1970s saw the battleground move to the courts. Various court cases (*Guadalupe* v. *Tempe, Diana* v. *State Board of Education, Larry P.* v. *Riles, PASE* v. *Hannon*) reviewed evidence that standardized test results are inappropriately used to assign minority group children to special educational placements. Standardized tests have been cited as discriminatory due to (1) *content bias*—the use of test material, language, or item types that are unfamiliar to children of certain backgrounds, or of scoring procedures that fail to account for language or cultural differences, and (2) *atmosphere bias*—test situation or examiner characteristics that have a detrimental effect upon a child's motivation or performance.

The issue of bias in assessment goes beyond testing as well. Studies have shown classification and placement decision-making by professionals in education to be influenced by physical appearance, prior expectations introduced by referral information, and previously-assigned disability labels. Concerns have also been raised about the fairness of assessment procedures across other dimensions, e.g., sex and SES.

In light of these concerns, Public Law 94-142 included the provision that

> Procedures to assure that testing and evaluation materials and procedures utilized for the purposes of evaluation and placement of handicapped children will be selected and administered so as not to be racially or culturally discriminatory. Such materials or procedures shall be provided and administered in the child's native language or mode of communication, unless it clearly is not feasible to do so, and no single procedure shall be the sole criterion for determining an appropriate educational program for a child.

But the federal law provides no definition of "racially or culturally discriminatory," nor guidelines to safeguard against such practices. While no one would take issue with the general principle that evaluation and placement should be biased towards none, the specific meaning of bias has been the subject of diverse opinions (see Flaugher, 1978; Cole, 1981).

A popular view has been to regard group differences in test scores or in assessment outcomes (e.g., proportion of a group assigned to special classes) as evidence of bias. In fact, the injunction against the use of IQ tests in California resulting from the celebrated *Larry P.* v. *Riles* case stipulated that, in order to be acceptable, an intelligence test must yield equivalent means for different racial/ cultural groups. This argument makes the assumption that differences in group scores reflect an artifact of the assessment instrument, rather than real and meaningful group differences.* According to this logic, it would be unacceptable for low-SES children to be identified and served at a higher rate than middle- and upper-SES children. Yet, it is to be expected that an economically-disadvantaged group will receive low test scores, and this appropriately signals the need for a relatively high rate of special educational services for this group. An assessment instrument that yielded similar scores for high SES and low SES children would probably not be sensitive to relevant differences in skills and achievement, and thus would be of limited value for distinguishing between high risk and low risk individuals.

Another approach is to define bias in terms of the mechanisms that are proposed to account for it, i.e., content bias and atmosphere bias. Identifying the dynamics of bias allows us to study how and to what extent biasing factors operate, and how they may be eliminated. With

---

*The sentiment that group differences in test scores are discriminatory and unacceptable appears to derive from the misconception that IQ tests and other cognitive measures are simply indicators of natural ability, and groups that perform poorly must therefore be less capable. In actuality, intelligence tests largely measure achievement, and cannot assess inate ability apart from the effects of prior learning, background experiences, and motivation.

regard to content bias, efforts to determine whether certain test items discriminate against members of a given culture or race have provided no clear evidence to this effect. Also, attempts to develop culture-fair tests, such as by eliminating culture-bound elements or using nonverbal tasks, have been largely unproductive. The general finding of much recent research using these and other approaches to identifying test bias is that "conventional tests are nearly always found to be largely unbiased" (Reschly, 1983, p. 75). This is not to say that research results contradict the fact that commonly used tests are heavily culture-laden. Rather, what may be tentatively concluded is that (1) minority groups are not necessarily penalized by test items with high mainstream-culture loadings relative to other items, and (2) that culture-laden tests, being relevant to educational objectives (which are themselves culturally bound), provide meaningful information that cannot be duplicated by culture-free tests. With regard to atmosphere bias, studies of test situation variables such as rapport, reinforcement, and examiner sex and race have not consistently shown effects upon test results, and in studies where effects have been demonstrated these have been of a relatively small magnitude (see Reschly, 1979; Sattler, 1970).

These findings on content and atmosphere bias have their limitations, however. First, they focus on tests, rather than on the overall assessment process. In so doing, various considerations that may affect educational decisions are disregarded. For example, the method of publicizing a screening program and the availability of child care services may affect the level of participation of low-SES parents. Or, professionals using clinical judgment to arrive at screening decisions may, consciously or unconsciously, make mental adjustments in interpreting results for a particular group and consequently over-predict or under-predict their educational prospects. Second, research studies tend to assume that tests will be selected, administered, and interpreted as per instructions and in accordance with recommended assessment procedures. As a result, they overlook the type of bias that is perhaps most prevalent—bias in decision-making due to inappropriate practices at any of the several stages of the assessment process.

Ironically, it is not the tests themselves, which have been the object of such controversy and condemnation, so much as inappropriate test use and interpretation that constitute the major sources of bias. Ysseldyke (1979), citing research showing that educational decisions are subject to bias due to diagnostically irrelevant pupil characteristics, contends that "if educators suddenly had *the* fair test, there would still be considerable bias in decision-making" (p. 156). He advocates, as have others, to guard against bias by responsible and informed professional practices throughout the assessment process. This typically includes guidelines such as (1) obtaining a wide array of information from multiple sources, (2) selecting reliable and valid instruments that are appropriate for the intended use and for the given population, (3) providing adequate testing conditions, (4) effectively establishing and maintaining rapport, (5) cultivating sensitivity to cultural, language, physical, and sensory differences, (6) involving professionals from multiple disciplines, as needed, in the assessment, and (7) adhering to procedural safeguards designed to insure that parents are informed and involved in the assessment process. (These points correspond in large part to the rules and regulations provided in the *Federal Register,* August 23, 1977, pp. 42474–42581, to expand upon the general provisions of P.L. 94–142.) Other recommendations include the use of state of the art measurement techniques such as criterion-referenced assessment, process assessment (see Meyers, Pfeffer, & Erlbaum, 1983), and dynamic assessment (see Lidz, 1983). It should be noted that these guidelines are no different from measurement and assessment practices that are recommended for use with all children.

Consistent with this emphasis upon the overall assessment process, and with its outcome in particular, the definition of bias that is generally endorsed by measurement experts is that of *fairness in use.* The essence of this definition is that assessment should be equally valid for all groups. This approach, which focuses on the accuracy of decisions that result from assessment, is particularly applicable to screening. A screening instrument may be considered free from bias if it makes referral decisions that are consistent with individuals' needs regardless of group membership. Since no identification measure is perfectly accurate, this means that a screening procedure is unbiased if over-referral and under-referral errors occur at similar rates for any given group within the screening population.

Thus, for the case of SES differences, the familiar pattern where preschool screening procedures refer higher percentages of low-SES than of high-SES children is not, in itself, evidence of bias. If this is consistent with group trends in prevalence of later educational problems, it is appropriate to make referrals and to provide services at a higher rate for the low-SES group (assuming, of course, that the "right" children are referred and served).

An example using MPSI validity data illustrates this point. As shown in Table 5-4, the MPSI referred 25 percent of low-SES children, but only 8 percent of high-SES children in the screening population. This was fairly consistent with criterion measure outcomes indicating that 13 percent of low-SES children, compared to 2 percent of high-SES children, experienced significant problems in kindergarten. Most important, the validity rates are fairly comparable for the two groups.

Table 5-4
MPSI Validity Data by SES Group

| | LOW SES | | |
| | Overall teaching rating | | |
MPSI	Moderate to severe problems	No major problems	Total
Refer	22	25	47
Pass	3	138	141
Total	25	163	188
	HIGH SES		
	Overall teaching rating		
MPSI	Moderate to severe problems	No major problems	Total
Refer	3	16	19
Pass	1	220	221
Total	4	236	240

(Note: lower hit rates are to be expected for the high-SES group, given the substantially lower problem base rate.)

In this same manner, the validity of the overall screening process for one group versus another can be compared. Evaluation results may indicate that the screening process tends to over-refer a given group, as indicated by a higher rate of over-referral errors and a lower rate of under-referral errors in comparison to the general population. If so, different decision rules would be needed for the group in question, in this case, a decision rule that referred fewer children.

An example of decision rules that differ by group is provided by the DIAL, which uses lower cutoff scores for males than for females so as to equalize referral rates. The implicit assumption in doing so is that the difference in referral rates that would result if the same decision rule were used (with more males referred than females) is inconsistent with actual needs; that is, the referral rates are equalized because males and females are presumed to require special services at a comparable rate. Follow-up evaluation of a DIAL screening sample, analyzed by sex, can best determine whether this is indeed the case.

Validation of screening procedures by group may also reveal a pattern of a different type: it may be discovered that a particular group is screened less accurately than the remainder of the population. The problem in this case is not a tendency toward over-referral or under-referral, but that the screening process predicts too poorly for the given group—resulting in higher rates of both over-referral and under-referral errors. This is not the same as assessment bias, where correcting a systematic inequity in the decision rule results in more consistent validity rates across groups. The screening process simply does not work as well for the given group. It may be necessary to use different screening procedures or to obtain additional screening information for this group in order to achieve a level of accuracy that is consistent with the rest of the population.

It has been proposed to this point that the hit rate model used to evaluate screening decisions can also be used to identify bias in screening. However, one cannot conclude the absence of bias from comparable hit rates between groups if the criterion measure, be it a standardized test, teacher rating, or evaluation outcome, is also biased. A screening procedure could appear to be unbiased when a particular group has a disproportionately high number of cases of inaccurately referred children, if the criterion measure misclassifies these same children as having problems. This illustrates (although, admittedly, without entirely resolving the dilemma) the need to guard against bias at all levels of decision-making, including follow-up assessment and criterion measurement.

Clearly, the issue of bias raises more questions than have been resolved. At present, methods for identifying and eliminating causes of bias are not all that advanced, and given the nature of the problem, are unlikely to be for some time to come. As with evaluation in general, however, some effort is far better than none and the imperative to address the matter is clear. Professionals can address the issue of screening bias on two levels: preventively, by promoting responsible assessment practices throughout the screening process, and, post hoc, by evaluating the validity of screening procedures and of the screening process for different groups.

THE LIMITS OF PREDICTION: HOW ACCURATE IS EARLY IDENTIFICATION?

Throughout this book, we have encouraged the reader to pay special attention to the decision-making accuracy of screening procedures. This was first introduced as a theoretical concern, i.e., Is the assumption justified that subsequent educational problems can be identified at the preschool age level? The hit rate model was then introduced as having practical significance in selecting screening procedures, in choosing among alternative decision strategies, and in evaluating the effectiveness of the screening process.

We have repeatedly made the point that some percentage of screening errors is unavoidable. Individual differences in rate of development, situational variations in human functioning, and imprecise definitions of developmental or educational problems all impose limitations upon our capacity to predict later school-age performance. The question is, What are the limits of prediction? At what point must we abandon heroic efforts to upgrade decision-making accuracy and accept that further efforts to approach the asymptote will be wasteful and unproductive?

Let us first review validity studies of developmental screening procedures in which follow-up interval is not a factor; that is, for concurrent validity studies. Two studies discussed in Chapter 4 reveal that a high degree of correspondence can be obtained between a screening measure and criterion measure administered at about the same time. Frankenburg, Camp, and Van Natta (1971) demonstrated high concordance between the Denver Developmental Screening Test and comprehensive measures of early development and intelligence (see Table 4-8). Almost all children (12 of 13) with intelligence test results in the below-70 range were identified as "abnormal" by the DDST, and 60 percent of DDST "abnormals" (12 of 20) proved to be in the below-70 range on the criterion measures. Concurrent validity of the Early Screening Inventory measured against the McCarthy Scales of Children's Abilities attained a similar high level: the ESI referred 17 of the 23 children with MSCA scores below 85, and 68 percent of the children classified as "refer" by the ESI were found to be in the MSCA high risk (below-85) group (see Table 4-10).

These high levels of concurrent validity are not surprising given the evidence that screening instruments can attain high test-retest reliability over short periods of time. After all, two measures that are highly similar in content should be able to produce results that correspond almost as highly as the same measure administered twice. A rather different situation applies, however, to efforts to classify children accurately (i.e., consistently) over longer periods of time. First, rates and patterns of developmental change are subject to individual differences. Second, there are differences in the nature of the functions assessed in moving from a developmental focus at the preschool level to an educational focus at school age.

An exhaustive survey of the research literature was conducted to find all instances in which early identification measures were validated against subsequent educational status. The predictors in this survey were not limited to screening procedures, but included any identification procedure (or set of procedures) that yielded classificational out-

Table 5-5
Summary of Early Identification Predictive Validity Studies Using Independently-Derived Decision Rules

Study	N	Screening sample	Prediction interval	Predictor	Criterion	Sensitivity	Specificity	Efficiency of referral*
Ferinden & Jacobsen (1970)	67	Kdg.	8 mos.	Evanston Early Identification Scale	Wide Range Achievement Test—Reading	.55	.79	.33
Ferinden & Jacobsen (1970)	67	Kdg.	8 mos.	Metropolitan Readiness Test	Wide Range Achievement Test—Reading	.45	.95	.63
Feshbach, Adelman, & Fuller (1974)	572	Kdg., IQ ≥ 90	15 mos.	deHirsch Index	Gates Reading Test	.26	.93	.61
Feshbach, Adelman, & Fuller (1974)	585	Kdg., IQ ≥ 90	15 mos.	Rating scale	Gates Reading Test	.30	.97	.83
Feshbach, Adelman, & Fuller (1977)	536	Kdg., IQ ≥ 90	2 yrs.	deHirsch Index	Cooperative Reading Tests	.38	.91	.32
Feshbach, Adelman, & Fuller (1977)	549	Kdg., IQ ≥ 90	2 yrs.	Rating scale	Cooperative Reading Tests	.46	.93	.46
Feshbach, Adelman, & Fuller (1977)	431	Kdg., IQ ≥ 90	3 yrs.	deHirsch Index	Cooperative Reading Tests	.29	.91	.25
Feshbach, Adelman, & Fuller (1977)	451	Kdg., IQ ≥ 90	3 yrs.	Rating scale	Cooperative Reading Tests	.43	.95	.49
Ireton & Thwing (1979)	287	Pre-Kdg.	1 yr.	Minnesota Preschool Inventory	Teacher ratings	.60	.89	.30
Lichtenstein (1982)	428	Pre-Kdg.	1½ yrs.	MPSI	Teacher ratings	.63	.93	.62

Study	N	Grade	Interval	Screening measure	Criterion measure			
Lichtenstein (1982)	428	Pre-Kdg.	1½ yrs.	DIAL	Teacher ratings	.54	.93	.59
Lichtenstein (1982)	296	Pre-Kdg.	2 yrs.	MPSI	Metropolitan Readiness Test	.56	.93	.62
Lichtenstein (1982)	296	Pre-Kdg.	2 yrs.	DIAL	Metropolitan Readiness Test	.46	.94	.61
Lindemann et al. (1967)	72	Pre-Kdg.	1–3 yrs.	Clinical interview	Teacher ratings	.31	.91	.50
Lindquist (1982)	351	Pre-Kdg.	1½ yrs.	DDST	Gates-MacGinitie Reading Test	.29	.89	.47
Satz, Friel, & Rudegair (1976)	151	Kdg. males	2½ yrs.	Abbreviated Satz Battery	Teacher rating, IOTA Word Recognition	.76	.71	.35
Stevenson, Parker, Wilkinson, Hegion, & Fish (1976b)	152	Kdg.	2½ yrs.	Teacher rating	WRAT, Stanford Achievement	.21	.93	.25
Wiske, Meisels, & Tivnan (1982)	78	Pre-Kdg.	1½ yrs.	ESI	Academic grades	.92	.72	.40
Wiske, Meisels, & Tivnan (1982)	85	Pre-Kdg.	1½ yrs.	ESI	Special services	.81	.72	.41
Wiske, Meisels, & Tivnan (1982)	60	Pre-Kdg.	2½ yrs.	ESI	Academic grades	1.00	.67	.32
Wiske, Meisels, & Tivnan (1982)	62	Pre-Kdg.	2½ yrs.	ESI	Special services	.81	.70	.48

*Proportion of referred children falling in criterion measure problem group, i.e., likelihood that "refer" outcome is accurate.

comes. (This was necessary because distinctions between screening and assessment procedures can be rather obscure, particularly in research studies.)

Several criteria were established for inclusion of studies in this survey. First, the studies were to involve young children, with identification procedures administered at kindergarten level or earlier. In all of the studies except one, the predictors were administered during the kindergarten year or within several months of school entry. The second criterion was that the prediction interval had to be of sufficient length, spanning at least one school year. Third, results had to be presented in classificational form so that hit rate tables could be constructed to summarize validity. For studies in which predictors or criteria were divided into more than two outcome categories, categories were combined so as to dichotomize measures as near as possible to the 15th percentile. Studies in which variables were only dichotomized near the mean, that is, in which referral rates or problem base rates were set near 50 percent, were ruled out as unrepresentative of early identification situations. Last of all, a minimum sample size of 50 children was established.

Before presenting survey findings, a caution of sorts is in order. Although it is of interest to compare the validity rates obtained with different types of early identification measures and with various specific instruments, it is generally inappropriate to make such comparisons from survey data because the studies vary in terms of sample composition, criterion measures, and follow-up intervals. The survey was primarily intended to provide a general sense of prediction hit rates, but could, perhaps, illuminate "suggestive" patterns if rather consistent differences between methods were found.

Tables 5-5 and 5-6 summarize the 16 longitudinal studies included in the survey, some of which reported results for more than one predictor, criterion, and/or follow-up point. Hit rates were computed for a total of 33 predictor-criterion pairings that met the conditions for inclusion in the survey.

One pattern that dominated survey results is that substantially higher hit rates were obtained in studies that used sample-specific decision rules as a basis for predictions; that is, in which cutoff points or other decision rules were devised "after the fact" so as to maximize the hit rates obtained in the particular study. Subsequent cross-validation of such decision rules is called for in order to get a true picture of decision-making accuracy. This is such a biasing factor that validity data based on sample-specific decision rules are presented in a separate table.

The need to distinguish between hit rates obtained with idepen-dently-derived decision rules (Table 5-5) and with sample-specific deci-sion rules (Table 5-6) may seem rather obvious when given special attention, but often forgotten in the excitement of apparent break-throughs in early identification. A particular case in point is the de Hirsch, Jansky, & Langford (1966) study that sparked high hopes for early prediction of reading failure. The remarkably high hit rates ob-tained in this study, i.e., sensitivity of .91 and specificity of .90, far outstripped validity rates obtained by any early identification pro-cedure previously—or since. The study involved many predictor vari-ables and relatively few children, both of which increase the likelihood that validity rates will "shrink" upon cross-validiation. The authors' later cross-validation study (Jansky & de Hirsch, 1973), using the same decision rules devised earlier, yielded so many errors that the original scoring system was revamped. (The data from the Janksy and de Hirsch study reported in Table 5-6 are based on a revised scoring system.) Other researchers (Eaves, Kendall, & Crichton, 1974; Fesh-bach, Adelman, & Fuller, 1974, 1977) who cross-validated the original de Hirsch battery and scoring system obtained similar results.

It is from the studies using independently-derived decision rules that we get a real sense of the highest levels at which we have been able to predict future educational status of young children. The results are humbling, indeed. Inspecting the validity data presented in Table 5-5, one finds that when sensitivity rates exceed .50, specificity rates are generally below .90 (meaning that over 10 percent of normal group children are referred) and often below .80 (over 20 percent of normals incorrectly referred). Furthermore, for most of these studies, predic-tion of high risk status proves to be substantiated by follow-up measure outcomes less than half of the time, i.e., efficiency of referral is gener-ally below .50. When efficiency of referral does surpass .50, it is rarely the case that sensitivity is also above .50, i.e., that more than 50 percent of target group children are identified. Interestingly, the only study in which both of these conditions were met involved predictions by two individual screening tests (see Lichtenstein, 1982 data in Table 5-5).

Some specific studies provided findings of interest. One study (Feshbach, Adelman, & Fuller, 1974, 1977) was conducted so as to provide direct comparisons between an observational predictor (a teacher rating scale) and standardized tests (the de Hirsch battery). Results showed a consistent advantage in favor of the teacher observa-tions. It should be noted, however, that the ratings were based on observations by kindergarten teachers over a period of eight weeks, an

Table 5-6
Summary of Early Identification Predictive Validity Studies Using Sample-Specific Decision Rules

Study	N	Screening sample	Prediction interval	Predictor	Criterion	Sensitivity	Specificity	Efficiency of referral*
Book (1974)	435	Kdg.	1 yr.	Metropolitan Readiness Test, Bender-Gestalt, Slosson Test	Reading level	1.00	.83	.33
Book (1974)	219	Kdg.	2 yrs.	Metropolitan Readiness Test, Bender-Gestalt, Slosson Test	Reading level	.94	.87	.54
Eaves, Kendall & Crichton (1974)	163	Kdg	2 yrs.	Modified deHirsch Index, teacher ratings	Recommended grade level	.63	.90	.60
Farrar & Leigh (1972)	1067	Ages 4–7	1 yr.	Lateralization, speech problems	Schonell Word Recognition	.66	.93	.61
de Hirsch, Jansky, & Langford (1966)	53	Kdg.	2 yrs.	de Hirsch Index	Gray Oral, Gates Reading Tests	.91	.90	.71
Ireton, Lun, & Kampen (1981)	287	Pre-Kdg.	1 yr.	Minnesota Preschool Inventory	Teacher ratings	.60	.97	.57
Jansky & de Hirsch (1973)	282	Kdg.	2 yrs.	Jansky Predictive Index	Gray Oral, Gates Reading Test	.77	.66	.58

Satz & Friel (1974)	473	Kdg. males	1½ yrs.	Satz battery	Teacher rating of reading level	.78	.86	.50
Satz, Friel, & Rudegair (1976)†	419	Kdg. males	2½ yrs.	Satz battery	Teacher rating, IOTA Word Recognition	.91	.66	.34
Stevenson, Parker, Wilkinson, Hegion, & Fish (1976a)	134	Pre-Kdg.	3 yrs.	Psychometric tasks	WRAT, Stanford Achievement	.33	.96	.45
Szasz, Baade, & Paskewicz (1980)	141	Kdg.	8 mos.	Human Figure Drawings (developmental scores)	Metropolitan Readiness Test	.40	.89	.61
Szasz, Baade, & Paskewicz (1980)	141	Kdg.	8 mos.	Human Figure Drawings (emotional scores)	Metropolitan Readiness Test	.67	.63	.45

* Proportion of referred chidren falling in criterion measure problem group, i.e., likelihood that "refer" outcome is accurate.
† The decision rule established with this sample was cross-validated on a separate sample. The cross-validated validity rates, reported in this same study, appear in Table 5.5

optimal type of situation for observational reports, whereas the comparison measure, the de Hirsch battery, has proved to be less valid than originally thought.

Studies predicting later school performance from measures of social-emotional adjustment are too few from which to generalize, but their results are, as might be expected, not very encouraging. Lindemann et al. (1967) found that preschool children whose maturity and adjustment were rated as poor on the basis of screening interviews with the child and the parent were as likely to be rated as achieving at a superior or satisfactory level as below average in the early grades. The study obtained teacher ratings of social-emotional adjustment as an additional criterion measure. The correspondence between preschool screening outcomes and this follow-up rating of adjustment was only slightly better than chance. (This was not included in Table 5-5 because results were reported by combining ratings of fair and poor into a single category that included 45 percent of the sample.) Szasz, Baade, and Paskewicz (1980) obtained respectable validity rates using Koppitz's (1968) emotional scoring system for Human Figure Drawings, but further analysis indicated that emotional scores were highly correlated with (and, thus, not appreciably different from) developmental scores, and that the two combined (by multiple regression) provided no improvement over either score used by itself. With these two studies, we are reminded of the measurement difficulties that plague the social-emotional area and impose even more severe limits than for early identification in general.

In summarizing survey results (keeping in mind the limited opportunities for fine-grained analysis), there were no clear trends reflecting an advantage for any particular type of early identification measure—for tests compared with observations or parent reports, for brief vs. length measures, for single measures vs. complete batteries, etc. But a striking and significant pattern emerges when validity data based on *post hoc* manipulations are excepted from prediction studies in general, namely, that early identification procedures administered at or before kindergarten level have not been shown to predict later school problems beyond a rather limited degree.

In reviewing the factors that work against classificational consistency over time at the preschool and early primary levels, this circumstance seems unlikely to change. Rates at which children develop vary; the relevant functions to be measured change in nature; children near the borderline between arbitrarily divided categories fluctuate between at risk and normal status. Technological advances in the measurement process simply cannot compensate for the uncertainties of trying to definitively classify a changing organism that interacts with changing environments at a single point in time. Given these circumstances, efforts to stretch the upper limits of predictions might be better directed towards devising more realistic ways of conceptualizing screening and early identification outcomes.

BEYOND SIMPLISTIC SCREENING DECISIONS

At least part of the reason why we are so limited in our ability to make accurate screening decisions about young children is because of the restrictive way in which screening outcomes are expressed. It has been repeatedly emphasized that screening is a decision-making process, the essence of which is to yield one or two outcomes, "refer" or "do not refer," which are intended to correspond to whether or not a child is in need of special services. The inadequacies of this two-category classification system have been touched on at numerous points throughout the book. Classifying chilaren who are near the borderline between "problematic" and "normal" status is a precarious and even arbitrary task. Classification decisions may depend upon definitions, assessment procedures, the decision-making process, and other factors that vary from program to program. Furthermore, children develop at various rates along a number of dimensions, so that their status may change over time in a way that confounds efforts at classification.

A two-category classification system, while highly inadequate for characterizing the development or educational status of the child, offers advantages of an administrative nature. A policy of providing special services only for a particular subset of the population (e.g., "handicapped children") requires that eligibility decisions be made. The assessment process then takes on the decision-making function of distinguishing between "problematic" and "normal" for purposes of documenting the need for services, allocating resources, enforcing procedural requirements, etc. Screening outcomes simply reflect the either-or logic that prevails throughout the service delivery system at an administrative level.

One respect in which the two-category classifcation system presents problems is that some children are so difficult to classify that a screen decision of either "pass" or "refer" is inadvisable. This may be because screening information is of questionable validity, or because a child's screening results place the child in the difficult-to-resolve borderline range. To refer all such children is generally unfeasible because of the excessive number of over-referral errors that would result. What is needed in such cases is a third category, a screening outcome of "cannot say."

This "questionable range" screening outcome can subsequently be resolved in any of several ways. One approach is to defer a screening decision for children in the questionable range, pending the collection of additional information during a second or even third stage of the screening process. This strategy of screening in multiple stages was introduced earlier as the successive hurdles approach. One might argue that the successive hurdles approach is little different from referring all children in the questionable range for further assessment, since both involve a continuation of the decision process at a later stage of sequential assessment. The important difference is that further screening, as opposed to further assessment, of children in the questionable range is less costly and elaborate, thereby making use of meaningful distinctions (i.e., refer vs. questionable status) made in the initial screening stage. Given the availability of a third option that calls for further screening, it becomes easier to reserve judgment and seek more information.

A second possibility is to rescreen the child at a later point in time. The nature and effect of this option will vary depending upon whether the second screening occasion is in the near future or further off in time. Rescreening as soon as possible is also similar to the successive hurdles approach in that an additional stage is added to the screening process. The critical distinction is that the successive hurdles approach involves collecting an additional set of data on the same occasion, whereas rescreening involves repeating the same process on a separate occasion. While the successive hurdle strategy is useful when initial screening results are insufficient, rescreening is the strategy of choice when initial screening information appears to be invalid but there is reason to believe that more valid responses may be obtained on another occasion in the near future.

Rescreening after a period of perhaps several months has a different connotation. It is not simply daily variability in behavior, or familiarity with the screening situation, that may yield more useful results. The passing of time allows the opportunity for developmental changes, or lack thereof, so that a child's uncertain status might resolve itself by becoming more, or less, of a concern than at the initial screening. The child might also mature with time so that behaviors that previously interfered with efforts to obtain valid screening results are no longer a problem. This approach might be referred to as a special case of periodic screening (special in that it is used only with a selected set of children) to distinguish it from rescreening soon afterwards.

The advantage of the strategies introduced to this point is that they offer scaled-down, cost-effective alternatives to comprehensive further assessment. There is some evidence to suggest that, for children with only marginal indications of apparent problems, such options are more suitable than a standard referral. The follow-up status of children with invalid screening test results was investigated in a validity study (Lichtenstein, 1978) with a suburban preschool screening sample. Of those children who were referred for further assessment because of invalid screening test results, only 10 percent (2 of 19) were placed in the preschool intervention program, as compared to 39 percent of referred children with valid screening results. Another relevant finding is that validity data on screening tests that include an intermediate decision category (i.e., DDST, DIAL, ESI) consistently show that although children scoring in the intermediate range are at higher risk than the population at large, they are far more likely to be classified as functioning within normal range than within problematic range by criterion measures (see Chapter 4 reviews).

What unfortunately is unavailable is research data indicating the hit rates obtained when intermediate range outcomes are resolved by rescreening. The children falling in this range are most likely to be those troublesome cases that confound prediction efforts in spite of extensive and elaborate assessment procedures. Rescreening may be as unproductive as comprehensive assessment at one point in time. In these instances, an alternative to assessing beyond the point of diminishing returns is to extend the decision process into the future through what may be called *ongoing assessment*. Ongoing assessment might involve having parents systematically observe and record developmental functions, or having a preschool teacher monitor the child's progress. On the basis of this information, a referral for more comprehensive assessment can be made at any point in the future that the child's functioning deteriorates to a clearly problematic level. This strategy, in effect, shifts the nature of the task from prediction to that of "continuous identification." The two requirements that appear most likely to impose limitations on this strategy are the need for motivated and capable "ongoing assessors," and the availability of a professional consultant to help set up the assessment process and interpret results.

How would evaluation of screening decisions be affected by the introduction of additional screening outcome categories? The hit rate model could be applied essentially as before. The 2×2 hit rate table can be expanded to any dimensions. The only drawback is that validity becomes harder to characterize with the proliferation of cells in the hit rate table. A recommended procedure is to calculate the likelihood of different criterion outcomes for each screening outcome category,

Table 5-7

Hit Rate Analysis for Three Screening Categories

DIAL Outcome	Teacher Rating			
	Moderate to severe problems	Mild problem	No problem	Total
Refer	20	10	17	47
Re-DIAL	1	4	7	12
OK	8	22	339	369
Total	29	36	363	428

For refer outcome:
    Probability of moderate/severe problems =   20/47   = .43
    Probability of mild problems   =   10/47   = .21
    Probability of no problem   =   17/47   = .36

For re-DIAL outcome
    Probability of moderate/severe problems =   1/12   = .08
    Probability of mild problems   =   4/12   = .33
    Probability of no problem   =   7/12   = .58

For OK outcome
    Probability of moderate/severe problems =   8/369   = .02
    Probability of mild problems   =   22/369   = .06
    Probability of no problem   =   339/369   = .92

(From Lichtenstein, 1982. With permission.)

which is analogous to using the "efficiency of referral" and "efficiency of non-referral" hit rates for a 2×2 table. To illustrate with the DIAL validity data in Table 5-7, we find that the probability that children classified "re-DIAL" will have problems in kindergarten is .42 (5 of 12), while the probability that they will have no substantial problems is .58. These results can also be broken down using all three criterion categories: for children classified "re-DIAL," the probability of evidencing moderate to severe problems in kindergarten is .08, the probability of mild problems is .33, and the probability of no problems remains .58. The "refer" and "OK" classifications can be similarly broken down by criterion outcome, as shown. This type of analysis provides insight into the extent of uncertainty of the status of children scoring in the intermediate range (in this case, extreme), and further investigation can indicate how successfully rescreening or further assessment is able to resolve the uncertainty.

The greater flexibility introduced by additional screening classifications serves to make the process more workable, but does not address the basic inadequacies of the classificational system itself. An identification process that leads to characterizing children's development or educational status in terms of a problem/no problem dichotomy is inconsistent with the objective of providing services according to identified needs. A great many children do not fall neatly into one or the other category; they may function well in some respects, but could still benefit from special attention to specific needs. However, a child must be ruled "eligible" (i.e., disabled or handicapped) before needs are addressed. The child who is just on the "normal" side of the cutoff is regarded as having no special needs, while an identified child who may have similar needs is eligible for a full complement of special services.

Extricating the identification process from the tyranny of arbitrary classifications would require restructuring our service delivery systems. A more productive approach from the standpoint of meeting children's needs (although less so from an administrative perspective) is to think in terms of a diverse set of service options, ranging from indirect and limited to direct and comprehensive, that may be matched to a child's individual needs. This might constitute a continuum of services that incorporates both special and "nonspecial" interventions, for example: (1) providing information on parent education materials and programs, (2) referral to a regular preschool program, (3) direct consultation with parents on child development and management, (4) training parents to implement an early intervention program in the home, (5) providing professional services directly to the child on a limited (i.e., non-daily) basis, and (6) placing the child in an intensive early intervention program. The concept of providing special services in a flexible and individualized manner is hardly new. This is the essential element of Hobbs' (1975) proposed service delivery model and of Massachusetts' Chapter 766 legislation, both of which are designed to transcend problems of classification.

How might availability of a continuum of service options impact upon the screening process? These diverse options reduce the necessity of making classificational distinctions in borderline cases. Children who have relatively minor service needs or who cannot be classified with any degree of certainty can be served on a limited basis as their progress is continually monitored. This bears a resemblance to the multiple levels of service formally incorporated into the special education implementation plans of many states. A critical distinction, however, is that these service delivery plans apply only within special education; that is, only for children formally classified as eligible by virtue of their handicapped status. As a result, services that are not encompassed (and reimbursed) under the special education rubric, particularly those that focus on prevention of problems rather than intervention, are commonly disregarded. If systems were to shift in the direction of offering a more diverse and less restrictive set of options that are not dependent upon formal classification, the identification process could become more flexible and individualized as well.

Consistent with proposals described earlier, screening and assessment might be regarded as more of a unified, continuous process. One might picture a series of stages in which children's needs for special services are progressively defined, with the process continuing only to the point where decisions can be made. A severely disabled child might pass directly from an initial, brief assessment to the final stage of devising an educational plan if the child is obviously best suited for a comprehensive preschool intervention program. A child in the questionable range might be assessed at several successive stages that result in limited services being offered on a tentative basis while periodic or ongoing assessment leaves open the possibility that more comprehensive service needs may be identified in the future.

Meanwhile, given that the great majority of screening programs operate within the traditional screening model, it is important to regard screening in a way that keeps simplistic decision options in perspective. Even though the primary objective of screening is to make referral decisions, the wealth of information obtained need not be disregarded or discarded. Various types of feedback, such as clarification of developmental phenomena, parenting suggestions, educational resources, and information on community services may be of great benefit to parents, particularly parents of children who are not referred from screening.* A worthy objective is to maintain a positive balance between maximizing the efficiency and effectiveness of the decision-making process, and attending to the immediate importance of interactions with parents and children in the course of screening.

SUMMARY

There is no guarantee that useful screening data will translate into accurate screening decisions. The value of alternative decision rules and interpretation strategies must be weighed in the course of designing an overall screening process. The process must then be subjected to systematic evaluation to determine whether the process works as intended.

The first piece in the decision-making puzzle is to estimate the expected base rate of children in the screening population with prob-

---

*This practice, however, may touch upon a sensitive area. Many school systems have a policy of avoiding "unnecessary" suggestions that, if formally recommended by school personnel, may obligate the school system to underwrite the cost.

lems to be identified. This provides initial guidelines in setting a target referral rate. Various strategies may be used to match actual referrals with this target rate, of which development of local norms over time is particularly effective.

The accuracy of the screening process and the appropriateness of program referral rates are evaluated through classificational comparison between screening and criterion measure outcomes. This is commonly represented by a 2 × 2 hit rate table, and summarized by pairs of validity rates (e.g., sensitivity and specificity) that together reflect both frequency of over-referral and of under-referral errors. Given evaluation data with which to compare alternative referral rates and their effect upon hit rates, the screener faces the prediction predicament of having to choose between over-referral and under-referral errors. The optimal balance between the two is a matter of judgment to be resolved by situational constraints and local priorities.

Subsequent decisions regarding interpretation of screening results involve choices between the additive and multiple cutoffs approaches to establishing decision rules, and the clinical and statistical methods for reaching final screening decisions. The logic for choosing one option as opposed to another depends upon program objectives and constraints, and the resulting process may purposefully combine different strategies.

It is essential to evaluate the consequences of using a given screening process, first, by determining whether children are referred at the rate intended and, second, by analyzing whether the right children were referred, and whether alternative procedures or strategies might accomplish the task more successfully. Various issues and problematic matters surface at this point: suitability of criterion measures, cross-validation, confounding effects of early intervention, and possible bias in the screening process.

In relying upon validity rates to evaluate how well particular screening procedures and screening programs fulfill their objectives, the question arises as to the level of screening accuracy that may possibly be attained. Predictive validity studies to date show that our capacity to predict the future educational status of preschool children is distinctly limited. The limitation is largely due to the continually changing nature of children's functioning and of situational demands, and is accentuated by the practice of characterizing children's developmental and educational status in terms of two discrete classifications, i.e., "problematic" and "normal." Recommendations to reduce the impact of these hazards include periodic or ongoing assessment of difficult-to-classify children, and adoption of more flexible identification and service delivery systems.

6

Preschool Screening and Beyond

At this point, we would like to reflect upon the state of the art in preschool screening. Its current standing will be considered in reference to the history of preschool screening and in relation to the key issues that are involved in screening. Alternative concepts and methods for enabling the development and learning of young children will then be considered.

REFLECTIONS ON PRESCHOOL SCREENING

The state of the art of preschool screening is better understood in the context of the history, or evolution, of preschool screening. This history is partly a history of assumptions that have not been clearly stated or adequately evaluated. The perceived need for preschool screening evolved from the recognition that many children who experience learning problems also suffer related developmental, sensory, physical, social-emotional, or family problems, conditions that appear to predate school problems and render children more vulnerable to school failure. It has been assumed that identification of these children prior to school entry can lead to interventions that reduce the risk of school failure or serious difficulty.

Historically, in medicine, the purpose of screening has been to tentatively identify diseases and problematic health conditions by administering brief screening tests. Frankenburg and Dodds (1967) extended this concept to screening for developmental abnormalities or deficits (i.e., mental retardation) by means of the Denver Developmental Screening Test. Introduction of this prototypic preschool screening instrument coincided with a landmark plan for implementing developmental screening on a nationwide scale—the Early and Periodic Screening, Diagnosis and Treatment (EPSDT) program. The EPSDT program was designed to provide early identification and treatment services for health and developmental problems for that population of children considered to be at increased risk by virtue of low socioeconomic status. It would be fair to say that developmental screening has assumed a secondary emphasis in this medically-oriented program. The Denver Developmental Screening Test was the most commonly used screening test in EPSDT. The DDST was also adopted early on by many preschool screening programs, and still enjoys considerable usage.

Public Law 94-142 shifted the focus towards identifying *educationally* handicapped children and providing them with remedial educational and related services. P.L. 94-142 is more broadly inclusive than EPSDT because (1) it extends special services to all preschool-age children and (2) it includes among the "handicapped," children with specific learning disabilities, as well as children with more serious physical, sensory, and mental or emotional handicaps.

Preschool screening, as typically implemented to fulfill the P.L. 94-142 mandate, combines elements of health screening with those of kindergarten roundup, the purpose of which is to determine the "school readiness" of all kindergarten-eligible children prior to kindergarten entry. In kindergarten roundup, the child's vision and hearing, speech and language functioning, and developmental status are the primary concerns, although medical history data is usually obtained and a preschool physical examination may be required. The kindergarten roundup/school-readiness approach has probably softened the ominous connotations of screening for disability and handicap.

Some school systems offer screening to younger children, and even infants, usually on an elective basis at the request of parents. There is also a trend towards mass screening at a younger age, moving down from prekindergarten level to focus on 3 and 4 year olds. In the state of Minnesota's preschool screening programs, 90 percent of the children screened are being screened about 15 months prior to kindergarten entry, usually between the ages of 3½ and 4½. With this shift, the issue of identifying children with current problems versus predicting future problems increases in importance.

In preschool screening, we are attempting to identify children with current developmental and other problems given the assumption that these problems will subsequently interfere with school performance if they are not remediated. For children with substantial problems or major handicaps, a typical pattern unfolds: identification occurs at an early point in time, and persistence of developmental problems, learning difficulties, and the need for special educational assistance predictably follow. But for young children with lesser degrees of "deviation" from developmental norms, none of these assumptions is secure. These children with borderline problematic functioning are likely to move in and out of the normal range over time. At older ages, some will display persistent developmental and learning problems, but the majority will function essentially within the normal range. The path that these children travel seems to have more to do with their parents' level of education, home environment, and economic circumstances than with their preschool borderline developmental status itself. Our capacity to make accurate predictions for these children with apparently mild developmental problems is severely limited.

Given the state of the art, how might we answer the question "Does screening work?" When asked, "Does psychotherapy work?" one psychologist replied, "Does a hammer work?" The implication is that "it depends . . . " on who is swinging the hammer, on what it is being used for, and on the properties of the particular hammer. In preschool screening, we can clarify what we are up to by asking, "who, is doing what, with whom, for what purpose, and with what results?" The public schools are now engaged in large scale screening programs of young children, usually ages 3–5, for the purpose of identifying and serving those children with developmental and educational problems. The question is, "Does the result match the intention?" Are accurate referrals made that lead to appropriate interventions that benefit significant numbers of children?

Elements and Issues

The variables of a preschool screening program that impact upon its effectiveness are many. It has been pointed out that administrative issues, from planning and organization, to outreach, to tracking, are as important as the content of screening, the validity of screening measures, and the qualifications of screeners. Technical considerations regarding test validity and the limits of prediction place humbling constraints on what we can reasonably expect to accomplish. Monetary and human resources set another kind of limit on our effectiveness. Let us review the key elements and issues that define responsible screening practices.

First of all, preschool screening is not an end in itself. The purpose of screening is to provide early intervention. Without the availability of early intervention resources, there is no point in beginning. Implicit in the identification-intervention link is the assumption that early childhood special education services are effective. Our answers to the questions "How early?" and "How effective?" obviously should affect decisions about when to screen.

Second, the goals of screening and the population to be screened should be clearly defined. Too often screening is undertaken in a vague manner, e.g., "we need to do preschool screening." A clear conception of a screening program's essential characteristics (who and why) allow the operational details (what, when, where, and how) to fall more readily into place. For example, if the intention is for early intervention to have a significant impact during the preschool age range, screening must be scheduled sufficiently in advance of school entry—perhaps a year or more.

Third, a clear system for organization and implementation of screening is essential. This overall system, or process, is more important than any single element or test within it. A comprehensive screening system includes a review of the child's current developmental, sensory, and physical status, plus environmental factors, plus relevant historical information. This information may be derived from testing or examination of the child, professional observation, and information provided by the parent. Planning also involves coordination with other programs or agencies that provide essential follow-up services.

Fourth, a comprehensive screening program requires the expertise of professionals from a number of disciplines. Screening is a task for several professions, not just one. Even in the area of developmental screening, early childhood teachers, speech-language clinicians, psychologists, special education specialists, social workers, and specialists in motor development all may be involved. Professionals involved in developmental screening should be knowledgeable about child development and developmental problems, about the uses, misuses, and limitations of tests (screening tests in particular), and about communication with children and with parents. They should have expertise specifically with the age level of the children who are being screened. The leadership or coordinating role in the screening should fall to a professional with administrative expertise plus the ability to relate well to other professionals and to parents.

Fifth, parent involvement in the process of preschool screening is critical to the development of working relationships between parents and school personnel. Publicity and outreach efforts directed toward parents of children who are eligible for screening must be clear and specific regarding the nature and purpose of the program. Parent information about the child's development, including parents' concerns, add both validity and credibility to the screening process. Misunderstanding and distrust are also minimized by actively involving the parent in the screening process in a meaningful way.

Sixth, turning to the measures used in development screening, it is critical to have an appreciation of their utility, limitations, and possible abuses. Utility is largely defined by the fact that screening is a decision-making process. Validity for making screening decisions is the single most important criterion applied in selection and evaluation of screening measures, which is reflected in the use of the hit rate model for validating screening outcomes. Early identification measures in general, and screening procedures in particular, simply cannot predict the future status of young children without making a disconcertingly-high percentage of errors.

Expectations placed upon screening procedures are often unrealistic, as evidenced by two particular myths. One is the myth that we are able to devise developmental screening tests that are very brief, simple to administer and score, and that have extremely high validity. This contradicts the basic rule that the briefer the test, the lower will be its reliability and validity. Nevertheless, there is a great demand for brief, high-performance screening tests. Test developers have attempted to rise to this occasion, and have produced commercial screening tests that "look good" or, as described, "sound good", but which may or may not achieve high levels of validity. It takes quite a bit of sophistication to "screen" the claims of test authors—which often hook into the pressing needs of test users—to identify instruments that are adequate for screening program use. A second myth is that the overall screening process can be refined to the point where every case of a child needing special educational services is accurately predicted. Screeners may be inclined to add more, and seemingly more sophisticated, screening measures and other types of information to the screening process in an effort to transcend the prediction predicament; that is, to identify those previously-missed children, without getting more over-referral errors in the bargain. But, as indicated by both empirical evidence and logic, the limits of prediction are rather inflexible, and heroic efforts to definitively classify those elusive borderline range cases tend to be a poor investment.

This brings us to the seventh point: screening is an economically-motivated system. The critical tension is that screening must be thorough enough to produce valid results, yet brief enough not to be prohibitive in cost. While we have proposed that an ideal screening process assembles a broad array of information about the child, this must be done cost-effectively and should not be pursued beyond the point of diminishing returns. Rather than devote excessive resources to assessing hard-to-classify young children at a single point in their development, recommended alternatives are to rescreen or reassess later, or to monitor their development over time.

Cost considerations frequently lead to the decision to use paraprofessionals or volunteers to assist in screening. However, the economic advantages of using nonprofessionals must take into account the critical need for professionals to train and supervise them. There is also some evidence to suggest that paid "volunteers" are more dependable and more responsive to training and supervision.

The commitment of federal, state, and local school system resources to early identification and intervention has continued, but variably and tenuously due to economic conditions. While the available resources necessarily shape the early identification process, there is a limit to the extent to which policies and programs can be adapted. Ethically, we would have to discontinue preschool screening if cost constraints were such that screening could not be conducted with adequate accuracy and consideration for participants.

Eighth, screening program outcomes should be the subject of evaluation. Documentation of screening results, referrals, and follow-up services provides the benchmarks by which the scope and effects of the program can be appreciated, and subsequently form the basis for systematic research. At a minimum, a school screening program needs to keep records of the number of children screened by age, the numbers and percentages of children who are identified and referred for evaluations, the numbers and percentages of children referred who are considered to have problems on the basis of evaluation, and the numbers of children in the first years of school who are considered to have learning problems and need special resources. From this information, data can be generated to evaluate the workability of the screening program and of the particular instruments used, and eventually to address the question of whether the results match program intentions.

Alternatives for Early Identification

It would be unfortunate if preschool screening came to be exclusively equated with mass screening of children at a given age, which is essentially kindergarten roundup under a new name. There is no single best way to accomplish the objectives of early identification. Several approaches have been tried, of which mass screening is perhaps the best known and most widely used at present. Depending upon the resources available and the commitment to early childhood services (both by professionals and by the community), alternatives for early identification may range from a bare bones approach to progressive new strategies.

The bare bones alternative would dramatically reduce short-term expenses, but may prove much more expensive in the long run. If we were to turn back the clock and abandon preschool screening and EPSDT, we would return to a system that might be called "natural screening" or "identification as usual." In this system, identification would depend upon an observant parent with concerns about his or her child's development seeking help, or upon recognition by a physician or other professional that the child was not developing normally. This method of identification could be enhanced by providing the public with information about child development and about early signs of developmental problems. Professionals involved in the care of young children could also be better educated about these issues.

A more focused approach would involve providing screening services only to child populations considered to be at risk by virtue of medical factors or economic circumstances. Or, we could provide these children and their families with easy access to quality medical care and preschool educational programs, and abandon screening as an isolated approach.

At a more comprehensive level, a way to serve educational needs while circumventing issues about labelling children is to provide preschool educational services for all 3–5 year olds. Children who have not attended an educationally-oriented program before they enter kindergarten are, in effect, educationally disadvantaged when they begin kindergarten. If children were enrolled in such programs, it would then be possible to review their developmental progress and their adaptation to a school-like environment in a highly valid manner, incorporating both the teacher's observations and the parent's knowledge of the child.

One particular alternative that we would now like to describe is a method of reviewing the development of young children that takes us beyond the medical-model approach of identifying children with disabilities, to that of promoting the healthy development of all children.

DEVELOPMENTAL REVIEW

A major limitation of developmental screening as currently practiced is that development is not like a disease entity, to be judged as present or absent. The medical-model approach to screening tends to do violence to both the nature and the complexity of the developmental process. Development describes the evolution of certain abilities and the processes that underlie this evolution. The rate of development of a particular ability, however, is not necessarily consistent over time. Nor does the rate of development in one area necessarily parallel the rate of development in another area. These observations suggest that, for young children, the "range of normal" is not easy for professionals to define, and account for our difficulties in predicting future functioning.

Parents wonder "How is my child doing?" and sometimes worry "Is my child normal?" with regard to their child's development. Information addressing these questions and concerns may be hard to come by, and parents may be left alone with their anxiety to deal with their children as best they can. At any given time, a child will be demonstrating a particular array of abilities and will be more or less adjusted to his or her environment. At the same time, the parent will be more or less satisfied about how the child is doing, possibly concerned or worried about the child's development or well-being, or at least have questions regarding the child.

What is needed then is a procedure for reviewing each child's developmental progress with parents, and for responding to their questions and concerns in a way that enables them to become better parents. This developmental review needs to assume a positive orientation that goes beyond the concept of "screening for defects." What parents need most is affirmation of their children's developmental achievements, and emotional support of their roles as parents. They also need information about child care and child development, and an opportunity to raise questions and express their concerns about their child. In addition, children and parents will need special assistance if the child is developmentally handicapped or has other problems.

Developmental Review is a method for reviewing the developmental progress of infants and preschool-age children. It serves a broader purpose than screening, although it includes a mechanism for identifying those children who are developmentally delayed. The purpose of Developmental Review is to review the child's progress with the parent (usually mother) in a way that is beneficial for parents of normally functioning, as well as developmentally disabled, children. The concept of developmental review is based upon the recognition that a child is as likely to be advanced in some areas of development, or even gifted, as it is that a child may be delayed in some areas, or even mentally retarded. The Developmental Review method stresses parent involvement by keying on the mother's description of her child's current behavior, and her questions and concerns, if any. It also includes observation of the child. Developmental Review has a clearly-defined clinical structure. The parent interview and the child observation are conducted according to a specified format, and with reference to a Developmental Map of milestones for the first five years.

The concept of Developmental Review emerged from a series of conferences on developmental screening sponsored by the American Association of Psychiatric Services for Children, under the auspices of the Department of Health, Education and Welfare, the outcome of which is described in a report titled "Developmental Review in the EPSDT Program" (Huntington, 1977). Developmental Review is conceived as an enabling process for both parents and children. It is designed to provide a mechanism by which all parents can be helped to understand better how their children are doing, and to obtain information and support that can enable them to be more effective and comfortable as parents. At the same time, it provides a mechanism by which those children with significant developmental delays and potential school problems can be at least tentatively identified.

From the initial contact with parents, the importance of parent involvement and the value of parents' observations of the child's functioning are stressed. Parents are informed, in words and by attitude, that "you know a lot about your child, and we need to know what you know about your child in order to understand your child." Parent involvement in the process of describing and understanding the child then serves as the bridge to the development of a working relationship or partnership between the parents and the professional. Communication is crucial every step of the way, keeping well in mind that parents put their egos on the line when they submit their child to the critique of others.

Developmental Review provides a mechanism for reviewing the child's current developmental achievements in order to appreciate how well the child is progressing in five areas of development: gross motor, fine motor, language, self-help, and social-emotional. Language development is broken down into expressive language, language comprehension, and speech articulation. This information is derived from both parental information and professional observation of the child. Parental information about the child is obtained first by means of a brief questionnaire and then through a structured interview. Positive attributes of the child as well as parental concerns regarding the child are solicited. Observation of the child by the professional is conducted in accordance with the guidelines provided. The interview with the parent and the observation of the child are accomplished with specific attention paid to the questions and/or concerns initially raised by the parent. In conducting the parent interview and the child observation, the evaluator refers to a Developmental Map, shown in Figure 6-1. The Developmental Map displays typically expected behaviors of children from birth to age 5. In the interview, the mother is first given a brief opportunity to describe the child's current development, in her own words. Next, depending on the parent's spontaneous description, the interviewer asks for additional description in each of the five areas, for example, "Tell me more about . . . " Finally, the interviewer asks about specific behaviors in each area from the Developmental Map at the child's age level. At the same time, the child is observed in a free play situation (perhaps off to the side, where blocks, paper and pencil, etc. are available). The child's developmental achievements are recorded on the Developmental Map.

The child's level of functioning in each area of development is categorized as "advanced, within age expectations, questionable, or delayed development" by comparing what the child is doing to the achievements of children within his or her age range and to the achievements of younger and older children. Guidelines for interpretation, as shown in Figure 6-1, appear on the reverse side of the Developmental Map. Developmental Review then includes the following data: the parent's questions and concerns, if any; the parent's description of the child's developmental activities; the professional's observations of the child; and the Developmental Map that records and pictures the child's developmental achievements.

The Developmental Review process and the Developmental Map were structured to make it easier for parents to appreciate their children's development. It was designed so that parents would be encouraged to learn about child development through the process, and become more confident parents. The end point of the Developmental Review is usually a discussion of results with the parents, and the provision of appropriate information and guidance. For those children with possible developmental problems, results are discussed with respect to the parents' questions or concerns (or lack thereof) about the child's development. Referral for follow-up evaluation is made when needed.

A pilot project (Stone, Ireton & Runquist, 1979) evaluated the efficiency of Developmental Review (time, ease of administration), its impact on parents, and, to some degree, its validity for identifying delayed children. The project was conducted in Minnesota, Ohio, and Texas, and included both urban and rural sites and public and private practice EPSDT providers. In some sites, it was possible to compare Developmental Review with the results of screening with the Denver Developmental Screening Test. A questionnaire for those conducting Developmental Review was completed by 28 professionals, of whom 74

DEVELOPMENTAL MAP OF THE FIRST FIVE YEARS

AGE	Gross Motor	Fine Motor	Language	Self-help	Social-Emotional	AGE
3	Lifts head & chest high	Clasps hands together	Vocalizes, coos, chuckles	Comforts self with thumb or pacifier	Social smile	3
	Supports head (no lag)	Reaches toward objects	Vocalizes spontaneously, social		Distinguishes mother from others	
	Rolls over back to front	Picks up toy with one hand			Initiates social contact	
6		Transfers toy from one hand to other	Wide range of vocalizations (Vowel sounds, consonant-vowel combinations)			6
	Sits alone—erect, steady without support			Feeds self cracker	Pushes things away he/she doesn't want	
		Picks up objects with thumb and finger grasp	Says mama, dada			
9	Crawls on hands & knees	Picks up small objects—precise thumb and finger grasp	Says mama, dada as names for parents	Holds own bottle or Drinks from a cup	Plays social games—peek-a-boo, pat-a-cake, bye-bye	9
	Stands alone well				Expresses several emotions clearly	
	Walks with support		Understands "no," "stop," etc.		Objects to separation	
12	Walks alone	Stacks two or more blocks	Uses 1 or 2 words as names of things or actions	Cooperates in dressing	Plays simple ball games	12
			Points to familiar things	Feeds self with a spoon		
	"Dances" to music	Scribbles	Points to parts of body		Hugs parent	
18	Runs well, rarely falls	Builds tower of four or more blocks	Uses words to express wants		Kisses with pucker	18
			Uses 2–3 word phrases or sentences	Eats with spoon, spilling little	Imitates adult activities	
	Kicks ball forward	Makes imitative (vertical, circular)	Names pictures of familiar objects		"Helps" with simple household tasks	
			Follows simple directions			
2-0	Rides tricycle, using pedals	Holds crayon with fingers	Uses pronouns for self & other	Puts on simple garment	Refers to self as I or me	2-0
		Handles small toys skillfully	Talks in sentences		Tells first & last name	
	Walks up & down stairs—one foot per step	Draws circle	Speech understandable ½ of time	Washes & dries hands	Plays with children	
			Tells use of familiar objects	Toilet trained	Shows sympathy	
3-0		Draws a person that has at least three parts	Tells stories about daily experiences	Washes & dries hands & face	Knows sex (own & opposite)	3-0
	Hops on one foot, without support	Draws a cross (+)	Knows 3 colors Understands concepts-big, little, etc.	Combs or brushes hair	Plays cooperatively with self	
			Understands 2–3 prepositions			
			Counts 4 objects, answers "how many"			
4-0	Hops—one foot, repeatedly	Draws a person that has at least six parts	Talks in sentences	Dresses & undresses without help, except for tying shoes	Plays role in "make-believe" play	4-0
	Skips		Completely understandable			
	Dances—skillfully	Draws square with good corners	Defines familiar words		Follows simple game rules	
	Good balance & coordination	Prints a few letters				
5-0	GM	FM	[1] EL S C	S-H	S-E	5-0

Summary:

[1] Expressive Language, Speech, Comprehension

Fig. 6-1. The Developmental Map used for Developmental Review.

INTERPRETATION - STEPS

1. Calculate the child's age by subtracting his birthdate from the date the Developmental Review was completed. See example below: The child has passed the age of 3 years, 1 month, but is not yet 3 years, 2 months. His age is recorded as 3-1. Drop the days after calculating the age, not before. For children under age two, the age is recorded in months. For example, a child whose age is calculated as 1 year, 7 months, is recorded 19 months.

	Year	Month	Day
Date Completed	1978	~~7~~ 6	~~8~~ 38
Birthdate	1975	5	14
Age	3	1	24

	Year	Month	Day
Date Completed	___	___	___
Birthdate	___	___	___
Age	___	___	___

2. Draw a horizontal line across the Developmental Map at the child's age level.

3. For each area of development, mark the individual items reported by the mother or observed in the clinic. It may be necessary to mark only the more mature items in each area rather than all items.

4. For each area of development, compare the child's behavioral age level to his actual age level. In this way, it is possible to appreciate whether the child's behavior is above, within or below age expectations.

5. Use the following developmental status categories to determine whether the child, in each area, is:

   A = Advanced - Displays behavior characteristic of children significantly older then himself--behavior above age interval.

   WA = Within age expectations - displays behavior at age interval or within age range (one interval below).

   (?)= Questionable development - Displays behavior at a level which is less mature than children significantly younger then himself. Fails to demonstrate behaviors within his age interval and fails to demonstrate behaviors at the next younger age interval. For example, a 13 month-old who is not walking (12-18 months) and not crawling (9-12 months).

   DD = Definitely delayed - Over 50% delayed, for example, a 2-year old who is not displaying the behavior of a 1-year old; example, a 2-year old who is not walking, a 4-year old who is not using word combinations, etc.

6. Record the classification in the space at the bottom of the Developmental Map. When in doubt, record two categories, for example: A/WA; WA/(?); (?)/DD. Underline ratings for those areas of development where the rating is either (?) or DD.

275

percent were nurses, and 17 percent physicians. The time to complete the procedure, including information gathering, interpretation, and follow-up discussion, averaged 38 minutes. Developmental Review procedures were rated as both more time-consuming and more comprehensive than the DDST. Practical utility for generating data for referral decisions was rated by the professionals as about the same, while parent acceptance as perceived by the professionals tended to be higher for Developmental Review.

Comments by participating professionals included the following: "The parents really like it . . . They enjoy having their opinions asked . . . This encouraged parents to talk . . . Some parents seem so eager to talk to a professional about their children . . . They appreciated receiving a copy of the Developmental Map." Overall effectiveness was rated as "useful or very useful" by 73 percent of professionals. Parents themselves (about 95 percent mothers) felt comfortable with the procedure, believed that their questions and concerns had been heard, and would recommend the procedure to other parents.

Validity data for the procedure are based on 599 children, of which 71 percent were English-spaking, 8 percent were Spanish-speaking, and 21 percent bi-lingual. Age range of the sample was fairly evenly distributed from birth through 5 years of age. Both sexes were represented equally. Incidence of delayed development was 6 percent for the group as a whole, and ranged from 0 to 22 percent across sites. Of the 28 children viewed as possibly delayed, 21 were boys and 7 were girls. For those children referred for follow-up evaluation, 70 percent were considered developmentally delayed, while the remaining 30 percent were not. The 6 percent incidence rate and the 70 percent accurate referral rate paralleled the rates in a comparison group of 928 children screened by the DDST.

This study of the efficacy and validity of the Developmental Review procedure was carried out under serious constraints and with limited training of the professionals who utilized the procedure (which consisted mainly of their being provided with the materials and instructions). The validity data are limited to follow-up of a small number of children, and do not include any evaluation of the incidence of under-referral errors, i.e., children with problems who were missed by the screening. Nevertheless, the results are promising in that they point toward hit rates that compare well to the DDST. The Developmental Review procedures show considerable promise for involving parents in the process and encouraging parents to be more aware of and more enabling of their child's development. The most meaningful conclusions at this point are that the concept and methodology are deserving of

serious consideration, but need refinement and, subseq
research to test their validity and utility.

The authors wish to stress that, at this point, the D
Review process is a prototype for a systematic means o
child's development. Neither the items of the Developm
the guidelines for interpretation of results should be taker
further research is done with this method. The logic a
Developmental Review could probably be used by profe
present form if the professional is knowledgeable about ea
development (i.e., milestones, and the range of normal
enced in working with young children.

Given the present narrowly-defined goals of mo
screening programs, it is unrealistic to expect that the D
Review method would be used *in toto*. However, it is our
concept of Developmental Review will at least affect
preschool screening is viewed, especially in terms of
parent information is regarded and the way a child's d
characterized. Furthermore, if future trends are in the
placing higher priorities on preventative services, on fa
ment in promoting child development, and on regarding
"special," the shift towards Developmental Review wil
one.

CONCLUSION

Preschool screening has been presented as a mear
rather than as an end in itself. It is part of an overall early
decision-making process, the ultimate objective of whic
children who have developmental, sensory, or physical
may interfere with school performance. In effect, we ma
tion that certain children will have problems in school, th
thwart the prediction by providing special services early
will ostensibly do the greatest good.

Aspects of this service model introduce questions a
bility, both on a practical and on a theoretical level. On a p
we have examined preschool screening programs as the
teristically implemented and have underlined the impor
ning and organization, of professional expertise and co
the procedures used to obtain screening information, of
used to translate screening information into screening dec
the need to evaluate program effectiveness. We have de

have developed preschool education programs that have enjoyed considerable success and parent support, but uncertainties of funding threaten the continued existence of such programs.

Another alternative, Developmental Review, addresses problematic aspects of the current screening approach by replacing the medical model with a developmental model. The emphasis is upon description of the child rather than classification, upon strengths and weaknesses rather than disabilities, and upon working collaboratively with families rather than providing services for families. While systems designed simply to funnel children into special education programs provide little of value for the majority of parents and children, Developmental Review can contribute to the healthy development of all children by fostering parent awareness, involvement, and effectiveness.

Having examined preschool screening as it is typically approached, we have outlined the essential elements of the process, noted its limitations, and proposed ways to improve the process. In doing so, we have accepted that the primary goal of preschool screening is to improve the delivery of special services to children with handicapping conditions. But, we have also attempted to step outside the system for a broader perspective that has led us to weigh the value of alternatives. As we strive to better meet the educational needs of handicapped children, we could also opt for promoting the healthy development of all children, as well as the development of their parents.

REFERENCES

Abeson, A, & Zettel, J The end of the quiet revolution: The Education for All Handicapped Children Act of 1975. *Except Child,* 1977, *44*, 114–128

Achenbach, TM, & Edelbrock, CS Behavioral problems and competencies reported by parents of normal and disturbed children aged four through sixteen. *Monogr Soc Res Child Dev,* 1981, *46* (1, Serial No. 188)

Ackerman, PR, & Moore, MG Delivery of educational services of preschool handicapped children. In T D Tjossem (Ed.), *Intervention strategies for high risk infants and young children.* Baltimore: University Park Press, 1976

Adelman, H, & Feshbach, S *Early identification of children with learning problems: Some methodological and ethical concerns.* Paper presented at the meeting of the Society for Research in Child Development, Denver, April 1975

Adelman, HS Predicting psycho-educational problems in childhood. *Behav Dis,* 1978, *3*, 148–159

Algozzine, B, & Ysseldyke, JE Special education services for normal children: Better safe than sorry. *Excep Child,,* 1981, *48*, 238–243

Alpern, GD, & Boll, TJ *Developmental Profile.* Aspen, Col.: Psychological Development Publications, 1972

Alpern, GD, Boll, TJ, & Shearer, M *Developmental Profile II.* Aspen, Col.: Psychological Development Publications, 1980

American Psychological Association, American Educational Research Association, & National Council on Measurement in Education. *Standards for educational and psychological tests.* Washington, D.C.: American Psychological Association, 1974

Anastasi, A *Psychological testing.* (4th ed.). New York: Macmillan, 1976

Barnes, KE *Preschool screening: The measurement and prediction of children at-risk.* Springfield, Ill.: Charles C. Thomas, 1982

Bayley, N Consistency and variability in the growth of intelligence from birth to eighteen years. *J Gen Psych,* 1949, *75*, 165–196

Bishop, D & Butterworth, GE A longitudinal study using the WPPSI and WISC-R with an English sample. *Br J Educ Psychol,* 1979, *49*, 156–168

Bloom, BS *Stability and change in human characteristics.* New York: John Wiley & Sons, 1964

Bolig, JR, & Fletcher, GO The MRT vs. ratings of kindergarten teachers as predictors of success in first grade. *Educ Lead,* 1973, *30*, 637–640

Boll, T, & Alpern, GD The Developmental Profile: A new instrument to measure child development through interviews. *J Clin Child Psychol,* 1975, *4*, 25–27

Book, RM Predicting reading failure: A screening battery for kindergarten children. *J Learn Disab,* 1974, *7*, 43–56

Bower, EM *Early identification of emotionally handicapped children in school* (3rd ed.). Springfield, Ill.: Charles C. Thomas, 1981

Bradley, RH, & Caldwell, BM Home Observation for Measurement of the Environment: A revision of the preschool scale. *Am J Ment Defic,* 1979, *84*, 235–244

Bradley, RH, Caldwell, BM, & Elardo, R Home environment, social status, and mental test performance. *J Educ Psychol,* 1977, *69*, 697–701

Brekstad, A Factors influencing the reliability of anamnestic recall. *Child Dev,* 1966, *37*, 603–612

Brewer, GD, & Kakalik, JS *Handicapped children: Strategies for improving services.* New York: McGraw-Hill, 1979

Bronfenbrenner, U *A report on longitudinal evaluations of preschool programs. Vol. II: Is early intervention effective?* (Office of Human Development Publication No. 76-30025). Washington, D.C.: Department of Health, Education, and Welfare, 1974

Buck, A, & Gart, J Comparison of a screening test and a reference test in epidemiological studies. *Am J Epidemiol,* 1966, *83,* 586–592

Buros, OK (Ed.). *The seventh mental measurements yearbook.* Highland Park, N. J.: Gryphon Press, 1972

Buroṣ, OK (Ed.). *Tests in print II.* Highland Park, N.J.: Gryphon Press, 1974

Buros, OK (Ed.). *The eighth mental measurements yearbook.* Highland Park, N. J.: Gryphon Press, 1978

Caldwell, BM & Bradley, RH *HOME (Home Observation for Measurement of the Environment) Inventory.* Homewood, Ill.: Dorsey Press, in press

Chang, A, Goldstein, H, Thomas, K, & Wallace, HM The Early Periodic Screening, Diagnosis, and Treatment program (EPSDT): Status of progress and implementation in 51 states and territories. *J Sch Health,* 1979, *49*, 454–458

Clarke, AM, & Clarke, ADB (Eds.) *Early experience: Myth and evidence.* New York: Free Press, 1976

Cochrane, A, & Holland, W Validation of screening procedures. *Br Med Bull,* 1971, *27*, 3–7

Cohen, S, Semmes, M, & Guralnick, MJ Public Law 94-142 and the education of preschool handicapped children. *Excep Child,* 1979, *46*, 279–284

Cole, NS Bias in testing. *Am Psychol,* 1981, *36*, 1067–1077

Coons, CE, Gay, EC, Fandal, AW, Ker, C, & Frankenburg, WK *The Home Screening Questionnaire reference manual.* Denver: Ladoca Publishing Foundation, 1981

Cronbach, LJ, & Gleser, GC *Psychological tests and personnel decisions.* Urbana, Ill.: University of Illinois Press, 1957

Davidson, JB, Lichtenstein, R, Canter, A, & Cronin, P *Directory of developmental screening instruments.* Minneapolis: Minneapolis Public Schools, 1977 (ERIC Document Reproduction Service No. ED 172 466)

de Hirsch, K, Jansky, J, & Langford, W *Predicting reading failure.* New York: Harper & Row, 1966

Denhoff, E, Hainsworth, PK, & Hainsworth, ML The child at-risk for learning disorder: Can he be identified during the first year of life? *Clin Pediatr,* 1972, *11*, 164–170

Divoky, D Is this screening test worth $1,319,638.50? *Learning,* May/June 1977, 66–72(a)

Divoky, D Screening: The grand delusion. *Learning,* March 1977, 28–34(b)

Doll, EA The Vineland Social Maturity Scale: Manual of directions. *Train Sch Bull,* 1935, *32*, 1–74

Doll, EA *Vineland Social Maturity Scale: Condensed manual of directions.* Circle Pines, Minn.: American Guidance Service, 1965

Doll, EA *Preschool Attainment Record manual* (Research ed.). Circle Pines, Minn.: American Guidance Service, 1966

Dopheide, W, & Dallinger, J Preschool articulation screening by parents. *Language, Speech, and Hearing Services in Schools,* 1976, *7,* 124–127

Drumwright, A *Denver Articulation Screening Exam.* Denver: Ladoca Publishing Foundation, 1971

Dunn, LM Special education for the mildly retarded. Is much of it justifiable? *Excep Child,* 1968, *35,* 5–21

Eaves, LD, Kendall, DC, & Crichton, JU The early identification of learning disabilities: A follow-up study. *J Learn Disabil,* 1974, *7,* 632–638

Ebert, E, & Simmons, K The Brush Foundation study of child growth and development. *Monog Soc Res Child Dev,* 1943, *8,* No. 2, 1–113

Edelman, MW Who is for children? *Am Psychol,* 1981, *36,* 109–116

Elliott, SN, & Bretzing, BG Using and updating local norms. *Psychol Sch,* 1980, *17,* 196–201

Farrar, J, & Leigh, J Factors associated with reading failure; A predictive Tasmanian survey. *Soc Sci Med,* 1972, *6,* 241–251

Ferinden, WE Jr., & Jacobson, S Early identification of learning disabilities. *J Learn Disabil,* 1970, *3,* 589–593

Feshbach, S, Adelman, H, & Fuller, W Early identification of children with high risk of reading failure. *J Learn Disabil,* 1974, *7,* 639–644

Feshbach, S, Adelman, H, & Fuller, W Prediction of reading and related academic problems. *J Educ Psychol,* 1977, *69,* 299–308

Flaugher, RL The many definitions of test bias. *Am Psychol,* 1981, *33,* 671–679

Frankenburg, W Selection of diseases and tests in pediatric screening. *Pediatrics,* 1974, *54,* 612–616

Frankenburg, WK, & Camp, BW (Eds.). *Pediatric screening tests.* Springfield, Ill.: Charles C. Thomas, 1975

Frankenburg, WK, Camp, BW, & Van Natta, PA Validity of the Denver Developmental Screening Test. *Child Dev,* 1971, *42,* 475–485

Frankenburg, WK, Camp, BW, Van Natta, PA, Demersseman, JA, & Voorhees, SF Reliability and stability of the Denver Developmental Screening Test. *Child Dev,* 1971, *42,* 1315–1325

Frankenburg, WK, & Dodds, JB The Denver Developmental Screening Test. *J Pediat,* 1967, *71,* 181–191

Frankenburg, WK, Fandal, AW, Sciarillo, W, & Burgess, D The newly abbreviated and revised Denver Developmental Screening Test. *J Pediat,* 1981, *99,* 995–999

Frankenburg, W, Goldstein, A, & Camp, B The revised Denver Developmental Screening Test: Its accuracy as a screening instrument. *J Pediat,* 1971, *79,* 988–995

Frankenburg, WK, Goldstein, A, Chabot, A, Camp, BM, & Fitch, M Training the indigenous nonprofessional: The screening technician. *J Pediat,* 1970, *77,* 564–570

Frankenburg, WK, & North, AF *A guide to screening for the Early and Periodic Screening, Diagnosis, and Treatment program under Medicaid.* U.S. Department of Health, Education, and Welfare, 1974

Frankenburg, WK, van Doorninck, WJ, Liddell, TN, & Dick, NP The Denver Prescreening Developmental Questionnaire. *Pediatrics,* 1976, *57,* 744–753

Gallagher, JJ, & Bradley, RH Early identification of developmental difficulties. In IJ Gordon (Ed.), *Early childhood education,* 71st Yearbook, Part 2. National Society for the Study of Education. Chicago: University of Chicago Press, 1972

Gesell, A *The mental growth of the pre-school child.* New York: Macmillan, 1926

Gesell, AL, & Amatruda, CS *Developmental diagnosis* (3rd ed.). New York: Hoeber, 1954

Goldfarb, W Psychological privation in infancy and subsequent adjustment. *Am J Orthopsychiatry,* 1945, *15,* 247–255

Goodenough, FL *Mental testing: Its history, principles, and applications.* New York: Rinehart, 1949

Goodwin, WL, & Driscoll, LA *Handbook for measurement and evaluation in early childhood education.* San Francisco: Jossey-Bass, 1980

Gottfried, AW, Guerin, D, Spencer, JE, & Meyer, C Validity of Minnesota Child Development Inventory in screening young children's developmental status. *J Pediat Psychol,* in press

Gottlieb, MJ, Zinkus, PW, & Thompson, A Chronic middle ear disease and auditory perceptual deficits. *Clin Pediatr,* 1979, *18,* 725–732

Graham, P, & Rutter, M The reliability and validity of the psychiatric assessment of the child: Interview with the parent. *Br J Psychiatry,* 1968, *114,* 581–593

Hainsworth, PK, & Hainsworth, ML *Preschool Screening System.* Pawtucket, R. I.: Early Recognition Intervention Systems, 1980

Hall, J, Mardell, C, Wick, J, & Goldenberg, D Final report: Further development and refinement of DIAL. *Resources in Education,* 1976. (ERIC Document Reproduction Service No. ED 117 200)

Harber, J Evaluating utility in diagnostic decision making. *J Spec Ed,* 1981, *15,* 413–428

Harrington, M *The other America: Poverty in the United States.* Baltimore: Penguin Books, 1962

Herrnstein, RJ IQ testing and the media. *The Atlantic Monthly,* August 1981, 68–74

Hildreth, G, Griffiths, H, & McGauvran, M *Metropolitan Readiness Test.* New York: Harcourt, Brace & World, 1964

Hobbs, N *The futures of children: Categories, labels, and their consequences.* San Francisco: Jossey-Bass, 1975

Hobbs, N Classification options: A conversation with Nicholas Hobbs on exceptional child education. *Excep Child,* 1978, *44,* 494–497

Hoepfner, R, Stern, C, & Nummedal, SG (Eds.). *CSE-ECRC preschool/kindergarten test evaluations.* Los Angeles: Center for the Study of Evaluation and Early Childhood Research Center, Graduate School of Education, University of California at Los Angeles, 1971

Holt, RR Yet another look at clinical and statistical prediction. *Am Psychol,* 1970, *25,* 337–348

Honzik, MP The constancy of mental test performance during the preschool period. *J Genetic Psychol,* 1938, *52,* 285–302

Hunter, C Classroom observation instruments and teacher inservice training by school psychologists. *Sch Psychol Monogr,* 1977, *3,* 45–88

Huntington, D *Developmental review in the EPSDT Program* (Department of Health, Education, and Welfare Publication No. 77-24537). Washington, D.C.: The Medicaid Bureau, 1977

Ilg. FL, & Ames. LB *School readiness: Behavior tests used at the Gesell Institute.* (New ed.) New York: Harper & Row, 1972

Hunt, JMcV *Intelligence and experience.* New York: Ronald Press, 1961

Ireton, H, Lun, K-S, & Kampen, M Minnesota Preschool Inventory identification of children at risk for kindergarten failure. *Psychol Sch,* 1981, *18,* 493–401

Ireton, H, & Thwing, E *Minnesota Child Development Inventory.* Minneapolis: Behavior Science Systems, 1974

Ireton, H, & Thwing, E Appraising the development of a preschool child by means of a standardized report prepared by the mother. *Clin Pediatr,* 1976, *15,* 875–882

Ireton, H, & Thwing, E *Minnesota Preschool Inventory.* Minneapolis: Behavior Science Systems, 1979

Ireton, H, Thwing, E, & Currier, S Minnesota child development inventory: Identification of children with developmental disorders. *J Pediatr Psychol,* 1977, *2,* 18–22

Ireton, H, Thwing, E, & Gravem, H Infant mental development and neurological status, family socioeconomic status, and intelligence at age four. *Child Dev,* 1970, *41*, 937–945

Jansky, J, & de Hirsch, K *Preventing reading failure: Prediction, diagnosis, intervention.* New York: Harper and Row, 1972

Jensen, AR How much can we boost IQ and scholastic achievement? *Harvard Educ Rev,* 1969, *39*, 1–123

Johnson, HW *Preschool test descriptions: Test matrix and correlated test descriptors.* Springfield, Ill.: Charles C. Thomas, 1979

Johnson, OG *Tests and measurements in child development: Handbook II.* San Francisco: Jossey-Bass, 1976

Johnson, OG, & Bommarito, JW *Tests and measurements in child development: Handbook I.* San Francisco: Jossey-Bass, 1971

Kaufman, AS Factor structure of the McCarthy Scales at five age levels between 2 1/2 and 8 1/2. *Educ Psychol Measure,* 1975, *35*, 641–656

Keogh, BK, & Becker, LD Early detection of learning problems: Questions, cautions, and guidelines. *Excep Child,* 1973, *40*, 5–11

Keogh, BK, & Smith, CE Early identification of educationally high potential and high risk children. *J Sch Psychol,* 1970, *8*, 285–290

Kirk, SA *Early education of the mentally retarded.* Urbana: University of Illinois Press, 1958

Kirk, SA *Educating exceptional children.* Boston: Houghton Mifflin, 1962

Kochanek, TT Early detection programs for preschool handicapped children: Some procedural recommendations. *J Spec Educ,* 1980, *14*, 347–353

Koppitz, EM *Psychological evaluation of children's Human Figure Drawings.* New York: Grune & Stratton, 1968

Kurtz, P, Neisworth, J, & Laub, K Issues concerning the early identification of handicapped children. *J Sch Psychol,* 1977, *15*, 136–139

Labeck, LJ, Ireton, HR, & Leeper, SD On-line computerized assessment of young children using the Minnesota Child Development Inventory. *Child Psychol Human Devel,* in press

Lazar, I, & Darlington, R Lasting effects of early education: A report from the consortium for longitudinal studies. *Monogr Soc Res Child Dev,* 1982, *47*(2-3, Serial No. 195)

Lessler, K Health and educational screening of school-age children—definition and objectives. *Am J Public Health,* 1972, *62*, 191–198

Lessler, K Some considerations pertinent to the health screening of children. The responsibility of pediatrics is much more than biological. *Clin Pediat,* 1973, *12*, 656–659

Lichtenstein, R *Comparative validity of alternative decision rules for a preschool developmental screening test.* Unpublished manuscript, 1978. (Available from author, Department of Educational Studies, University of Delaware, 19711)

Lichtenstein, R *Classificational methods for the psychometric evaluation of screening procedures.* Paper presented at the meeting of the Society for Research in Child Development, San Francisco, March 1979

Lichtenstein, R *Identifying children with special educational needs via preschool screening: Binet revisited.* Doctoral dissertation, University of Minnesota, 1980 (a)

Lichtenstein, R *Minneapolis Preschool Screening Instrument.* Minneapolis: Minneapolis Public Schools, 1980 (b)

Lichtenstein, R Comparative validity of two preschool screening tests: Correlational and classificational approaches. *J Learn Disabil,* 1981, *14*, 68–73

Lichtenstein, R New instrument, old problem for early identification. *Excep Child,* 1982,

49, 70–72

Lichtenstein, R Predicting school performance of preschool children from parent reports. *J Abnorm Child Psychol,* in press

Lidz, CS Dynamic assessment and the preschool child. *J Psychoeduc Assessment,* 1983, *1*, 59–72

Lindemann, E, Rosenblith, J, Allinsmith, W, Budd, L, & Shapiro, S Predicting school adjustment before entry. *J Sch Psychol,* 1967, *6*, 24–41

Lindquist, GT Preschool screening as a means of predicting later reading achievement. *J Learn Disabil,* 1982, *15*, 331–332

Mann, AJ, Harrell, A, & Hurt, M, Jr. *A review of Head Start research since 1969.* Washington D.C.: George Washington University, Social Research Group, 1978

Mardell-Czudnowski, CD Validity and reliability; Studies with DIAL. *J for Special Educators,* 1980, *17*, 32–45

Mardell, C, & Goldenberg, D *Developmental Indicators for the Assessment of Learning (DIAL).* Edison, N.J.: Childcraft Education Corp, 1975

Mardell-Czudnowski, C, & Goldenberg, DS Personal communication, February 18, 1983

Matusiak, I *Preschool screening for exceptional education needs in a large urban setting.* Milwaukee: Milwaukee Public Schools, 1976

McCall, RB Nature-nurture and the two realms of development: A proposed integration with respect to mental development. *Child Dev,* 1981, *52*, 1–12

McCall, RB, Hogarty, PS, & Hurlburt, N Transitions in infant sensorimotor development and the prediction of childhood IQ. *Am Psychol,* 1972, *27*, 728–748

McCarthy, D *McCarthy Scales of Children's Abilities.* New York: Psychological Corporation, 1972

McCarthy, D *McCarthy Screening Test.* New York: Psychological Corporation, 1978

McShane, M *The utility of parent reports in clinical practice and research with children.* Unpublished manuscript, 1973. (Available from H. Ireton, Mayo Box 381, University of Minnesota Health Sciences, Minneapolis, MN 55455)

Meehl, PE *Clinical versus statistical prediction.* Minneapolis: University of Minnesota Press, 1954

Meehl, PE, & Rosen, A Antecedent probability and the efficiency of psychometric signs, patterns or cutting scores. *Psychol Bull,* 1955, *52*, 194–216

Meisels, SJ *Developmental screening in early childhood: A guide.* Washington D.C.: National Association for the Education of Young Children, 1978

Meisels, SJ Personal communication, March 1, 1983

Meisels, SJ Prediction, prevention and developmental screening in the EPSDT program. In HW Stevenson & AE Siegel (Eds.), *Child development and social policy.* Chicago: University of Chicago Press, in press

Meisels, SJ, & Wiske, MS *Eliot-Pearson Screening Inventory.* Medford, Mass.: Tufts University, 1976

Meisels, SJ, & Wiske, MS *Early Screening Inventory.* New York: Teachers College Press, 1983

Mercer, JR *Labeling the mentally retarded: Clinical and social system perspectives on mental retardation.* Berkeley: University of California Press, 1973

Meyers, CE, Orpet, RE, Attwell, AA, & Dingman, HF Primary abilities at mental age six. *Monogr Soc Res Child Dev,* 1962, *27*, No. 1

Meyers, J, Pfeffer, J, & Erlbaum, V Process assessment: A model for broadening assessment. *J Spec Educ,* in press

Mitchell, JV Jr. (Ed.) *Tests in print III.* Lincoln, Neb.: Buros Institute of Mental Measurements, in press

Moore, RS, & Moore, DN *Better late than early.* New York: Reader's Digest Press, 1975

National Diffusion Network. *Educational programs that work* (7th ed.). San Francisco: Far West Laboratory, 1980

Novack, H, Bonaventura, E, & Merenda, P A scale for early detection of children with learning problems. *Excep Child,* 1973, *40*, 98–105

Novick, J, Rosenfeld, E, Bloch, DA, & Dawson, D Ascertaining deviant behavior in children. *J Consulting Psychol,* 1966, *30*, 230–238

Nurss, JR, & McGauvran, ME *Metropolitan Readiness Tests.* New York: Harcourt Brace Jovanovich, 1976

Office of Special Education, State Program Implementation Studies Branch. *Second annual report to Congress on the implementation of Public Law 94-142: The Education for All Handicapped Children Act.* U.S. Department of Education, 1980

Paget, K & Bracken, B (Eds.) *The psychoeducational assessment of preschool children.* New York: Grune & Stratton, 1982

Pyles, MK, Stolz, HR, & Macfarlane, JW The accuracy of mothers' reports on birth and developmental data. *Child Dev,* 1935, *6*, 165–176

Quay, H Patterns of aggression, withdrawal, and immaturity. In H. Quay & J. Werry (Eds.), *Psychopathological disorders of childhood.* New York: John Wiley, 1972

Ramey, CT, Stedman, DJ, Borders-Patterson, A, & Mengel, W Predicting school failure from information available at birth. *Am J Ment Defic,* 1978, *82*, 525–532

Ramsey, PH, & Vane, JR A factor analytic study of the Stanford Binet with young children. *J Sch Psychol,* 1970, *8*, 278–284

Read, KH *The nursery school* (6th ed.). Philadelphia: W.B. Saunders, 1976

Reschley, DJ Nonbiased assessment. In GD Phye & DJ Reschley (Eds.), *School psychology: Perspectives and issues.* New York: Academic Press, 1979

Reschly, DJ Legal issues in psychoeducational assessment. In GW Hynd (Ed.), *The school psychologist: An introduction.* Syracuse: Syracuse University Press, 1983

Robb, GP, Bernardoni, LC, & Johnson, RW *Assessment of individual mental ability.* Scranton: International Textbook Company, 1972

Robbins, LD The accuracy of parental recall of aspects of child development and of child-rearing practices. *J Abnorm Soc Psychol,* 1963, *66*, 261–270

Rojcewicz, S, & Aaronson, M Mental health and the Medicaid screening program. In TD Tjossem (Ed.), *Intervention strategies for high risk infants and young children.* Baltimore: University Park Press, 1976

Rubin, RA, & Balow, B Measures of infant development and socioeconomic status as predictors of later intelligence and school achievement. *Dev Psychol,* 1979, *15*, 225–227

Rubin, RA & Balow, B Infant neurological abnormalities as indicators of cognitive impairment. *Dev Med Child Neurol,* 1980, *22*, 336–343

Rubin, RA, Balow, B, Dorle, J, & Rosen, M Preschool prediction of low achievement in basic school skills. *J Learn Disabil,* 1978, *11*, 664–667

Rutter, M The long-term effects of early experience, *Dev Med Child Neurol,* 1980, *22*, 800–815

Salvia, J, & Ysseldyke, JE *Assessment in special and remedial education.* (2nd ed.) Boston: Houghton Mifflin, 1981

Sarff, L *A comparison of DIAL variables to chronological age and the Peabody Picture Vocabulary Test variables.* Doctoral dissertation, Walden University, 1974

Sattler, J Racial "experimenter effects" in experimentation, testing, interviewing, and psychotherapy. *Psychol Bull,* 1970, *73*, 137–160

Sattler, JM *Assessment of children's intelligence and special abilities* (2nd ed.). Boston: Allyn and Bacon, 1982

Satz, P, & Friel, J Some predictive antecedents of specific reading disability: A preliminary two-year follow-up. *J Learn Disabil,* 1974, *7*, 437–444

Satz, P, Friel, J, & Rudegair, F Some predictive antecedents of specific reading disability: A two-, three- and four-year follow-up. In Guthrie, J (Ed.), *Aspects of reading acquisition.* Baltimore: Johns Hopkins Press, 1976

Sawyer, J Measurement and prediction, clinical and statistical. *Psychol Bull,* 1966, *66,* 178–200

Skeels, HM A study of the effects of differential stimulation on mentally retarded children: A follow-up report. *Am J Ment Defic,* 1942, *46,* 340–350

Skeels, HM Adult status of children with contrasting early life experiences: A follow-up study. *Monog Soc Res Child Dev,* 1966, *31,* No. 3

Soeffing, MY BEH officials identify and discuss significant federal programs for the handicapped. *Excep Child,* 1974, *40,* 437–442

Sontag, L, Baker, C, & Nelson, V Mental growth and personality: A longitudinal study. *Monogr Soc Res Child Dev,* 1958, *23,* No. 2, 1–143

Southworth, LE, Burr, RL, & Cox, AE *Screening and evaluating the young child: A handbook of instruments to use from infancy to six years.* Springfield, Ill.: Charles C. Thomas, 1981

Spitz, RA, & Wolf, KM Anaclitic depression: An inquiry into the genesis of psychiatric conditions in early childhood, II. In A Freud, et al. (Eds.), *The psychoanalytic study of the child. Vol. II.* New York: International Universities Press, 1946, 313–342

Stangler, SR, Huber, CJ, & Routh, DK *Screening growth and development of preschool children: A guide for test selection.* New York: McGraw-Hill, 1980

Stanley, JC, & Hopkins, KD *Educational and psychological measurement and evaluation.* Englewood Cliffs, N.J.: Prentice-Hall, 1972

Stevenson, HW, Parker, T, Wilkinson, A, Hegion, A, & Fish, E Longitudinal study of individual differences in cognitive development and scholastic achievement. *J Educ Psychol,* 1976, *68,* 377–400 (a)

Stevenson, HW, Parker, T, Wilkinson, A, Hegion, A, & Fish, E Predictive value of teachers' ratings of young children. *J Educ Psychol,* 1976, *68,* 507–517 (b)

Stone, N, Ireton, H, & Runquist, M *Procedures for the assessment and review of development: A field study.* Unpublished report for the Early and Periodic Screening, Diagnosis and Treatment Program of The Health Care Financing Administration, 1979, (HCFA contract #77-500-0032)

Strully, CF *Test analyses: Screening and verification instruments for preschool children. Volume I.* Harrisburg, Pa.: Pennsylvania State Department of Education, 1977 (ERIC Document Reproduction Service No. ED 135 856)

Sturner, RA, Funk, SG, Thomas, PD, & Green, JA An adaptation of the Minnesota Child Development Inventory for preschool developmental screening. *J Pediat Psychol,* 1982, *7,* 295–306

Szasz, C, Baade, L, & Paskewicz, C Emotional and developmental aspects of human figure drawings in predicting school readiness. *J Sch Psychol,* 1980, *18,* 67–73

Telegdy, GA A factor analysis of four school readiness tests. *Psychol Sch,* 1974, *11,* 127–133

Terman, LM *The measurement of intelligence.* Boston: Houghton Mifflin, 1916

Terman, L, & Merrill, M *Stanford-Binet Intelligence Scale.* Boston: Houghton Mifflin, 1960

Thorndike, RL, & Hagen, E *Measurement and evaluation in psychology and education.* (3rd ed.). New York: John Wiley & Sons, 1969

Tobiessen, J, Duckworth, B, & Conrad, G Relationships between the Schenectady Kindergarten Rating Scales and first grade achievement and adjustment. *Psychol Sch,* 1971, *3,* 29–36

Vopava, J, & Royce, J *Comparison of the long-term effects of infant and preschool programs on academic performance.* Paper presented at the Annual Meeting of the American Educational Research Association, Toronto, March, 1978

Walker, DK *Socioemotional measures for preschool and kindergarten children.* San Francisco: Jossey-Bass, 1973

Walker, DK, & Wiske, MS *A guide to developmental assessments for young children.* (2nd ed.) Massachusetts Department of Education, Early Childhood Project, 1981

Wallbrown, FH, Blaha, J, & Wherry, RJ The hierarchical factor structure of the Wechsler Preschool and Primary Scale of Intelligence. *J Consult Clin Psychol,* 1973, *41*, 356–362

Weber, CU, Foster, PW, & Weikart, DP An economic analysis of the Ypsilanti Perry Preschool project. *Monogr High/Scope Educ Res Found,* 1978 (No. 5)

Weintraub, F Understanding the individualized education program (IEP). *Amicus,* March 1977, 23–27

Wenar, C The reliability of developmental histories. *Psychosom Med,* 1963, *25*, 505–509

Wenar, C, & Coulter, J A reliability study of developmental histories. *Child Dev,* 1962 *33*, 453–462

Werner, EE, Bierman, JM, & French, FE *The children of Kauai: A longitudinal study from the prenatal period.* Honolulu: University of Hawaii Press, 1971

Westinghouse Learning Corporation/Ohio University. *The impact of Head Start: An evaluation of the effects of Head Start on children's cognitive and affective development.* Washington D.C.: Office of Economic Opportunity, 1969 (ERIC Document Reproduction Service No. ED 036 321)

White, SH, Day, MC, Freeman, PK, Hartman, SA, & Messenger, K *Federal programs for young children: Review and recommendations.* Cambridge, Mass.: Huron Institute, 1973

Wiggins, JS *Personality and prediction: Principles of personality assessment.* Reading, Mass.: Addison-Wesley, 1973

Wilson, J, & Jungner, G *Principles and practices of screening for disease.* Geneva: World Health Organization, 1968

Wirt, RD, Lachar, D, Klinedinst, JK, & Seat, PD *Personality Inventory for Children.* Los Angeles: Western Psychological Services, 1977

Wiske, MS, Meisels, SJ, & Tivnan, T Development and validation of the Early Screening Inventory: A study of early childhood developmental screening. In NJ Anastasiow, WK Frankenburg, & AW Fandal (Eds.), *Identifying the developmentally delayed child.* Baltimore: University Park Press, 1982

Woodcock, RW, & Johnson, MB *Woodcock-Johnson Psycho-Educational Battery.* Boston: Teaching Resources, 1977

Yarrow, MR Problems of methods in parent-child research. *Child Dev,* 1963, *34*, 215–226

Ysseldyke, JE Implementing the "protection in evaluation procedures" provisions of P.L. 94-142. In *Exploring issues in the implementation of P.L. 94-142: Developing criteria for the evaluation of protection in evaluation procedures provisions.* (Position papers developed for Department of Health, Education and Welfare, Bureau of Education for the Handicapped.) Philadelphia: Research for Better Schools, 1979

Zehrbach, RR *Comprehensive Identification Process.* Bensenville, Ill.: Scholastic Testing Service, 1975 (a)

Zehrbach, RR Determining a preschool handicapped population. *Excep Child,* 1975, *42*, 76–83 (b)

Zigler, E, Abelson, WD, Trickett, PK, & Seitz, V Is an intervention program necessary in order to improve economically disadvantaged children's IQ scores? *Child Dev,* 1982, *53*, 340–348

Zigler, E, & Valentine, J (Eds.) *Project Head Start: A legacy of the war on poverty.* New York: Free Press, 1979

Zinkus, PW, & Gottlieb, MI Patterns of perceptual and academic deficits related to early chronic otitis media. *Pediatrics,* 1980, *66*, 246–253

Appendix

AUTHOR/PUBLISHER ADDRESSES FOR PRESCHOOL SCREENING INSTRUMENTS

ABC Inventory
    Educational Studies and Development
    1357 Forest Park Road
    Muskegon, Michigan 49441

Assessment of Children's Language Comprehension
    Consulting Psychologists Press
    577 College Avenue
    Palo Alto, California 94306

Bankson Language Screening Test
    University Park Press
    300 North Charles Street
    Baltimore, Maryland 21201

Basic School Skills Inventory—Screen
    PRO-ED
    5341 Industrial Oaks Boulevard
    Austin, Texas 78735

Burks' Behavior Rating Scale
    Western Psychological Services
    12031 Wilshire Boulevard
    Los Angeles, California 90025

California Preschool Social Competency Scale
    Consulting Psychologists Press
    577 College Avenue
    Palo Alto, California 94306

Child Behavior Rating Scale
    Western Psychological Services
    12031 Wilshire Boulevard
    Los Angeles, California 90025

Classroom Behavior Inventory
    Dr. Earl S. Schaefer
    University of North Carolina
    Chapel Hill, North Carolina 27514

Comprehensive Identification Process
    Scholastic Testing Service, Inc.
    Bensenville, Illinois 60106

Cooperative Preschool Inventory, Revised Edition
    Educational Testing Service
    Box 995
    Princeton, New Jersey 08540

Daberon: A Screening Device for School Readiness
    Daberon Research
    4202 SW 44th Avenue
    Portland, Oregon 97221

Dallas Pre-School Screening Test
    Dallas Educational Service
    P.O. Box 1254
    Richardson, Texas 75080

Del Rio Language Screening Test
    National Educational Laboratory Publishers, Inc.
    P.O. Box 1003
    Austin, Texas 78702

Denver Articulation Screening Exam
    LADOCA Publishing Foundation
    East 51st Avenue at Lincoln Street
    Denver, Colorado 80216

Denver Developmental Screening Test
    LADOCA Publishing Foundation
    East 51st Avenue at Lincoln Street
    Denver, Colorado 80216

Denver Prescreening Developmental Questionnaire
    LADOCA Publishing Foundation
    East 51st Avenue at Lincoln Street
    Denver, Colorado 80216

Developmental Activities Screening Inventory
    Teaching Resources Corporation
    50 Pond Park Road
    Hingham, Massachusetts 02043

Developmental Indicators for the Assessment of Learning (DIAL)
    Childcraft Educational Corporation
    20 Kilmer Road
    Edison, New Jersey 08817

Developmental Profile II
    Psychological Development Publications
    Box 3198
    Aspen, Colorado 81612

Developmental Tasks for Kindergarten Readiness
    Clinical Psychology Publishing Company
    4 Conant Square
    Brandon, Vermont 05733

Developmental Test of Visual-Motor Integration
    Follett Publishing Company
    1010 West Washington Boulevard
    Chicago, Illinois 60607

Early Detection Inventory
    N.E.T. Educational Service Center, Inc.
    3065 Clark Lane
    Paris, Texas 75460

Early Screening Inventory
    Teachers College Press
    1234 Amsterdam Avenue
    New York, New York 10027

Expressive One-Word Picture Vocabulary Test
    Academic Therapy Publications
    20 Commercial Boulevard
    Novato, California 94947

Florida KEY: A Scale to Infer Learner Self-Concept
    Bureau of Educational Research
    University of Mississippi
    University, Mississippi 38677

Hannah-Gardner Test of Verbal and Nonverbal Language
    Functioning
    Lingua Press
    P.O. Box 293
    Northridge, California 91324

Home Screening Questionnaire
    LADOCA Publishing Foundation
    East 51st Avenue at Lincoln Street
    Denver, Colorado 80216

Inventory of Language Abilities
    Educational Performance Associates
    463 Westview Avenue
    Ridgefield, New Jersey 07657

Inventory of Readiness Skills
    Educational Programmers, Inc.
    P.O. Box 332
    Roseburg, Oregon 97470

Joseph Preschool and Primary Self Concept Screening Test
    Stoelting Company
    1350 South Kostner Avenue
    Chicago, Illinois 60623

Kaufman Developmental Scale
    Stoelting Company
    1350 South Kostner Avenue
    Chicago, Illinois 60623

Kaufman Infant and Preschool Scale
    Stoelting Company
    1350 South Kostner Avenue
    Chicago, Illinois 60623

Kindergarten Questionnaire
    Ms. Evelyn Perlman
    10 Tyler Road
    Lexington, Massachusetts 02173

Lexington Developmental Scale
    United Cerebral Palsy of the Bluegrass, Inc.
    P.O. Box 8003
    Lexington, Kentucky 40503

McCarthy Screening Test
    Psychological Corporation
    757 Third Avenue
    New York, New York 10017

Minnesota Preschool Inventory
    Behavior Science Systems, Inc.
    Box 1108
    Minneapolis, Minnesota 55440

Minneapolis Preschool Screening Instrument
    Prescriptive Instruction Center
    Minneapolis Public Schools/Special Education Division
    254 Upton Avenue South
    Minneapolis, Minnesota 55405

Motor Free Visual Perception Test
    Academic Therapy Publications
    20 Commercial Boulevard
    Novato, California 94947

Movement Skills Survey
    Follett Publishing Company
    1010 West Washington Boulevard
    Chicago, Illinois 60607

Northwestern Syntax Screening Test
    Northwestern University Press
    1735 Benson Avenue
    Evanston, Illinois 60201

Peabody Picture Vocabulary Test—Revised
    American Guidance Service, Inc.
    Publishers' Building
    Circle Pines, Minnesota 55014

Pennsylvania Preschool Inventory
    Pennsylvania State Department of Education
    Box 911
    Harrisburg, Pennsylvania 17126

Photo Articulation Test
    Interstate Printers & Publishers
    19-27 North Jackson Street
    Danville, Illinois 61832

Pictorial Test of Bilingualism and Language Dominance
    Stoelting Company
    1350 South Kostner Avenue
    Chicago, Illinois 60623

Preschool and Kindergarten Performance Profile
    Educational Performance Association
    463 Westview Avenue
    Ridgefield, New Jersey 07657

Preschool Attainment Record, Research Edition
    American Guidance Service, Inc.
    Publisher's Building
    Circle Pines, Minnesota 55014

Preschool Behavior Rating Scale
    Child Welfare League of America, Inc.
    67 Irving Place
    New York, New York 10003

Preschool Language Assessment Instrument
    Grune & Stratton, Inc.
    111 Fifth Avenue
    New York, New York 10003

Pre-School Screening Instrument
    Stoelting Company
    1350 South Kostner Avenue
    Chicago, Illinois 60623

Preschool Screening System
    Early Recognition Intervention Systems
    P.O. Box 1635
    Pawtucket, Rhode Island 02862

Primary Self-Concept Inventory
    Teaching Resources Corporation
    50 Pond Park Road
    Hingham, Massachusetts 02043

Pupil Behavior Inventory
    Dr. Norma Radin
    School of Social Work
    University of Michigan
    Ann Arbor, Michigan 48109

Riley Motor Problems Inventory
    Western Psychological Services
    12031 Wilshire Boulevard
    Los Angeles, California 90025

Riley Preschool Developmental Screening Inventory
    Western Psychological Services
    12031 Wilshire Boulevard
    Los Angeles, California 90025

School Behavior Checklist
    Western Psychological Services
    12031 Wilshire Boulevard
    Los Angeles, California 90025

School Entrance Checklist
  Educator's Publishing Service
  75 Moulton Street
  Cambridge, Massachusetts 02138

School Readiness Checklist—Ready or Not?
  Research Concepts
  1368 East Airport Road
  Muskegon, Michigan 49444

School Readiness Survey
  Consulting Psychologists Press
  577 College Avenue
  Palo Alto, California 94306

Screening Speech Articulation Test
  Communication Research Associates
  P.O. Box 110212
  Salt Lake City, Utah 84111

Screening Test for Auditory Comprehension of Language
  Teaching Resources Corporation
  50 Pond Park Road
  Hingham, Massachusetts 02043

Slosson Intelligence Test
  Slosson Educational Publications
  P.O. Box 280
  East Aurora, New York 14052

Test of Early Language Development
  PRO-ED
  5341 Industrial Oaks Boulevard
  Austin, Texas 78735

Tree/Bee Test of Auditory Discrimination
  Academic Therapy Publications
  20 Commercial Boulevard
  Novato, California 94947

Vane Evaluation of Language Scale
  Clinical Psychology Publishing Company
  4 Conant Square
  Brandon, Vermont 04733

Verbal Language Development Scale
  American Guidance Service, Inc.
  Publisher's Building
  Circle Pines, Minnesota 55014

Vineland Social Maturity Scale
  American Guidance Service, Inc.
  Publisher's Building
  Circle Pines, Minnesota 55014

To obtain ERIC documents:
  ERIC Document Reproduction Service
  Computer Microfilm International Corporation (CMIC)
  3030 N. Fairfax Drive, Suite 200
  Arlington, Virginia 22201
  Telephone: (703)841-1212

Index